COMMANDING BOSTON'S IRISH NINTH

Patrick R. Guiney as major or lieutenant colonel of the Ninth Massachusetts. Photo courtesy of College of the Holy Cross Rare Books—Special
Collections and Archives.

Commanding Boston's Irish Ninth

*The Civil War Letters of
Colonel Patrick R. Guiney,
Ninth Massachusetts
Volunteer Infantry*

edited by
CHRISTIAN G. SAMITO

FORDHAM UNIVERSITY PRESS
New York
1998

Copyright © 1998 by Fordham University Press
All rights reserved
LC 97–38443
ISBN 0–8232–1812–0
ISSN 1044–5315
Irish in the Civil War, no. 6

Library of Congress Cataloging-in-Publication Data

Guiney, Patrick R. (Patrick Robert), 1835–1877.
    Commanding Boston's Irish Ninth : the Civil War letters of Colonel
Patrick R. Guiney, Ninth Massachusetts Volunteer Infantry / edited by
Christian G. Samito.
        p. c.m. -- (Irish in the Civil War, ISSN 1044–5315 : no. 6)
    Includes bibliographical references (p.) and index.
    ISBN 0–8232–1812–0
    1. Guiney, Patrick R. (Patrick Robert), 1835–1877--
Correspondence. 2. United States. Army. Massachusetts Infantry
Regiment, 9th (1861–1864) 3. United States--History--Civil War, 1861–
1865--Personal narratives. 4. United States--History--Civil War, 1861–
1865--Participation, Irish American. 5. Boston (Mass.)--History--Civil
War, 1861–1865. 6. Irish Americans--Massachusetts--Boston--
Correspondence. I. Samito, Christian G. II. Title. III. Series.
E513.5 9th.G85 1998   97–38443
973.7'444--dc21   CIP

Printed in the United States of America

CONTENTS

SERIES EDITOR'S PREFACE

It would be easy to stereotype the Irish experience in the Civil War. Most Irish-Americans in 1861 were poor, uneducated, urban-dwelling Catholics who had recently fled the horrors of famine Ireland. They voted overwhelmingly Democratic, opposed Lincoln's election, and had no sympathy with those who advocated rights for blacks. If they threw themselves into the war effort, their reasons for doing so were not those of the Lincoln administration. Yet such generalizations overlook important Irish actors in America's greatest drama. Christian Samito's edition of the letters of Col. Patrick Robert Guiney of the Ninth Massachusetts Volunteer Infantry vividly tells the story of one such Irishman. Colonel Guiney may have been typical in his Irish courage on the battlefield, but in most ways his story is distinctive.

When the war began Guiney was a well-educated, successful Boston attorney. His law practice had allowed him to move to a comfortable suburb and to maintain his wife and young daughter in a style to which few recent Irish immigrants could aspire. Though he had previously been a Democrat, shortly after the war began he became a staunch supporter of Lincoln and the Republicans. Unlike most Irishmen in the army he criticized Democratic generals like McClellan who did not press the enemy hard enough. He entertained far more liberal views on racial issues than most Irishmen and he openly welcomed the end of slavery. His outspoken support for the Republican prosecution of the war not only separated him from the Irish community in Boston; it set many of the men in his own regiment against him.

Guiney's story is a valuable reminder that the Civil War—and even the comparatively narrow slice of the Irish role in the war—was much more complex than popular legend would have it. Postwar memoirs and regimental histories often conveniently forgot about the war's cowards and shirkers, just as they often passed silently over episodes of trouble within the regiments. But stories of heroes and sacrifice, of unity and comradeship, tell only half-truths. Samito's edition of Col. Guiney's letters describes the real contributions of a hard-fighting Irish regiment in the Army of the Potomac, but it also reveals some of the more personal battles that took place within the regiment and within the Boston Irish community that sent this regiment to the front. Most of all, it tells the story of a courageous Irish-American officer who dared to differ with his countrymen on the war and the difficulties he endured for doing so.

A horrible head wound finally ended Guiney's military service in 1864, but he had already suffered a deeper emotional wound from the opposition he had received from his own Irish-American community. His example demonstrates both the existence of a powerful consensus among the Irish on the issues of the war and of at least one remarkable man who risked his career to challenge it.

LAWRENCE FREDERICK KOHL

PREFACE

I did not expect to find an extensive collection of Civil War letters when I entered the Rare Book Room in Dinand Library at the College of the Holy Cross. Since Holy Cross predates the Civil War, I thought the college might possess a few official documents or perhaps some scattered correspondence in its collection. Instead, I found a stack of letters written during three years of active field service by Patrick R. Guiney. Upon reading them, I was impressed with the sentiments, eloquence, and information expressed in Guiney's letters. His words and deeds inspired me to begin this project.

Guiney attended Holy Cross for a year. In 1910 his daughter, Louise Imogen Guiney, donated his library "in loving memory to my father's Holy Cross." Louise Guiney achieved eminence as a poet, and following her death in 1920, Father Michael Earls began collecting her letters, manuscripts, and books. At present, Holy Cross holds most of the surviving letters written by Patrick R. Guiney and his daughter and all the letters used in this volume are located there, unless otherwise noted.

Several people assisted me in the course of my work, and I wish to acknowledge their help. At Holy Cross, Rare Book and Special Collections Curator James M. Mahoney proved invaluable during this project. His good spirits, sense of humor, and constant eagerness to help made it a pleasure to work in the archives. The Reverend Paul J. Nelligan, S.J., archivist, and the rest of Dinand Library's staff went out of their way to assist me in any possible way. The Reverend Gerard R. Reedy, S.J., president of Holy Cross, granted permission and gave words of encouragement in my endeavor to publish Guiney's letters, and Professor Stephen Ainlay and the Center for Interdisciplinary Studies and Special Studies Special Programs Subcommittee provided me with some funding.

Professor Lawrence F. Kohl of the University of Alabama provided me with many valuable ideas and research leads and greatly aided in producing this volume.

I am grateful to Henry Roberts, who provided me with important information, along with a copy of a diary written by Timothy
Regan of the Ninth Massachusetts Volunteers, presently owned by
Kenneth Pluskat. Kevin McLaughlin came across a note Guiney
wrote in the hospital following his wounding at the Wilderness
and quickly brought it to my attention. The informative conversa-
tions we shared, and their interest and enthusiasm in both the
Ninth Massachusetts and my project, are greatly appreciated.

I would like to thank Sister Anne Gabrielle of the Sisters of
Notre Dame; James E. Fahey, Military Archivist at the United
States Naval Shipbuilding Museum, Massachusetts Military Research Center; Peter Drummey, Massachusetts Historical Society;
and the staffs of the National Archives, Library of Congress, Massachusetts State Archives, and Boston Public Library for assisting
me to locate and utilize various documents in their respective
collections. The Reverend David Maris helped by translating a
German passage from the Cologne *Gazette*, and Joel Villa, Killian
MacCarthy and Kenneth Cooper provided me with their expertise
in photography.

I should also like to thank my parents and family for their love,
support, and financial assistance, and for patiently enduring my
frequent digressions into the nineteenth century.

Finally, I will always be thankful for my many friends from Holy
Cross, among both professors and students. You have given me
many happy years and continue to do so, and you will always be
dear to my heart. Guiney attended the school when it was only a
few years old, and its spirit remained a source of pride and fond
recollections throughout his life. During my time at Holy Cross,
the same sense of community, intellectual growth, and cherished
friendships continues. In this I feel a connection with Patrick R.
Guiney which has, in no small way, inspired me to research his
life, his letters, and his cause.

In the course of editing these letters, I have silently corrected
the few spelling mistakes Guiney made, except in cases of proper
names of locations (e.g., Fort Munroe; Sharpsburgh). On the
whole, he was very accurate in his spelling and most of the errors
seemed to be "slips of the pen." To leave them in place seemed
to me an undue and unnecessary distraction from Guiney's eloquence.

PROLOGUE:
THE DRUMS OF WAR

Crowds of people filled the heart of Boston, watching a thousand uniformed Irishmen parade away from the columned State House. After hostilities erupted at Fort Sumter, Americans rallied to defend nation, state, home, and sweetheart. Throngs of volunteers came forth to participate in what they expected would be a short, glorious war to either win the independence of the Confederacy or restore the Union. As the Ninth Massachusetts Volunteer Infantry left Boston that early summer's day, a spirit of patriotism and anticipation united those who had gathered.

One of the regiment's citizen soldiers was Patrick Robert Guiney, a young lawyer living near Boston with his beautiful wife and beloved infant daughter. His wife undoubtedly stood in the crowd, craning her neck for one last glimpse as he marched by, anxious at the prospect of time spent apart and the realization that he was destined for the seat of war. The Irishman soon came to appreciate that, contrary to early expectations, this conflict would be long and arduous. In a little over a year's time he rose in rank to command the Ninth Massachusetts and would eventually attain the honorary rank of brigadier general for gallant service in the field—along with a debilitating head wound that shattered his health and cost him an eye.

Guiney was born on January 15, 1835, in Parkstown, County Tipperary, an agricultural region of southern Ireland. He was baptized on April 27th, the son of James Guiney and his Scottish wife, born Judith Macrae or Magrath. At the age of seven, young Patrick joined his father to emigrate to the United States, forced out of Ireland due to troubles with a landlord. The boy and his father went first to New Brunswick, Canada, and then on to Maine. Here they experienced the discrimination some native-born Americans practiced against the Irish, when a hotel owner would not allow the Guineys to enter. Within a year, Patrick's mother and younger brother William joined them and the family settled in Portland, Maine.[1]

In boyhood, young Patrick endured much work and little youthful leisure. He walked three and a half miles to a rope factory where he performed monotonous labor as a wheel-boy. Upon reaching fourteen, Guiney became apprenticed to a machinist in the Essex Shop in Lawrence, Massachusetts, where he remained for half a year. A young man now, he returned to Portland for a three-year apprenticeship in the machine shop of the Portland Company. The labor did not appeal to the growing intellectual nature of the boy, and he attended grammar school in Portland with the dream of attending college someday.[2] Furthermore, he later recounted a feeling of loneliness in his youth, writing that he "had no one to tell the secrets of my soul to. I say <u>secrets</u>, not <u>sins</u> . . . the yearnings and aspirations of my heart." Part of this stemmed from the distance between the boy and his mother. Guiney's only daughter later recalled her as cold, stoic, and unsympathetic to the desires of her son.[3]

Guiney found release upon entering the College of the Holy Cross, a Jesuit school founded upon the hills of Worcester, Massachusetts. He entered the school October 20, 1854, joining a student body that numbered forty-two by year's end. He enjoyed his time spent at Holy Cross, later remembering fondly that "it was the Alma Mater of a few full minds and of many empty stomachs." However, his funds began to run low after a year. The president of the college, the Reverend Peter Blenkinsop, S.J., privately approached the young man and offered to arrange matters so that he could continue, but Guiney did not want to accept such charity.[4]

---

[1] Louise I. Guiney, "Patrick Robert Guiney," in *The Holy Cross Purple*, vol. 3, no. 1 (June 1896), 37–38. *The Pilot*, March 31, 1877. Grace Guiney to Fr. William Luccy, August 19, 1959. Birth Certificate for Patrick Robert Guiney, signed by William Breen, March 21, 1963, in Dinand Library Rare Book Room, College of the Holy Cross. James Bernard Cullen, ed., *The Story of the Irish in Boston* (Boston: James B. Cullen & Company, 1889), p. 245.

[2] Louise I. Guiney, "Patrick Robert Guiney," 38. Sketch of "Our Candidate," *General Guiney's Scrapbook*, in Dinand Library Rare Book Room, College of the Holy Cross, p. 5. Hereafter cited as Guiney scrapbook.

[3] Patrick R. Guiney to Louise I. Guiney, December 5, 1876. Louise I. Guiney, "Patrick Robert Guiney," 38.

[4] Louise I. Guiney, "Patrick Robert Guiney," 38–39. Holy Cross Registration Book. Of the forty two students, two were from Canada, four from California,

For a while, Guiney thought he would enjoy working in theater. He later recalled, "I was possessed with the idea of becoming an actor on the dramatic stage. I applied to a celebrated manager for a chance, and placing his hand tenderly on my head, he asked, 'do you think you can become a great actor?' I stammered that I did not know. 'Find that out first,' said he, 'for it is better to be a slave than a poor actor.' That interview cured me. I never went on the stage."[5]

Instead, he went back to Portland to study law under Judge Charles Walton, who later served in the United States Congress and on the Maine State Supreme Court.[6] Admitted to the bar on April 24, 1856, Guiney also put his eloquent writing to use as an assistant editor for the Lewiston *Advocate* in Maine. In September 1858 he relocated to Boston, where he served as a lawyer and wrote articles for the Boston *Times*. Although not much is known of their courtship, Guiney fell deeply in love with and married Jeannette Margaret Doyle on January 8, 1859, in the old Cathedral in Boston. She was a relative of the Right Reverend James Doyle, Bishop of Kildare and Lighlin. The Guineys quickly established residency in Roxbury, an independent town outside Boston at that time.[7]

Guiney became involved in public affairs and won election in 1859 to serve on the Common Council of Roxbury. On March 22, 1860, Guiney joined the Irish Charitable Society of Boston, an organization founded in 1737 by Bostonians of Irish ancestry.[8] By the late 1850s the organization had become a "wining and dining club" for middle- and upper-class Irish. While it still provided small donations to Irish families in need, a sizeable portion of the society's budget went to fund its yearly St. Patrick's Day celebration at the posh Parker House, where it also held its quarterly

---

and two from Cuba—a surprising geographic assortment. Between January and June 1855 another ten students arrived.

[5] Patrick R. Guiney to Louise I. Guiney, March 8, 1877.

[6] Louise I. Guiney, "Patrick Robert Guiney," 39. United States Congress, *Biographical Directory of the American Congress 1774–1927* (United States Government Printing Office, 1928), p. 1664. Walton served as a Republican in Congress from March 4, 1861 to May 26, 1862, when he accepted appointment as an associate justice on the state supreme court, a position he held for the next 25 years.

[7] Louise I. Guiney, "Patrick Robert Guiney," 39. *The Pilot*, March 31, 1877. Patrick R. Guiney Pension Record, National Archives, Washington, D.C. *The Catholic News*, August 2, 1930.

[8] Notes of Rev. William Lucey, S.J., Dinand Library Rare Book Room, College of the Holy Cross.

meetings.[9] Meanwhile, the young couple began a family. Their first-born son died in infancy, but Louise Imogen Guiney, born in Roxbury on January 7, 1861, grew up to become an eminent poet.

When the Civil War broke out, loyalty to his adopted state and country welled up in Guiney. In its time of need, he joined in defending the Union he had grown to cherish. Over the course of his service, Guiney wrote a series of beautiful letters to his wife. They run from June 4, 1861 to April 7, 1864 and discuss all aspects of life in the regiment and army, from training to combat duty, from camp under a starry sky to receiving absolution from the regimental chaplain before going into battle. In reading Guiney's words, one can have a fuller appreciation of what motivated civilians to volunteer to fight a war and of the privations they suffered in service to their country. Furthermore, the personality of an Irish Catholic soldier shines through, and Guiney's intense love for his wife and infant child, anxiety for the victorious conclusion of the war, and the burdens of leadership are common themes in his writing.

Above all, Guiney's political views comprise his most interesting aspect, as they set him apart from the majority of his Irish-American comrades. In several episodes, Guiney experienced opposition motivated by animosity at his divergence from the political tenets traditionally held by most Boston Irish. Originally a Democrat, like virtually all his countrymen, Guiney's later support for Lincoln, Republicanism, and the abolition of slavery created great tension between Guiney and several of his officers and even in the Boston community. Guiney often wrote of these difficulties, which became a major theme of his correspondence.

In his first surviving letter Guiney missed Jennie and Louise and expressed misgivings in parting with his family, fearing that perhaps he was too rash in enlisting. Throughout the war he agonized over their financial security and general well-being, yet honor and belief in the cause for which he fought kept him from resigning. He wrote, "the cause in which we are enlisted is truly a good and grand one—one that will entitle those who labor in the

---

[9] Oscar Handlin, *Boston's Immigrants 1790–1880: A Study in Acculturation* (Cambridge: Belknap Press of Harvard University, rev. and enl. ed. 1979), pp. 155, 160. Cullen, *The Story of the Irish in Boston*, pp. 40–41.

achievement of its success to the gratitude and remembrance of the present, as well as of unborn generations—one that of itself compensates by its sublimity and goodness for all which may be sacrificed in its defense."[10]

Despite longing to be reunited with his family, Guiney displayed an early enthusiasm for service and constantly reassured his wife that he would survive the war, that fortune would smile upon him. He acted as a typical soldier, reading a great deal to pass the time in camp, lonely without his wife, and waiting for constant letters from her. Overall, his greatest wish was for a rapid, victorious conclusion to the war and for his awaited homecoming.

Guiney also wrote about issues in his regiment and army and expressed many fascinating and astute opinions on military operations and high ranking-officers. He had critical assessments of the Ninth's Colonel Thomas Cass and Lieutenant Colonel Cromwell Rowell and scorned some officers who joined not to fight but to loaf. The letters describe the rivalries, ambitions, and schemes men attempted in an effort to advance in this, and probably all other, units. Guiney was a man of action who constantly desired vigorous, goal-directed activity. Even as Major General George B. McClellan's popularity peaked, Guiney criticized his slowness and realized that, despite his intelligence, McClellan did not have the "Genius" to conduct the war. Instead, Guiney wanted to push the Rebels, defeat them in battle, and end the war once and for all; he became exasperated at lost opportunities and unnecessary defeats. Furthermore, Guiney displayed an astute sense of how the war should be fought; while others called for a drive to capture Richmond, he saw the destruction of the Confederate army as the real Federal objective. Similarly, Guiney mirrored Lincoln's sentiment that Pennsylvanian George Meade would fight well in his own state during the Gettysburg campaign and believed that the entire Army of the Potomac would be inspired to shatter the Confederate invasion of a loyal Union state.

Guiney's letters are all the more illuminating and important in that they were written by a man very different from those he commanded. Beneath his seemingly smooth rise from first lieutenant to colonel, tension with several of his officers and with the

---

[10] Patrick R. Guiney to Jennie Guiney, Arlington Heights, Va., July 31, 1861.

Boston Irish community plagued Guiney's tenure in command. Most Irish-Americans living in Boston at that time were poorly educated laborers living in slums. They became staunch Democrats with tremendous hostility toward Lincoln, Republicanism, and the blacks whose cause abolitionists promoted. Guiney, by contrast, was an educated lawyer, living in a Boston suburb, who came to support the Lincoln administration and liberation of blacks from the shackles of slavery. Not content to remain silent with his liberal views, Guiney professed his beliefs in word and deed, and made clear his political stance and individuality of thought. The political cohesion of the Irish-American community is illustrated by its treatment of one who broke from its ranks. In order to fully appreciate his situation and its significance, however, one must look to the Irish immigration of the 1840s, the interaction between American society and these newcomers, and the subsequent political effects thereof.

The potato rot which struck Ireland in 1845 caused great famine in an already impoverished land and stimulated emigration, especially to the United States. Prior to 1840 the number of immigrants landing in Boston reached four thousand only once, and most of the newcomers were westward-bound. However, by 1850 the Irish population in Boston had grown to thirty-five thousand, and swelled past fifty thousand by 1855.[11] These impoverished Irish immigrants needed immediate employment upon landing in Boston, a condition that precluded the luxury of choosing a job or learning a trade. General aversion toward hiring the Irish except for manual work, coupled with their lack of capital, literacy, or skills, led the newcomers to rely heavily on unskilled positions.[12]

These Irish-Americans spurred Boston's industrial growth by providing a cheap labor pool, and the number of industrial employers doubled in the decade between 1845 and 1855 and again from 1855 to 1865. The textile industry flourished, aided by the availability of immigrants willing to learn tailoring and work for wages unacceptable to a proper tailor. While Boston had 473 tailors in 1845, five years later it had over 1,547, more than a thou-

---

[11] Handlin, *Boston's Immigrants*, pp. 45, 51–52.

[12] Edward M. Levine, *The Irish and Irish Politicians* (Notre Dame: University of Notre Dame Press, 1966), pp. 58–59. Handlin, *Boston's Immigrants*, pp. 60, 61.

sand of whom were Irish. When Boston experienced a building boom, Irishmen filled out the construction crews.[13]

Irish-American laborers found both their wages and working conditions to be low, and as more immigrants flowed in there was increased competition for a limited number of jobs. Despite working fifteen-hour days, seven days a week, many workers needed supplementary earnings from their wives, sons, and daughters in order to meet expenses. Initially, even the Civil War did little to ameliorate these conditions, until enough men had been drawn into the army and the industrial stimulation provided by the massive Union war effort created an equilibrium between the supply and the demand for laborers.[14]

Most of the Irish immigrants suffered in terrible living conditions, unable to remove their families to the calm streets and spacious dwellings of suburban Roxbury or Dorchester. Many settled in the clogged North End and Fort Hill slums, where landlords allowed buildings to grow dilapidated rather than make repairs. The Irish took over these sectors and created their own community. Lacking the money to move away, this close contact with their countrymen enticed many subsequent newcomers to gravitate to the stifling tenements. A few Irish-Americans relocated to the South End after the extensions of Washington, Harrison, and Suffolk (Shawmut) Streets and the introduction of horsecars running down to Roxbury in 1856. However, these were almost wholly limited to educated tradesmen, and Irish representation in the suburbs was limited. Similarly, the opening of street railroads in 1858 made Roxbury more accessible, but only to prosperous groups.[15]

In the North End and Fort Hill districts, people pressed into small rooms and dank cellars. One North End house sheltered a family of nine living in one room, while another had fifteen people in three attic rooms. In Fort Hill, some three- to six-story buildings housed forty to a hundred inhabitants. Putrid air and

---

[13] Handlin, *Boston's Immigrants*, pp. 63, 74, 76.

[14] Thomas H. O'Connor, *Fitpatrick's Boston 1846–1866* (Boston: Northeastern University Press, 1984), p. 83. Handlin, *Boston's Immigrants*, pp. 61, 86.

[15] As early as 1850, 40 percent of Roxbury's population were foreigners or children of foreigners; however, they were primarily non-Irish immigrants. Handlin, *Boston's Immigrants*, pp. 91, 93–94, 99. Levine, *The Irish and Irish Politicians*, p. 58.

contaminated, undrained water fostered diseases such as cholera, smallpox, dysentery, and consumption in epidemic proportions. The unsanitary conditions led to a high mortality rate among children, who suffered high incidence of pneumonia, bronchitis, and intestinal disorders.[16]

The hard labor and low quality of life led to great indulgence in alcohol. In 1846 there were 850 liquor dealers in Boston; by 1849, 1,200 bars existed in the city. By 1850, Irish-Americans operated 900 of 1,500 such establishments, and a survey conducted by the city marshal in November 1851 found that nearly half of Boston's groggeries were concentrated in the North End and Fort Hill districts. Such places were popular for their cheap whiskey, for providing an opportunity for people to gather and socialize, and as centers of political activity.[17]

The Democratic party of the 1850s supported unrestricted immigration and freedom from interference in religious and social concerns. Democrats attacked what they viewed as a Republican attempt to intervene in all facets of life: nativist limits on immigration, the restriction of individual and collective ethnic conduct found to be incompatible with their views, and the violation of personal liberty by state intrusion into people's conduct and beliefs. The Republicans were seen as attempting to impose their puritanical beliefs on everyone by attacking Catholicism, tampering with slavery, and promoting prohibition of alcohol.[18]

The Irish turned out as staunch supporters of the Democrats and remained hostile to the reform impulses that evolved into the Republican party. Such movements as the nativist hostility toward immigrants, pro-temperance activism, and abolitionism were partly the manifestation of northern, native-born Protestants' fears. Their notion of moral stewardship joined with a view that the state should have wide authority to direct the economic life

---

[16] Robert H. Lord, John E. Sexton, and Edward T. Harrington, *History of the Archdiocese of Boston* 3 vols. (New York: Sheed & Ward, 1944), 2: 453–54. Handlin, *Boston's Immigrants*, p. 115. O'Connor, *Fitzpatrick's Boston*, p. 84.

[17] Dennis P. Ryan, *Beyond the Ballot Box: A Social History of the Boston Irish, 1845–1917* (Rutherford, N.J.: Fairleigh Dickinson University Press, 1983), p. 85. Thomas H. O'Connor, *The Boston Irish: A Political History* (Boston: Northeastern University Press, 1995), p. 65. Handlin, *Boston's Immigrants*, p. 121.

[18] Joel H. Silbey, *A Respectable Minority: The Democratic Party in the Civil War Era 1860–1868* (New York: W. W. Norton, 1977), pp. 24–25.

of the country. Abhorrence of Rome, the papacy, and Catholics unified the Protestants against Irish immigrants and led to a nativist demand that ethnic groups renounce both their cultural roots and their clannishness, though not necessarily their values, in order to assimilate into American Anglo-Saxon culture.[19]

Some Protestant Yankees, observing Catholics arriving on their shores, felt fear and animosity toward these Europeans and their foreign culture and religion. The Irish maintained particularly strong ties to their old country and a close sense of community in their adopted land, and this reinforced nativist hostility toward the newcomers. Concern over Irish-American loyalty to foreign religious leaders such as the pope, their strong interest in events in their mother country, and clamors for United States involvement in Ireland's quest for independence strengthened such Yankee perceptions.[20] The Democrats absorbed these immigrants, especially in urban areas, while many Northern Protestants abandoned the party in favor of the nativist American, or Know-Nothing, party. These rejectionists felt the Democrats had grown unconcerned of the immigrant threat, or worse, welcomed them as a source of new votes. Not surprisingly, Protestant groups less affected by the Catholic influx remained more loyal to the Democratic party.[21]

A number of Radical Republicans opposed the nativist wing of the party, viewing it as preoccupied with a minor issue which detracted from the principal mission of the party, combatting slavery. The editor of the radical *National Era,* Gamaliel Bailey, attacked Know Nothingism as irreconcilable with civil and religious liberty. While content for nativists to cast their ballots for Republican candidates, William H. Seward remained unwilling to make concessions on abolitionism or the rights of foreigners in

---

[19] Eric Foner, *Free Soil, Free Labor, Free Men The Ideology of the Republican Party Before the Civil War* (New York: Oxford University Press, reprint 1995), pp. 227–29. The question of Cuba's annexation serves to illustrate this loathing of Catholicism. John P. Hale and other Republicans opposed it not only on an antislavery motivation, but on the grounds that most of Cuba's population was Catholic, while the United States was rooted in and maintained on the principles of Anglo-Saxon Protestants.

[20] O'Connor, *The Boston Irish,* pp. 69–70. Levine, *The Irish and Irish Politicians,* p. 63.

[21] Silbey, *A Respectable Minority,* pp. 15, 17.

order to gain their votes. Nonetheless, while the 1856 Republican platform did not support nativism the party was still associated with the movement.[22]

The Irish resented governmental attempts to control alcohol consumption. Even while trying to cope with the problems of drunkenness in the Irish-American community, the Catholic Church opposed state interference in this matter. Religious fervor permeated the prohibitionists, who, deeming drinking to be impious and contrary to God, tried to use government to "annihilate sin." The first prohibition law passed in Maine in 1851, but by 1855 the Democrats recaptured control of that state's legislature by capitalizing on ethnic hostility against another similar act passed by the Republican legislature elected a year earlier. Elsewhere, temperance movements met with such opposition that state Republican parties stopped discussing the issue.[23] Meanwhile, some reformers blamed the Irish for the failure of the Maine acts and, linking the Irish and their religion to the vice of drinking, vowed to oppose Catholicism.[24]

A variety of reasons led Irish-Americans to maintain hostility to both abolitionists and their cause. The Irish felt dismay at the prospect of millions of freed slaves migrating north, intensifying competition for already scarce jobs and driving out white laborers.[25] During the Civil War, *The Pilot*, an influential Boston newspaper that served the city's Irish population, questioned,

> . . . where the white find it difficult to earn a subsistence, what right has the negro to either preference, or to equality, or to admission?

---

[22] Foner, *Free Soil, Free Labor, Free Men*, pp. 233–35, 249. William Seward became popular with the Irish because of his position on financial aid to Catholic schools while governor of New York. In January 1840 he began a two-year controversy by proposing to give some funding to the schools, but the money was never appropriated. He later served as Secretary of State under Presidents Abraham Lincoln and Andrew Johnson. Florence E. Gibson, *The Attitudes of the New York Irish Toward State and National Affairs 1848–1892* (New York: Columbia University Press, 1951), p. 106.

[23] *Massachusetts Anti-Liquor Law; with an Analysis and Exposition* (Boston: State Temperance Committee, 1852). *Address of the State Temperance Committee to the Citizens of Massachusetts on the Operation of the Anti-Liquor Law* (Boston, 1853). Foner, *Free Soil, Free Labor, Free Men*, pp. 241–42. Handlin, *Boston's Immigrants*, p. 134.

[24] Levine, *The Irish and Irish Politicians*, p. 93.

[25] *The Pilot*, July 20, 1861; February 15, 1862. Handlin, *Boston's Immigrants*, p. 133. Ryan, *Beyond the Ballot Box*, p. 130. The July 20, 1861 edition of *The Pilot*

. . . What has the African done for America? What great or even decent work has his head conceived, or his hands executed? We pity his condition; but it is unjust to put him in the balance with the white laborer. To white toil this nation owes everything; but to black, nothing.[26]

Amidst the scorn aimed at them, the Irish could find solace in the existence of a social class beneath them. Living in the slums of Boston themselves, Irish-Americans viewed blacks not with fraternal sentiments as another oppressed group, but as a peril to their jobs.[27] Many blacks, in turn, felt hostility toward the Irish, as immigrants drove free African-Americans out of the job market. While blacks composed the majority of servants in New York City in 1830, two decades later the number of Irish domestics alone outnumbered the city's total black population ten to one. These African-Americans, angered at losing their jobs, derisively referred to the Irish as "white niggers."[28]

When the Irish patriot Daniel O'Connell urged his countrymen in America to oppose slavery in the interest of liberty, many Irish-Americans attacked his stance and argued that their obtaining equality with Protestant Yankees took priority. Irish in both America and Ireland adored O'Connell, who had participated in the antislavery activism which resulted in England's emancipation of slaves in the British West Indies. On May 9, 1843, O'Connell gave a speech in Dublin in which he attacked slavery as a "black spot" and a "damning stain," a crime which "a just Providence will sooner or later avenge." Irish-Americans resented these remarks, as well as a subsequent petition he addressed to them urging their opposition to slavery; *The Pilot* criticized O'Connell's interference with a domestic issue.[29]

---

emphatically declared, "The white men of the free states do not wish to labor side by side with the Negro."

[26] *The Pilot*, August 16, 1862.

[27] Levine, *The Irish and Irish Politicians*, p. 60. O'Connor, *The Boston Irish*, p. 81. Silbey, *A Respectable Minority*, p. 82.

[28] Joseph M. Hernon, Jr. *Celts, Catholics & Copperheads* (Columbus: Ohio State University Press, 1968), p. 65.

[29] Rice further argues that, due to nativism and anti-Catholic prejudice, Irish-Americans were afraid of being laid open to the charge of European domination. Madeleine Hooke Rice, *American Catholic Opinion in the Slavery Controversy* (New York: Columbia University Press, 1944), pp. 80–83. Mary Alphonse Frawley, S.S.J., *Patrick Donahoe* (Washington, D.C.: The Catholic University of America Press, 1946), p. 127. Levine, *The Irish and Irish Politicians*, p. 96. Hernon, *Celts, Catholics & Copperheads*, pp. 59–61.

While insisting that slaveowners treat their slaves justly and charitably, the Catholic Church did not find the institution contrary to divine or natural law.[30] Madeleine Hooke Rice found that "Ecclesiastical leaders, mindful of conflicts between church and civil authorities in the Old World, were fearful of tendencies toward greater centralization of governmental powers in the United States. Convinced that slavery was a matter of local concern, they quite generally advocated state rather than federal control."[31]

The anti-Catholic stance of most abolitionists, partially motivated by the immigrants' pro-slavery bias, further insured Irish-American hostility to the movement. As early as 1839, *The Pilot* warned that many abolitionists were "bigoted and persecuting religionists . . . [desiring] the extermination of Catholics by fire and sword."[32] Abolitionist goals and strategy, such as that preached by William Lloyd Garrison, were viewed as a threat to the nation's safety and adverse to Irish values. *The Pilot* reported to a Catholic population which already saw abolitionists as opponents of religion, public order, and the Union. Freesoilers, also known as Black Republicans, were seen as being in "direct conflict with the Constitution."[33]

Irish views on temperance and abolitionism furthered nativist hostility, which was exacerbated by their dramatic expansion as part of the voting population. From 1850 to 1855, the Irish accounted for almost half of the total increase in Massachusetts' population, and while the native-born vote grew 14.7 percent, the foreign-born vote, comprised mostly of Irish, exploded at 194.6 percent.[34] Extreme nativists in the 1855 Massachusetts legislature moved to exclude foreigners from voting or office-holding rights completely. The state's Know-Nothing governor, Henry Gardner, proposed a twenty-one-year period following naturalization before newcomers could receive suffrage. The legislature adopted

[30] Hernon, *Celts, Catholics & Copperheads*, p. 66.

[31] Rice, *American Catholic Opinion in the Slavery Controversy*, p. 114.

[32] *The Pilot*, September 23, 1839.

[33] Hernon, *Celts, Catholics & Copperheads*, p. 59. Ryan, *Beyond the Ballot Box*, p. 130. Rice, *American Catholic Opinion in the Slavery Controversy*, pp. 78, 93, 95, 109. *The Pilot*, May 31, 1856, quoted in Rice, p. 95.

[34] Nonetheless, a lack of leadership, funding, and organized political machines at this point prevented Irish-Americans from fully taking advantage of their electoral power. O'Connor, *The Boston Irish*, p. 70.

this measure, along with acts mandating a literacy test for voting and the disbandment of foreign militia companies. Two more passages were required before the provision became an amendment to the state constitution. The 1856 legislature reduced the waiting period from twenty-one to fourteen years. In 1857, radical Republicans were able to lower the period to two years and the people of Massachusetts voted in favor of the amendment in an 1859 referendum. Additionally, the immigrants' overwhelming support of Democratic urban political machines further fostered Republican antagonism toward them, and some Freesoilers blamed the Irish vote for the defeat of their 1856 presidential candidate, John C. Frémont.[35]

Against nativism and abolitionism, Democrat Stephen Douglas was a heavy favorite of the Irish in the 1860 presidential contest. The New York *Irish American* endorsed Douglas, and *The Pilot* expressed the opinion that no Catholic should vote for Lincoln.[36] Nevertheless, Lincoln and the Republicans emerged victorious and firmly in control of government, at least in the North. By 1860 they controlled fourteen of eighteen governorships above the Mason-Dixon line, 102 of 146 Northern seats in the United States House of Representatives, and twenty-nine of thirty-six Northern seats in the Senate.[37]

Few expected an enthusiastic Irish-American response when Lincoln called for volunteers to help quash the rebellion after the South fired on Fort Sumter. After all, they had opposed Lincoln and denounced reform; they had remained loyal to the Democratic party, and had supported the South and the institution of slavery. However, many Irish in the North remained patriotic citizens of their adopted land, devoted to the Union and to the Constitution that governed it. The *Irish American* claimed,

> For us . . . our duty . . . is clear and well-defined. Our standing in this community, the freedom and equality we proudly claim . . . come to us directly from the whole Union, to which our first alle-

[35] A number of Radicals urged total defeat of the suffrage measure, and Republicans in the western United States feared that the measure, if it passed, would hamper efforts to attract German voters to the party. Handlin, *Boston's Immigrants*, p. 204. Foner, *Free Soil, Free Labor, Free Men*, pp. 230–31, 250–51. Hernon, *Celts, Catholics & Copperheads*, p. 64.

[36] Frawley, *Patrick Donahoe*, p. 168. O'Connor, *Fitzpatrick's Boston*, p. 186. Gibson, *The Attitudes of the New York Irish*, p. 105.

[37] Silbey, *A Respectable Minority*, p. 18.

giance is due, under the guarantees of the Constitution which we have sworn to uphold.[38]

Some viewed the war as an opportunity to increase the patriotism of both the populace in general and the Irish-American community in particular, and to reinvigorate the spirit of civic virtue. On November 2, 1861, *The Pilot* argued,

> The war of the North is a just one. . . . This same war has already made us love our country better than ever we did before; it will correct the corruption of all our political proceedings; and at the end of it we shall be contupled in spirit and in ability to defend the integrity of the Republic against any foe.[39]

The Catholic Church's emphasis that government must be lawfully established helped preclude Irish-American support of the illegitimate government of the Southern revolt against the Constitution. Furthermore, England's pro-Confederate sentiments antagonized Irish support for the Rebels. When the *Trent* affair erupted in late 1861, caused by Federal Captain Charles Wilkes's forcible removal of Confederate envoys from the British ship, the *Irish American* welcomed the prospect of war with Britain. Similarly, some members of the Irish Brigade embraced the possibility of conflict and greeted the news "[w]ith a wild and joyous feeling," imagining Irish exiles envisioning "the revivification of 'Erin, our mother and discrowned queen.' "[40] Of course, sectionalism played a major role in determining loyalties, and many a Southern Irishman served in the Confederate ranks during the war.

The Irish Charitable Society unanimously adopted resolutions denouncing any "principle or movement that would dissever these United States" and, after affirming their "love for the Union and Constitution," summoned all Irish to support the

---

[38] *Irish American*, April 20, 1861.

[39] *The Pilot*, November 2, 1861.

[40] *The Pilot* (June 8, 1861) printed: "When England takes part with the South, she can have no possible good object in view. . . . When we Irish are side by side with England in any quarrel, we *must* be in the wrong. It is the natural instinct of our race to hate the English side, and take the other; and if the southern States of America have England for their backer, they must look on it as a thing of fate to have Ireland for their foe." *The Pilot*, October 26, 1861. *Irish American*, January 11, 1862. Handlin, *Boston's Immigrants*, pp. 208–209. O'Connor, *Fitzpatrick's Boston*, p. 187.

Union regardless of sectional preferences.[41] Following the bombardment of Fort Sumter, Irish-American newspapers announced their support of the Union. While criticizing Northern fanatics for antagonizing the South, the *Irish American* argued that secession was unjustifiable and called upon its readers to support the Union. *The Pilot* announced in January 1861 that "Catholics have only one course to adopt, only one line to follow. Stand by the Union; fight for the Union; die for the Union."[42]

Nevertheless, articles in *The Pilot* consistently stressed that Irish volunteers went forth in support of the Union and not to free the slaves. The July 20, 1861 edition of the newspaper declared that "Not one volunteer in a hundred has gone forth . . . to liberate slaves."[43] In the summer of 1862 the anti-black feelings of the Irish-Americans erupted into riots in several cities; for example, two to three thousand Irishmen assaulted blacks in Brooklyn on August 4, 1862.[44]

The Emancipation Proclamation created a maelstrom of Irish hostility toward Lincoln and the Republican party. *The Pilot* assessed the administration as "incompetent, fanatic, radical" and noted widespread Irish sentiments that Lincoln had betrayed them to the anti-Catholic abolitionist movement. According to *The Pilot*, Emancipation would harden the Southern will to fight, postpone the war's conclusion, and result in hordes of freed blacks streaming north to take jobs from white laborers. The newspaper proclaimed in May 1863 that "the Irish spirit for the war is dead!" and, in September, observed that "At one time we did support Lincoln . . . he changed, and so have we." The New York *Irish American* concurred, condemning the Emancipation as giving "to the South the strongest incentive to fight with greater desperation than ever" and stating that it signified Lincoln's surrender to radical abolitionism.[45]

---

[41] Cullen, *The Story of the Irish in Boston*, p. 32.

[42] *Irish American*, November 17, 1860. *The Pilot*, January 1, 1861. *The Pilot* concurred that "fanaticism for the negro compelled the South to revolt. . . ." *The Pilot*, April 4, 1863.

[43] *The Pilot* further asserted, "The white men of the free states do not wish to labor side by side with the negro."

[44] Hernon, *Celts, Catholics & Copperheads*, p. 19.

[45] *The Pilot*, October 4, 1862; December 13, 1862; January 17, 1863; May 30, 1863; September 19, 1863. *Irish American*, January 10, 1863, quoted in Gibson, *The Attitudes of the New York Irish*, pp. 142–43.

The Pilot supported Major General George B. McClellan as the Democratic candidate for President in 1864. According to the paper, Lincoln was alternately a "boob" or a cunning Mephistopheles. Only if the Democrats captured the White House could the restoration of the Union be achieved, as they would not be vindictive in accepting the South's return. *The Pilot* further argued that "the Democratic party . . . has been . . . the only hope and refuge to which the oppressed of Ireland could flee" and claimed, "the opposition . . . has distinguished itself by . . . its narrow bigotry . . . and its open hatred for the rights of the poor and laboring classes." While the *Irish American* did not support the peace movement, it endorsed McClellan in August and went so far as to deem him "the most untrammelled candidate ever presented, on an unblemished record . . . his only Mentors the voices of the Fathers of the Republic. . . ."[46] Dale Baum calculated that Massachusetts Irish-Americans "preferred McClellan to Lincoln at a rate of nine to one." While Irish-born voters comprised 10 percent of the Massachusetts electorate in 1864, they provided 37 percent of McClellan's vote versus a mere 2 percent for Lincoln.[47]

Guiney greatly differed from the majority of Irish by supporting Lincoln and the causes for which he stood. As early as September 1861 Guiney repudiated his support of the Democrats and wrote, "The sordid misers who are not accumulating in these novel times, and the craven Democrats who rot in office and starve out of it, are trying all over the country to get up an opposition to the government."[48]

Furthermore, Guiney realized the wrongs of slavery and agreed in principle with the abolitionists. In July 1861 he wrote his wife that "slavery curses the land in which it is."[49] Near Big Bethel, Virginia, at the end of March 1862, five black females entered

---

[46] *The Pilot,* June 25, 1864; September 3, 1864; October 15, 1864; and November 5, 1864, quoted in O'Connor, *Fitzpatrick's Boston,* p. 209. Gibson, *The Attitudes of the New York Irish,* p. 165. *Irish American,* November 12, 1864. The November 12 edition was distributed in advance of its usual time, so as to reach people before the November 8 election.

[47] Dale Baum, "The 'Irish Vote' and Party Politics in Massachusetts, 1860–1871," *Civil War History,* vol. 26, no. 2 (March 1980), 122.

[48] Patrick R. Guiney to Jennie Guiney, Arlington Heights, Va., September 1st, 1861.

[49] Patrick R. Guiney to Jennie Guiney, Washington, D.C., July 14, 1861.

the Ninth's picket line while Guiney was on duty and he proudly proclaimed, "In the name of old Ireland and Massachusetts, I set you free." In thanking a company that presented him with a sword in late August 1862, Guiney mentioned "Irish devotion to the vindication and establishment of human liberty," presumably for both Irish-Americans and the slaves. In a speech supporting Ulysses S. Grant's candidacy for president in 1868, Guiney said that the "seething despotism . . . of human slavery was menacing and shaking this Republic . . . " before the Civil War erupted.[50]

Guiney openly expressed his sentiments, and these political views and support for Lincoln caused him trouble within the Ninth Massachusetts. By February 1863 a saddened Guiney wrote, "I find but very few whose views are congenial to me. I am weary of expressing my opinions. I would like to serve on to the end—to the triumphant end—but how painful in the midst of men who are constantly talking down the government!"[51] While campaigning for Lincoln during the 1864 election, Guiney admitted, "the great bulk of my countrymen differ with me in politics, as they have a perfect right to do, and I differ with them, as I have an equally perfect right to do. . . ." After the war, Guiney noted in a speech, "During the war I held opinions and spoke them on public matters, as you well know. These opinions did me no good at the time. Indeed, they were not agreeable to my dearest friends, as I had occasion to know."[52]

Several incidents illustrate the hostility some Irish-Americans felt at Guiney's political outspokenness, as well as the jealousy occasioned by his swift rise to command. The most serious occurred when, upon assuming command of the regiment following Cass's death, Guiney faced a conspiracy of eleven officers who designed to replace him with another. The clique sent a petition to Governor Andrew criticizing Guiney for his absence from the battle of Malvern Hill on July 1, 1862. They ignored the fact that, at the time, Guiney was extremely ill with malaria which rendered

---

[50] *The Pilot*, April 26, 1862; September 13, 1862. Draft of one of Guiney's speeches in support of Ulysses S. Grant and written in Guiney's hand, located in the Rare Book Room of Dinand Library, College of the Holy Cross.

[51] Patrick R. Guiney to Jennie Guiney, Head Quarters 2nd Brigade, February 11, 1863.

[52] Patrick R. Guiney to Editor of the *Boston Journal*, Boston, September 27, 1864 in Guiney scrapbook, 3. Guiney scrapbook, 10, 13.

him unable to move without help and confined him to an ambulance. One newspaper noted, "Col. Guiney, being a gentleman as well as a soldier, was outside of a certain grog-house ring at the North End of Boston, which undertook to control the regiment. These men fomented dissatisfaction among the officers and finally induced eleven of them to bring charges against Col. Guiney, the substance of which was that he was 'suddenly taken ill' before the battle of Malvern Hill. . . ." In 1864, when Guiney campaigned in support of Lincoln's re-election bid, the issue was resurrected in retaliation. The article's defense of the colonel continued: "Guiney's only sin is that he unites with nine out of ten of the soldiers of our army and the great bulk of the loyal population of the North in advocating the election of President Lincoln. For this, those worn-out lies are paraded again in the columns of the [Boston] *Courier*."[53]

The North End slum, as a Democratic stronghold, proved to be troublesome to Guiney in this incident and throughout the war. The petitioners' ringleader, Captain Timothy O'Leary, was a resident of Salem, but he had close ties to the North End; in February 1863 his friends there gave O'Leary a sword and belt.[54] People associated with the North End continually antagonized Guiney throughout the war with public criticism, letters to Governor Andrew, and general disdain. For example, in the spring of 1863 Guiney disciplined two non-commissioned officers for absence without leave by reducing their rank, putting them in the guard house for a night, and having them tied for a day, labelled "skulker." North-Ender Eneas Smyth retaliated by requesting various inquiries of this action and by penning a vicious assault on the Ninth Massachusetts' commander, in which he deemed Guiney a "political and skedaddling Colonel." Guiney wrote that "the unarmed traitors of the North End encourage them [i.e., officers opposing him] in seeing hostility to me because I am for the government in all its measures—and they know that I am." Guiney further recognized the slum as a stronghold of the Copperhead movement, which opposed Lincoln and prosecution of the war, advocating a compromised peace instead.[55]

[53] Guiney scrapbook, 11–12.
[54] *The Pilot*, February 21, 1863. Guiney scrapbook, 2.
[55] Boston *Post*, April 17, 1863. Patrick R. Guiney to Jennie Guiney, Head Quarters 2nd Brigade, February 26, 1863. Patrick R. Guiney to Jennie Guiney, Log-House at Camp, April 13, 1863.

There were also socioeconomic factors in this situation. Dennis P. Ryan wrote that "Irish students who matriculated from Boston College, Holy Cross College in Worcester, or Harvard were an unusually ambitious lot." In addition, many Irish-Americans living in the slums and tenements of the North End and Fort Hill districts felt hostility toward those who moved upward.[56] Guiney arrived in America before the mass immigration of the famine Irish which started in 1845. Although financial reasons prevented his graduation from Holy Cross, Guiney did become a lawyer successful enough to move to the Roxbury suburbs and to enjoy membership in the Irish Charitable Society. Among the underprivileged as a youth, Guiney had achieved a measure of success and wealth which eluded most Irish-Americans. He looked down on lower-class behavior and wrote in 1862, "What do I care for a drunken rabble?"[57] Guiney's status as an educated lawyer gave him job security, and no reason to fear the emancipation of the slaves. The coupling of his intellectual enlightenment and his economic condition directly resulted in Guiney's political views. This no doubt antagonized members of the North End already angered by Guiney's political sentiments.[58]

Another complication came from the intrigues of officers and outsiders seeking to control advancement within the regiment, something which greatly bothered Guiney. Boston Irish leaders such as Patrick Donahoe and Bernard S. Treanor sought to pro-

---

[56] Ryan, *Beyond the Ballot Box*, p. 73. Levine, *The Irish and Irish Politicians*, p. 103.

[57] Patrick R. Guiney to Jennie Guiney, Head Quarters 9th Massachusetts, November 30, 1862.

[58] The professions of those who petitioned Governor Andrew following Guiney's promotion indicate that social and economic differences worsened the tensions between him and the other officers. Of the nine signers whose occupations are known at the time of mustering in, only one, a law student, was involved in professional work. Among the other jobs held by members of the clique were bootmaker, tanner, blindmaker, shoemaker, clerk, custom house worker, and gasfitter; ringleader Timothy O'Leary was a tailor. Similarly, two other chronic troublemakers for Guiney, Captains James F. McGunnigle and John C. Willey, were a bootmaker and a turnkey, respectively. On the other hand, one of his earliest friends in the regiment was a professional, a physician named Edward Fitzgerald. See the muster roll printed in Daniel George Macnamara, *The History of the Ninth Regiment Massachusetts Volunteer Infantry* (Boston: E. B. Stillings & Company, 1899). Hereafter cited as Macnamara, *Ninth Regiment*. See also *Massachusetts Soldiers, Sailors, and Marines in the Civil War, and Marines in the Civil War* 8 vols. and index, compiled and published by the Adjutant General of Massachusetts, 1931–1937. Information on the Ninth Massachusetts is available in volume 1.

mote their candidates for various commissions. Timothy Regan, a
member of the Ninth Massachusetts, wrote in his diary that "not
always has merit had anything to do with . . . promotions, the
influence of friends at home being 'the power behind the
throne.' "[59] Officers within the regiment tried to engineer promotions for their cronies as well. Regan noted, "I am satisfied that
the Colonel is not to blame, but that it is the doings of some of
the captains who send for their friends to join the companies with
a view of promoting them to be noncommissioned officers, and
then to engineer them into lieutenancies."[60]

Guiney may have felt wearied and troubled that his political
views led to personal attacks against him. Nonetheless, he remained unbowed and continued in his outspoken support of the
cause for which he fought and of its leader, Abraham Lincoln.
While at home soon after receiving his horrible head wound at
the Wilderness, Guiney gave a speech at a pro-Lincoln rally of
Union supporters in Roxbury before the 1864 election. The meeting convened at a packed Institute Hall in Roxbury, and throngs
waited outside in a vain attempt to gain admission. Upon Guiney's
introduction, a number of Democrats present began hissing to
show their disfavor of his views, but the audience drowned out
the disrupters with three ringing cheers for Guiney and a round
of applause. Some wanted to eject the protesters, but Guiney
asked them not to touch the offenders. He continued with his
speech, stating that he once felt proud to be a Democrat but
could not support them under traitorous leaders. Guiney also remarked that Stephen Douglas, so popular among Irish-Americans

---

[59] Timothy J. Regan diary, January 28, 1862. Hereafter cited as Regan diary.
William L. Burton, *Melting Pot Soldiers: The Union's Ethnic Regiments* (Ames: Iowa
State University Press, 1988), pp. 131–35. An example of this meddling came
during the formation of the second Massachusetts Irish regiment. Patrick Donahoe supported Francis Parker for its commander while Bernard S. Treanor
criticized Donohoe's choice, and claimed that he could submit the name of a
gentleman from among 25 Irish nationalists. Irishmen from New York contacted
Governor Andrew with their opinion that he should staff the regiment with New
York Irish and push to get it attached to Brigadier General Thomas F. Meagher's
Irish Brigade. Andrew announced plans for two new Irish regiments, one of
which could go to the Irish Brigade, in an effort to placate the various parties.
The Twenty-eighth and Twenty-ninth Massachusetts Infantry Regiments went to
New Yorkers William Montieth and Thomas J. Murphy, respectively, and Andrew
soothed a dissappointed Parker by assigning him command of the Thirty-second
Massachusetts.

[60] Regan diary, October 26, 1862.

in the 1860 election, would have supported the present government. He then quoted Irish hero Daniel O'Connell's loathing
of slavery. Concluding with a critical recounting of McClellan's
military career, he received thunderous applause for his speech.[61]

Soon afterward, Guiney gave a similar oration at Dorchester on
October 4, 1864. He happily noted that here, men were "allowed
to come forward with their voices for the Union and speak in
peace and without disturbance." Guiney then attacked slavery as
an evil which "simmered, and burned into the very vitals of the
nation, until, at last, it raised up armies to fight against our Republic," and deemed it the "strength of the rebellion." He again
invoked O'Connell's opposition to slavery and reviewed McClellan's military record, criticizing his waste of time in sieges (referring to Yorktown) and blaming his slowness for the Second
Manassas debacle. McClellan and the Democrats, Guiney said, desired no more than the restoration of the Union, while Republicans wanted to combat those who perpetrated "a great crime
against the human race." He also said that any man who acted to
weaken the government "will have committed a crime for which
a life of penance cannot expiate."[62]

After the war, Guiney maintained that he "was the only member of that regiment [the Ninth Massachusetts] who called himself a Republican."[63] The issue of his support of Lincoln followed
him as well. In late 1866, an article in *The Pilot* called the Colonel
a "high-minded, honorable man," but also noted "He opposed
General McClellan, which we are sorry for. . . ."[64]

Guiney's situation, that of an enlightened and educated Irishmen holding political views different from the bulk of his countrymen, parallels that of Thomas Francis Meagher. A New York
lawyer, Meagher became a popular lecturer. He was the only Irishman of national prominence to support the Lincoln administration in the 1864 election, a stance that seriously crippled his
popularity among the Irish community. American Catholics
called him a "Red Republican," a term used for those committed
to promoting atheism and disrupting social order, morality and

---

[61] Guiney scrapbook, 2.
[62] *Daily Advertiser,* October 7, 1864 in Guiney scrapbook, 12–13.
[63] Guiney scrapbook, 10.
[64] *The Pilot,* October 13, 1866.

religion.[65] Guiney and Meagher shared a friendship, no doubt largely based and sustained on their similar political views. Included in this volume is a telling letter from Meagher to Guiney, in which Meagher unleashed a scathing criticism of the Democratic party and of the Irish who blindly followed its traitorous course. Several ethnic periodicals published the letter and fiercely attacked its author. The *Irish American* criticized his "uncalled for and unwarranted attack upon our countrymen" and wrote of Meagher, "It is not an enviable position for one for whom a better fate might have been hoped; but it is of his own choosing. . . . [B]etween him and the people who loved and trusted him once he has opened a gulf he never can bridge over." Another edition lamented a pro-Lincoln speech he gave:

> In General Meagher's fall from the high position he once held in the esteem and affection of his countrymen, we see only a subject for regret; our indignation at his unprovoked attack upon our people has long since subsided into contempt, and we have no desire to add a deeper tint to an act that has gone so far to darken the record of a life, of which the promise was once so fair.[66]

Guiney did not suffer such a fate. After the war, he maintained a prominent position among the Irish-American community and participated in political events. However, that is a matter to be discussed in the epilogue of this book. First, here are his letters—the writings of a civilian at war and an officer in command. They reveal not only the experiences and thoughts of a Boston Irish Catholic soldier, but also the hidden tensions within that immigrant community. Guiney's significant views and observations not only illuminate his personal independence of thought, but also the political landscape which he tried to improve.

---

[65] Hernon, *Celts, Catholics & Copperheads*, pp. 105–106. Rice, *American Catholic Opinion in the Slavery Controversy*, p. 91.

[66] Thomas Francis Meagher to Patrick R. Guiney, New York, October 7, 1863. *Irish American*, October 15, 1864; November 12, 1864.

1861: ". . . a cause bright and grand as the Sun."

With Lincoln's call for volunteers to quash the Southern rebellion, Thomas Cass offered Massachusetts Governor John A. Andrew his services in organizing a regiment. Born in Farmley, Queen's County, Ireland in 1821, Cass arrived with his parents in America when he was nine months old. After education in Boston, he married and by age twenty he owned merchant ships trading in the Azore Islands and held stock in the Tow-Boat Company. With strong loyalties to the Democratic party, he served as an officer of his Boston ward. Cass joined a predominantly Irish militia group, the Columbian Artillery, and enjoyed rapid promotions to become its commander. However, nativist hostility led state officials to disband the unit, which met unofficially and without state pay or arms thereafter. In the present national crisis, Cass used its former members as the nucleus of a volunteer regiment, with himself as its colonel. Patrick Donahoe, editor of The Pilot, *supported the effort, promoted recruitment in his weekly periodical, and served as treasurer of a citizen's committee convened for the purpose of raising funds to furnish the regiment.*[1]

Many Boston Irish heeded the call to arms sweeping across the North and enlisted in Colonel Cass's unit, initially designated the Thirteenth Massachusetts Volunteer Militia. The Irishmen initially gathered at Faneuil Hall and used the historic structure as their barracks. The steamer Nellie Baker *transported the men to the open air of Long Island in Boston Harbor on May 12, 1861 to begin their training; at this time, Guiney was First Lieutenant of Company I under Captain Bernard S. Treanor.*[2]

A three-mile spit of land in Boston Harbor, Long Island had witnessed military action before. In June 1776 a naval battle between revolutionary forces and the British occurred offshore, and Commodore William Bainbridge advised its fortification in 1814, an action which helped save Boston, lying six miles away, from attack during war with the British.[3] *Now, the new recruits went to the southern side of the island and received instruction at Camp Wightman, named after Boston's mayor. Amid green,*

---

[1] Patrick Donahoe, born in Munnery, County Cavan, Ireland, on March 17, 1814, took over the failing Boston diocese newspaper in 1834. In partnership with Henry Devereaux, he renamed it *The Pilot*, added political and Irish news to its religious focus, and turned it into a successful publication. *The Pilot*, July 27, 1861. O'Connor, *Fitzpatrick's Boston*, pp. 16–17, 169, 194. Cullen, *The Story of the Irish in Boston*, pp. 227–30.

[2] Macnamara, *Ninth Regiment*, pp. 6–10.

[3] Patrick J. Connelly, *Islands of Boston Harbor 1630–1932* (Dorchester, Mass.: Chapple Publishing Company, Ltd, 1932), pp. 20–21.

spacious fields, the troops engaged in company and battalion drill, guard mounting, picket duty, daily dress parades, bayonet charges, and much double-quick marching.

Reports of difficulties in the Irish regiment led Governor Andrew to send George D. Wells, a Harvard Law School graduate, to judge the situation.[4] *On May 16, Wells sent Andrew a private letter advising that no more Irish be sent to Long Island, lest it result in "strife + bloodshed." He found the Irishmen to be "a fine body as a whole," but they needed adequate officers in order to become an efficient military unit. While Cass and some officers were "good men," many others were "ignorant—vicious—vile." He questioned whether it was it wise to allow "the sweepings of our jails" to elect "officers of their own stripe." Wells reported that the men "have no respect for their officers, + care nothing for their authority," and believed the regiment should not be sent to Washington or Baltimore, lest it tarnish the reputation of Massachusetts. As an example, Wells cited an incident in which he observed a "sentry . . . patrolling with bare feet + a pipe in his mouth. . . ." Wells felt the Irish could be turned into good soldiers, but he recommended that Andrew investigate the situation in person. In particular, Wells thought the governor should consider giving the regiment a different set of officers or breaking it up and distributing its companies to other units, so that the men would "be overcome by superior force + feel that they* must *obey."*[5]

Difficulties also emerged with Colonel Cass, who proved "arbitrary in his manner, and severe in his decisions and discipline as a commanding officer."[6] *At Andrew's request, Bernard Treanor wrote a lengthy letter assessing some of the officers of the regiment and recent incidents of camp. Although Cass had long been involved in peacetime militia groups, a possibly biased Treanor found that the colonel "does not understand battalion movements," and further, he lacked "the necessary power and pa-*

---

[4] George D. Wells was commissioned lieutenant colonel of the First Massachusetts Volunteer Infantry on May 22, 1861, and mustered out to date on July 30, 1862, to receive promotion as colonel and commander of the Thirty-fourth Massachusetts Volunteer Infantry. He received a wound on May 15, 1864 at New Market, Virginia and was killed on October 13, 1864 near Cedar Creek. He received a posthumous brevet promotion to brigadier general to date October 12, 1864. *Massachusetts Soldiers, Sailors,* 1: 2; 3: 590.

[5] George D. Wells to Governor John A. Andrew, Boston, May 16, 1861. Original located in the Andrew collection, Massachusetts Historical Society, Boston, Massachusetts.

[6] Macnamara, *Ninth Regiment,* p. 183.

tience of imparting his own knowledge to others." Treanor further commented,

> *His commands are given in such a manner—so quick—that but few understand them, and then the officers receive abundance of oaths and curses for not performing movements which he understands at best but very imperfectly. . . . A multiplicity of the most undignified acts of various kinds— Censuring rudely the officers if anything is wrong with the men, and then telling the men, if they make complaints of anything, that the fault is with their own officers, convince every one capable of judging that his habitual manner is anything but that of a gentleman. . . .*

Treanor also recalled an incident in which Colonel Cass rushed at a soldier who was smoking while being drummed out of the regiment and "with his own hand, [Cass] snatched, or knocked, the pipe out of the man's mouth."[7]

Many of the difficulties were eventually overcome as Colonel Cass worked to enforce discipline and to forge his unit into a potent, effective weapon. With time and training, the rough Irish civilians began to master their drills and hold themselves with a more military bearing. Colonel Cass specifically trained the regiment in double quick drills, and the men would let out a loud Irish yell when they charged with bayonets. The Irishmen practiced the manual of arms frequently and took pride in their proficiency in handling their weapons. An occasional competition even occurred, such as when Lieutenant James McCafferty defeated his challenger, Sergeant-Major John Teague, in a drill contest. On Sundays the men rested, with the exception of guard-mounting and dress parade. Family members, friends, and sweethearts visited the men, and the day was spent in pleasantries until the sorrow of farewell. They were unsure which would be the final Sunday before the regiment went off to defend Washington.[8]

Camp Wightman
June 4th 1861

My Darling:

Since I received your affectionate note of Sunday eve I have realized more than ever the possible rashness of my resolution to

---

[7] B. S. Treanor to Governor John A. Andrew, Camp Wightman, Long Island, June 10, 1861. Original located in the Andrew collection, Massachusetts Historical Society, Boston, Massachusetts.

[8] Macnamara, *Ninth Massachusetts*, pp. 11–14.

volunteer. I care not for myself, but for you and my little Darling, my mind is occupied with heavy thoughts—I might say misgivings, as to the future. Compensation, at present, I fear is out of the question. Government is proverbially slow. It will be so in this case. Some months may elapse before payment is made. In the mean-time what will you do Darling? I know not what to say to you. It is too late for me to recede, I cannot—I would be over-whelmed with shame if I did so. I cannot entertain the thought. But my forebodings as to your welfare and that of my little angel cause me to tremble, and they will do so until I know that you both are out of danger. I expect a small sum of money by Sunday next. If I get it, Darling, I will send, or, if you are down here, give it to you.

In relation to Mr. [William] Gaston; I went to see him—he thought matters would be all right.[9] He submitted your claims to a committee having in charge the volunteer fund and, doubtless, the matter has been settled ere this.[10] You must go and see him. He seemed very kindly disposed.

You will exert yourself to share in this fund—it is not charity—it belongs to families of volunteers. This is the only way open to us at present, until government pays up. Do your business quietly letting no one know. Be sure and call to see Mr. Gaston. He will do all he can in the matter.

My Darling, as for myself, I am well and I would say happy were

---

[9] William Gaston served as a member of the Roxbury Common Council from 1849 to 1853 and as that body's president from 1852 to 1853. He went on to become mayor of Roxbury (1861–62) and mayor of Boston (1871–72). *A Catalogue of the City Councils of Boston 1822–1890; Roxbury 1846–1867; Charlestown 1847–1873* (Boston: Rockwell and Churchill, 1891), pp. 168–69, 205–207, 211–12.

[10] On May 23, 1861, the Massachusetts legislature approved an act in aid of the families of volunteers. The statute allowed towns to raise money, including by taxation, to be applied under the direction of the mayor, aldermen, or city council for the assistance of the wives and children of those mustered into the state militia or army of the United States. Reimbursements were to be provided to towns and cities from the state treasury at one dollar per week for the wife and one dollar per week for each child or dependant parent of such volunteers, given that the entire sum would not exceed twelve dollars per month for the dependants of a single soldier. The Roxbury city government clearly moved quickly to set up such a fund. *Acts and Resolves Passed by the General Court of Massachusetts in the Year 1861* (Boston: William White, Printer to the State, 1861), pp. 649–50.

it not for the plight in which you are. I have everything necessary for me. When I do go, I trust I "Go where Glory waits me."

I will try and send you a pass before Sunday. God Bless You Darling.

Your Husband

On June 11, the Thirteenth Massachusetts Volunteer Militia mustered into United States service as the Ninth Massachusetts Volunteer Regiment. Colonel Cass replaced Company D's Captain James J. Pendergast with Guiney, newly promoted to captain. The company initially resisted the change, but soon accepted Guiney. William W. Doherty and John H. Rafferty served under Guiney as the company's first and second lieutenants, respectively.[11]

The troops ate off the land until June 12, when they received their first army rations. Colonel Cass heard of the mens' discontent with their food allotment and attempted to stretch supplies by providing thinner soup and weaker coffee. The increase in amount at the expense of quality failed to fool the disgruntled troops, who reluctantly accepted the situation.[12] *On June 24 the regiment returned via the* Nellie Baker *to Boston's Long Wharf and paraded through the city to the State House, where Governor Andrew presented the men with a Bay State flag and declared that the nation knew no distinction "between its native-born citizens and those born in other countries"—a far cry from the discrimination previously experienced by the immigrants. Passing huge throngs watching from the streets, the Irish soldiers proceeded to Boston Common, where Mayor Joseph Wightman and other city dignitaries reviewed the regiment. Cass delivered a brief oration for which he received cheers and the Ninth accepted a silk American flag and a green silk Irish flag donated by the widow of ex-Mayor Harrison Gray Otis. Donahoe presented Cass with ten bags containing a hundred dollars of gold each, to help outfit the regiment, and*

---

[11] Regan diary, June 11, 1861. Macnamara, *Ninth Regiment*, pp. 10–11, 17–18. William W. Doherty resigned as first lieutenant on November 1, 1861. John H. Rafferty of East Cambridge was commissioned first lieutenant of Company A on November 2, 1861, and was killed at Malvern Hill, July 1, 1862. *Massachusetts Soldiers, Sailors,* 1: 640, 643.

[12] Macnamara, *Ninth Regiment*, 21–22.

the men reboarded the Nellie Baker *to return to Long Island.*[13] *Despite this display of Irish patriotism for their adopted land, elements of nativist hostility existed in the crowd that watched the regiment depart, as one onlooker commented to another, "There goes a load of Irish rubbish out of the city."*[14]

With excitement and anticipation, the Ninth Massachusetts left for Washington, D.C. the next day.[15] *Guiney's Company D, along with Captain James E. Gallagher's Company A, Captain William Madigan's Company C, and Lieutenant Colonel Cromwell G. Rowell—in all, 204 men—boarded the steamer* Cambridge *at 2:30 in the afternoon; the rest of the regiment travelled aboard the* Pembroke *and the unarmed* Ben DeFord.[16] *By June 27th, the vessels drew near Virginia and passed Cape Charles that evening. The ships anchored near Fort Monroe at five the next morning, and Colonel Cass visited that impregnable Federal stronghold with his staff officers later that day.*[17] *The following letter, written on board the ship, has very shaky handwriting. Guiney mentions that the steamer was rocking in wavy water, although his hand may have quivered from a bout of seasickness.*

On Board the Cambridge in
sight of Fort Monroe
June 28th /61

My Dear Jennie:

As we will land in a few minutes I have but time to say a few words. I was quite sea sick part of the way but I am well now. On

---

[13] Regan diary, June 24, 1861. Macnamara, *Ninth Regiment*, pp. 22–25. O'Connor, *Fitzpatrick's Boston*, pp. 194–95. Cullen, *The Story of the Irish in Boston*, p. 228.

[14] *The Pilot*, August 24, 1861.

[15] *The Pilot*, July 13, 1861. Regan diary, June 25, 1861. Macnamara's narrative mistakenly places the departure date at June 26. Macnamara, *Ninth Regiment*, p. 25.

[16] Lieutenant Cromwell G. Rowell, a Boston policeman, resigned his commission on October 23, 1861. Captain James E. Gallagher was a bricklayer and resigned his commission on July 9, 1862. Before the war, Captain William Madigan was a Boston printer; he was killed in action on June 27, 1862, at Gaines' Mill. *Massachusetts Soldiers, Sailors*, 1: 617, 620, 635.

[17] *The Pilot*, July 13, 1861. Macnamara, *Ninth Regiment*, pp. 25-27. Sergeant Michael A. Finnerty, a clerk from Milford, served as a correspondent for *The Pilot*. His first article was printed on July 13, 1861 under his signature; subsequent articles were simply signed "M. A. F." Guiney refers to Colonel Cass's role in editing these letters. After Guiney assumed command of the regiment following

the whole we have had a pleasant voyage. The officers of the ship are very gentlemanly and attentive. I can see from here a Rebel Battery on the shore—but if they knew when they are well off they will let us alone. We are ready for them. However, we do not anticipate any trouble until we are going up the Potomac to Washington. Then we expect a brush. We have plenty of ammunition and cannon on Board. The next time I write to you it will be from Washington. We will be there tomorrow.

I have every comfort thanks to your kindness and foresight. I would like to say other and sweet words to you but I must wait another opportunity. I mail this at Fort Monroe. Love to friends, to Lizzie and little angel. God protect you and me and little Julia.[18]

Your Husband

[On the side is written:]
Father Scully, Col. Cass and all the staff officers are on board the Ben Deford anchored just above here—the major is on board the Pembroke just behind. We have had her in tow for the past two days and let go of her this morning. Write to me at Washington unless I direct you differently.

The ship is rocking so I cannot write plain.

Guiney

The little flotilla carrying the regiment entered the Potomac River later on June 28th. A large steamer, the Quaker City, *passed by and warned Colonel Cass to proceed cautiously near Matthias Point, informing the colonel that Southerners had occupied it and probably fortified it with artillery. The day before, Commander James H. Ward had attacked the position with his side-wheel steamer* Thomas Freeborn *and two smaller*

Cass's death, *The Pilot* did not maintain a correspondent with the Ninth. Following Cass's death, Finnerty wrote that he would resign, but he remained in service and eventually became captain of Guiney's old Company D on March 30, 1863. Patrick R. Guiney to Jennie Guiney, Arlington Heights near Washington, D.C., August 1, 1861. *The Pilot,* August 2, 1862. *Massachusetts Soldiers, Sailors,* 1: 664.

[18] Guiney often refers to Louise as "Loolie," but it appears, from the context, that "Julie" also is Louise.

vessels under Lieutenant Chaplin. Ward landed a force and drove the Confederate skirmishers in, but had to retreat upon striking the Rebel main body, at the cost of his own life and four wounded. Cass issued ammunition to his men and planned to land at Matthias Point if attacked, but as the regiment passed the position on June 29th, the Rebels provided no opposition.[19] The regiment's only casualty so far was a nineteen-year-old farmer, Private Owen W. Garland of Company E, who fell overboard and drowned in the early hours of the day.[20]

Later on the 29th, the flotilla steamed by George Washington's home at Mount Vernon, inspiring many of the regiment to feel that he gazed upon them as they traveled to preserve the Union he helped create.[21] That evening the ships reached their destination, the nation's capital. The Massachusetts Irishmen debarked at the Wharf and bivouacked nearby. The next day, June 30, President Abraham Lincoln welcomed the regiment and addressed the men, an incident which Guiney relates in the following letter with surprisingly little commentary. He probably had not converted to the staunch Republicanism which would mark his political views in the coming months.[22]

Washington, D.C.
July 2nd 1861

My Dear Jennie:

When I was at Fort Monroe I wrote to you and hope you received my note. From Fort Monroe we came up the Potomac river. On our voyage up we anticipated trouble. The day before we came up the river an engagement took place and the gallant commander of the U. S. Boat "Freeborn" lost his life by a rebel rifle shot. We were obliged to pass up the river at the same point, and, of course, we were already for resistance. The place is called Matthias' Point. When we came there we had the ships cannon growling at the rebel Batteries within sixty feet of us; but they did

---

[19] Macnamara, *Ninth Regiment*, pp. 27-28. Michael H. Macnamara, *The Irish Ninth in Bivouac and Battle* (Boston: Lee and Shepard, 1867), p. 36. Hereafter cited as Macnamara, *Bivouac*.

[20] *The Pilot*, July 13, 1861. Macnamara, *Ninth Regiment*, p. 29. *Massachusetts Soldiers, Sailors*, 1: 646.

[21] *The Pilot*, July 13, 1861.

[22] Macnamara, *Ninth Regiment*, pp. 29–30.

not fire upon us. However we gave them a couple of bomb-shells as momentos of our regard. The shells made them fly some. We could see them running to and fro. Then we approached the famous Acquia Creek and many other points of Rebel strength but their receptions at each were extremely cold. If they attacked us it was the intention to land our troops at some distance from the attacking point and, while the ship's cannon were paying their respects to the batteries, to advance upon the enemy's rear and, with fixed bayonets, to give them "down the banks." However we sailed on, and arrived at Washington on last Saturday morning; but the ship in which I was, was run ashore by a blundering officer, who had charge of the wheel. So we were obliged to go up to Washington in a small river boat. Having landed in the city we were placed in the yard of the Arsenal, where we slept all night, on the grass—and under a most beautiful bed curtain all bespangled with the diamonds of heaven. I slept well. Next morning we took up line of march for Virginia and pitched our tents here about three miles outside of Washington on a splendid Hill. Jennie, this is a beautiful place. I wish you could be here to enjoy it with me. It is one of those choice places which a pleasure party would seek to bathe themselves in refreshing shades—under lofty and waving trees. I am delighted with the location of our camp. It is grand. Only think of me wandering out of a fine brilliant moonlight evening amid all the natural beauties of such a place, and then think of me looking around through the hundred valleys and hills which hold within and upon them one hundred and twenty five thousand men who have all left "Dear ones at home," and draw their swords from motives of a noble patriotism to fight for our Republic, and you must have some idea of my feelings and musings when I am alone here enjoying an evening walk.

We do not expect to be here long—the probability is that we will advance farther into Virginia in a few days. The struggle is growing hot around here. I was out this morning making a scout with my company in the woods. The company broke into three parties and after sending two parties off under command of sergeants (sorry to say I have no lieutenants whom I would trust in such a position), I went off with about twenty of my men and entered a dense wood where it was said a few forlorn rebels were lurking. By my directions the three parties met at a stated point outside of the wood, we went through but met no one, yet we heard some sharp rifle shots not far off. We immediately swung off towards the place where the firing was going on and we found there another company of our Regmt. carrying off two of their number who had been shot by the rebels—not fatally I trust—one of them was struck with rifle ball in the leg and the other in the ankle. This indicates that the rebels were lying down in ambush. As soon as we got to the camp a skirmishing party was formed and have just left here to clear out the woods. They are in command of Lieut. [Philip E.] Redmond of my friend's [Captain Edward] Fitzgerald's company.[23] I hope he will return safe but I am afraid he will not as the rebels are notorious for selecting officers for targets to shoot at.

My brother James came to visit me today, he having seen my name in one of the Washington papers—he belongs to the First Regmt. Maine volunteers and is in camp one mile from here.[24] I have been anxiously enquiring for the Illinois Regmts. trying to find your brother James but I cannot find out where they are.

My Darling—I send you twenty dollars which is all I can get hold of at present. You must pray for me, that is all you can do for me now and when you do pray mingle the success of the cause in which I am engaged with my name. For whatever betides the soldiers I feel sure that very few of us care to return unless we are triumphant. A few days I think will bring about stirring events— Congress meets day after tomorrow and it is expected that after Congress meets, the President will advance the troops as far south as is consistent with health. By the way, I had the honor of conversing with "Old Abe" himself and shaking Sec. [of State William H.] Seward by the hand.[25] President Lincoln is a man of consider-

---

[23] A Salem physician, Captain Edward Fitzgerald resigned to date from September 3, 1861. Twenty-one-year-old Salem currier Lieutenant Philip E. Redmond was cashiered February 28, 1862. He re-enlisted and was mustered in on August 14, 1862, and died of disease on September 17, 1863, as second lieutenant of Company K. *Massachusetts Soldiers, Sailors*, 1: 649, 652, 655.

[24] James Guiney of Lewiston, Maine served in one of the regiments called upon by Lincoln to serve three months, the First Maine. When it disbanded, he enlisted and served a term as private in Company K, the "Lewiston Zouaves" of the Tenth Maine Regiment, and later served as a private of Company A of the Twenty-ninth Maine. John M. Gould, *History of the First-Tenth-Twenty-ninth Maine Regiment* (Portland: Stephen Berry, 1871), pp. 15, 332, 618.

[25] William H. Seward served two terms as governor of New York and in 1848 won election to the United States Senate. As one of the founders of the Republi-

able western intellect but he is ten times a homlier man than I expected he was.

Jennie, it may be some time before I can write to you again—I do not know how it will be. Kiss my little Darling for me ten times and remember me to Lizzie.

Affectionately yours
P. R. Guiney

P.S. Direct your letter to me—9th Regmt. M. V. U. S. A. Washington, D.C. and it will be sent out here put on—Capt. Co. "D"

P. R. G.

Washington, D.C.
July 9th 1861

My Darling:

Your welcome blessed little note came to me yesterday. I had written to you before I received yours and sent by Adam's Express Company. I hope you received it. Capt. Fitzgerald of Salem left here for home yesterday. I do not know whether he intends to return or not. On the 5th inst. as he and I were coming home to camp from Washington we were fired at by one or more rebels from a wood. Col. Cass who was just ahead of us was also fired upon in the same place. But happily we all escaped without injury. We were entirely unarmed, having just been over the Potomac paying a friendly visit to the N. Y. 69th.

I found [Major Thomas Francis] Meagher and Col. [Michael] Corcoran [of the Sixty-ninth New York] in good spirits and glad

---

can Party, Seward embraced abolitionism but eschewed nativism. Although considered a leading Republican candidate for the presidential election of 1860, Seward did not receive the nomination. He went on to serve the Lincoln administration as an effective secretary of state and continued in this capacity during Andrew Johnson's administration. Allen Johnson and Dumas Malone, eds., *Dictionary of American Biography* 22 vols. and index (New York: Charles Scribner's Sons, 1928-37), 16: 615-21.

to see me.[26] I do not think much of their Fort Corcoran.[27] It is a dangerous experiment. There is no rebel city, town, or village which its guns can harm. It cannot harm the rebels at all unless they come up to it on the easterly side which movement is very improbable. While if in the chances of war it should fall into hostile hands, down goes Washington in a few hours. It looked to me like an unintentional menace upon the city. However this is simply my opinion.

It is exceedingly hot here I assure you. I stand the heat very well. We expect to be put into a Brigade with 1st Regmt. M. V. and sent on further in a few days. However our address will still be Washington. Lieut. [Patrick T.] Hanley of Capt. [Christopher] Plunkett's Co. [B] was accidentally hurt the other day but is recovering.[28] Plunkett tendered his resignation to the government, but

---

[26] Guiney's friend, the Irish-born Thomas Francis Meagher, was an active partisan of Irish liberty. In the winter of 1862 he organized the "Irish Brigade" and received appointment as its brigadier. Meagher and his Irishmen served in many of the Army of the Potomac's battles, and performed especially bravely in charging Marye's Heights at Fredericksburg, where the brigade suffered severe casualties. Meagher also served in the western theater under Major General William T. Sherman from 1864 until the end of the war. In peacetime he held a government post in the territories, and served as acting governor of the territory of Montana until his accidental death by drowning on July 1, 1867. Michael Corcoran emigrated from Ireland to the United States, and joined the Sixty-ninth New York Militia as a private. By the outbreak of the war he had risen to become its colonel, and was captured while leading his regiment at the battle of First Manassas; later exchanged, he received promotion to brigadier general. In December 1863 Corcoran was riding with Meagher when his horse fell, killing him. Ezra J. Warner, *Generals in Blue: Lives of the Union Commanders* (Baton Rouge: Louisiana State University Press, 1964), pp. 93–94, 317–18. Hereafter cited as *Generals in Blue.*

[27] Fort Corcoran was in northern Virginia, close to the southern bank of the Potomac River, near the Aqueduct Bridge. The construction of several other Federal works further inland rendered it even more unnecessary. *Official Military Atlas of the Civil War* (Washington, D.C.: Government Printing Office, 1891), Plate 7.

[28] Guiney consistently misspelled this name as "Hanly" throughout his letters. A Boston cooper, Patrick T. Hanley rose from lieutenant to the rank of lieutenant colonel, and received a brevet promotion to colonel of volunteers to date March 13, 1865. During a double-quick drill, Lieutenant Hanley's Company B had to jump over a ditch. Hanley held his scabbard (with sheathed sword) in his left hand while jumping, but the sword leapt out of the scabbard and stuck into the opposite bank of the ditch, hilt first. The sharp point struck the lieutenant's left leg above the knee as he landed, passing seven inches diagonally through his flesh. Hanley removed it with his right hand, and made a full recovery under the care of Assistant Surgeon P. A. O'Connell. Captain Christopher Plunkett of Company B was a Boston clerk and salesman, and he resigned his commission

finally withdrew it. He seems to be uneasy about matters at home. Poor Plunkett, with all his extravagances, is a genial companion and I would be sorry if he should leave us. I miss Fitzgerald very much and if Plunkett left I would be quite lonesome.

My Darling, I can hardly say anything to you by way of advice as to what you shall do in future. I have every confidence in your judgment. You can take no step upon the foot-print of which I will not invoke blessings. I <u>think</u> it would be well for you to visit Portland, Maine. O! Darling, how my heart bounds at the thought of meeting you again in peace and love, and under happier circumstances. Until we do so meet may God preserve us <u>both</u>. Little Julia, my eyes moisten at thinking of her. Love to Mr. Campbell and wife and Lizzie—

Your Husband

Washington, D.C.
July 14th 1861

My Dear Jennie:
I sent you a half finished letter this morning.[29] I was obliged to do so because the letter carrier was waiting for it at the door.

I think that I closed my description of the people here with a reference to the exposition of the Ladies' shoulder blades. The men who belong about here are worse looking than the Ladies. They seem to be simple and generally uneducated. In looking at the people—at the splendid country which surrounds them—its fertility—its elegantly sloped hills, and undulating valleys—the genial sky and the full, ever-flowing rivers—I cannot help coming to the conclusion that, say what we will to the contrary, slavery curses the land in which it is. If the northern people had this climate, this soil—these facilities, this place would be a terrestrial paradise

---

on August 7, 1861. He re-enlisted on August 14, 1862 and rose to first lieutenant on January 8, 1863. After losing his right arm by a twelve-pound solid shot on May 23, 1864 at North Anna River, he mustered out on June 21, 1864 as lieutenant of his old Company B. *Massachusetts Soldiers, Sailors*, 1: 628, 630, 637. Macnamara, *Bivouac*, p. 252. Macnamara, *Ninth Regiment*, p. 34.

[29] This letter is missing from the Guiney Collection at the College of the Holy Cross.

in ten years. Everything here except nature herself seems to me to be sluggish.

Washington itself, excepting the Capitol and government buildings, may be said to resemble a half grown tree withered by a premature extraction of sap.[30]

I understand to-day that our regiment is to be stationed at the Arsenal in Washington as part of the force reserved for the defence of the city. This arrangement will save us the trouble of fighting as, in my opinion, the rebels will never be able to attack it. My brother was here to see me to-day and says his regiment is going home soon as their term of enlistment has almost expired.[31] Jennie, if you knew how anxiously I awaited the distribution of the mail to-day you would have sent me a letter—I know you would.

Capt. Fitzgerald is at home for a few days—I sent him your address—he will call upon you. Welcome him for he is a noble man, and my friend.

There was quite a battle a short distance from here last evening and the rebels were routed as they ought to be.

I saw a Boston paper to-day which gave an account of a meeting of Laborers who were out of employment in Roxbury.[32] I see that the authorities broke it up. It struck me that preaching on a street corner was a poor process by which to get employment. Let me know who got it up. How is Campbell? Mulrey? Minton? Does any of them call to see you? How is Mr. and Mrs. O'Donnell who have been so kind to you? How is Miss Crespy who is so dear to us? How is sister Lizzie? How is that sweet little angel of ours, whose plump, loveable, darling face so often meets me in my day thoughts, and night dreams—our own cherub? How is yourself my dear wife?

---

[30] Timothy Regan visited Washington while on a pass and agreed with Guiney's assessment. "If all the public buildings were taken out of it, there would nothing be left but a dirty looking country town," he wrote, "where cows, hogs, mules, and hungry looking dogs are allowed to run loose wherever they please." Regan diary, July 12, 1861.

[31] Guiney is referring to James Guiney, who served at the time with the First Maine Infantry. Scheduled to serve only three months, the unit started for home on July 31, 1861 and mustered out in Portland on August 5, 1861. Most of the men re-enlisted into the Tenth Maine Infantry. For more information, see footnote 24. *First-Tenth-Twenty-ninth Maine Regiment*, p. 660.

[32] About 40 to 50 unemployed Irishmen, mostly boys, assembled for an organized street meeting in Roxbury on the morning of July 10, 1861. The gathering quickly broke up without violence or incident. Roxbury *City Gazette*, July 11, 1861.

It is unnecessary for me to say to you, Darling, to think well—act nobly—trust to God, and be hopeful of the future. God bless you.

Guiney

Will write again when I get yours.

Washington, D.C.
July 15, 1861

My Dear Wife:

I am very much engaged to-day being what is called "Officer of the day" having charge of the whole encampment. Yet, on account of an item which I see in the papers which you so thoughtfully sent me, along with your most gratifying letter, (all of which I have just received,) I am willing to neglect my official duties for a few moments to set you right upon the supposed perils of being shot at.

As far as I am concerned Jennie, I had just as Life a bullet would come within an inch of me as within a mile—what's the difference? It doesn't hurt me in either case. There is no such thing as danger in War. A man is either shot or not shot. I was not shot! That's enough, Darling, for you and me.

My cap was not torn by the shot referred to; I suppose the report arose from the fact that when the bullet whizzed by, I took off my cap jocosely to see if there was a hole in it. Several soldiers who belonged to a New Hampshire Regmt. were standing near and they thought from seeing me take off the cap that I had been struck. This, I think was the origin of the report.

Fitzgerald and I had considerable fun over it when we found we were not hit. We looked in the direction from which the ball came and good-naturedly but loudly dared the rascal to show his nose. He didn't show it, and so much the better for us. We went on our way laughing at the bad aim and ungallant behavior of one who would deprive a lady of her husband. It's all right. Don't be alarmed Jennie. The bullet is not cast, and never will be, that will shoot me. This may seem to you like overconfidence in me. But I feel so, anyhow. I had a letter from Fitzgerald this morning.

He seems in good spirits and much pleased with his visit to you. He says the baby is fat and beautiful, on this last remark he simply shows his cultivated taste. Of course she is. How could she be otherwise Jennie? I will leave it to you.

I am quite well myself. Hanley is recovering. All the boys well. Plunkett is as full of jokes and larks as ever. I am glad you intend to write to me so often. Send me Roxbury + Boston papers once in a while.

I do not regard this as an answer to your letter—I will write again in a day or two—this is only a scrap. I like to be writing to you so much—It brings you so near to me.

Kiss little Darling for me and be sure and have no tears in the ceremony. Be of splendid cheer.

Farewell Darling
Guiney

July 16th, 1861

My Dear Jennie:

I open the letter which I had written yesterday, to enclose in it a word or two to-day. The last I said to you about our future movements I think was that we were to go to the Arsenal in city of Washington. That is contradicted this morning. It is said now on good authority that we are to cross the Potomac river and advance down into Virginia. By the way, the rebels are getting used up so fast that I fear we will have no one to advance upon. What a sweep our troops are making on the other side of the river! When the flag of our country flashes upon the rebels on the battlefield, they become abashed and cowardly. I suppose you get full account of Battles fought around here. I sincerely think that the people of Massachusetts have earlier intelligence of what occurs here than we who are here say within a distance of five miles of the place of occurrence. The newspapers here are miserable. If we should be sent down [to] Virginia, I will let you know. Of course, you will direct letters as before and they will reach me wherever I go.

If we should remain here a few days I will send you a description of the manner in which I live. If I convey in it the facts as they are, I am sure the letter will be grotesque.

Good bye Love. Love to Campbell.

                                        Guiney

During the Federal defeat at First Bull Run, the Ninth Massachusetts stood in readiness to reinforce the Union army. The Irishmen started to advance into their first major fight when Brigadier General Joseph K. Mansfield, military commander of the District of Columbia, personally revoked the regiment's marching orders.[33] Guiney recounts this in a letter which seems to have been started on July 21 and completed the next morning.

The debacle at First Bull Run depressed the North and shattered the illusion that the war would be swift and with few casualties. On July 22, Lincoln called youthful Major General George B. McClellan from western Virginia to take command of the forces near Washington and forge them into an organized, effective army.

                                        Washington, D.C.
                                        July 21st 1861

My Dear Jennie:

I hasten to write a few words to you this morning in answer to your letter of the seventeenth inst.

I received the articles which you sent by Capt. Fitzgerald. They fit nicely. You are so thoughtful Darling—these things are just what I wanted. I was punished from wearing my old stiff uniform. God Bless You.

I have been unwell for the last three days with a dangerous sore throat. It was a relapse of an illness about which I wrote to you before. The reason why I ventured out so soon after my first illness was on account of complaints made by Col. Cass that when

---

[33] *The Pilot*, August 10, 1861. Regan diary, July 22, 1861. William C. Davis, *Battle at Bull Run* (Baton Rouge: Louisiana State University Press, 1977), pp. 6, 11. Joseph Mansfield later assumed command of the Federal XII Corps on September 15, 1862. Two days later, at Antietam, he led his troops forward to attack Major General "Stonewall" Jackson's Southerners after the repulse of Major General Joseph Hooker's I Corps, when a bullet struck him in the chest and left him mortally wounded. Warner, *Generals in Blue*, pp. 309-10.

my company was out in Battalion drill in charge of my Lieutenants some serious mistakes were made by them, owing entirely to
the inefficiency of the officers. I wished to remedy this and went
out contrary to Surgeon's orders. I, of course, had to strain my
voice in giving orders, and in this way I became again prostrate.
Last evening about seven o'clock my throat broke on the inside
and I began to recover, but still I was very weak. At 9 o'clock last
night we received orders to advance towards Manassas Junction.
The Colonel, Fitzgerald and all my friends here advised me to stay
here in the camp. In fact the Surgeon ordered me to stay, but
no—I was determined to go with my company. I did go with them
to the surprise of everybody who knew how sick I was. I knew I
could walk about three miles anyhow and then if my strength gave
out I had two of my ablest men appointed to carry me. This may
seem to you like imprudence. But Jennie, I had rather die on the
road than remain behind on such an emergency. Well, we went
on about two miles and the order for our advance was countermanded by an U. S. officer [presumably Mansfield] who rode up
to us in the darkness of the night. So we returned to camp. I stood
the tramp first rate and felt better for the exercise.

The reason we were ordered to advance I suppose to be this:
Yesterday, we heard the booming of cannon in the direction of
Manassas Junction and everybody was in great suspense to hear
the news. Towards evening a messenger came in from battle to
Washington with news that our troops were repulsed and were
retreating. On the receipt of this news the War Department immediately issued orders for our advance to re-inforce the federal
troops. Just as we were about to cross the Potomac over the famous Long Bridge at midnight news of a more cheering character
came and consequently we are restrained here for the present.[34]
However we are ordered to be in constant readiness to move and
do not be surprised if my correspondence should suddenly break
off. I suppose you will read, before you receive this, an account of
the great battle. The gallant 69th N. Y. did splendidly and
Meagher and his Zouaves charged like tigers upon the enemy.
But the poor fellows were badly cut up—You will get an account

---

[34] The Long Bridge crossed the Potomac River from Washington, D.C. to
northern Virginia. *Official Military Atlas of the Civil War*, Plate 7.

of details in Boston papers. We have all sorts of rumors here this morning. One says that Meagher is taken prisoner—another is that Col. Corcoran is killed.[35] It will be several days before the whole truth will be known. It is said that when the 69th were sustaining a tremendous onset from the enemy—Col. Corcoran exclaimed—"Where is the Massachusetts Ninth?"[36] We only wish we had been there to answer him.

Close as we are to these scenes, we are not posted as well upon the details of them, as the people of Mass. are. There is so much excitement here—and no news-papers.

I promised to send you a description of camp-life but I fear I will not have sufficient time to do so. All well here to-day and I am strong as a Derrick.

Direct your future letters to me, "Washington, D.C. or elsewhere."

Mention company and Regmt. (I wish I had room to say something about baby.)

Darling, God Bless You.
Guiney

P.S. Call and see Geo. W. Searle attorney, on Court St. (opposite Court House) and inquire if any of my cases have been disposed of and ask him to write to me.[37] I received a letter from Mr. Mulrey. Tell him if we are left here a day or two I will write to him. My regards to Campbell—Lizzie and kiss for baby.

P. R. G.

---

[35] Corcoran had been wounded and captured, and would remain a Confederate prisoner until the following August. Warner, *Generals in Blue,* p. 94.

[36] The Sixty-ninth New York charged up Henry Hill twice, and was repulsed both times. Davis, *Bull Run,* p. 218. Finnerty recalls Colonel Corcoran's statement in his dispatch. *The Pilot,* August 10, 1861.

[37] Born in Salem, Massachusetts on January 26, 1826, George W. Searle received his education at Philips Andover Academy. He studied law, was admitted to the bar in 1847, and wrote several legal treatises; he died in 1892. William T. Davis, *Professional and Industrial History of Suffolk County in Three Volumes. Volume I: History of the Bench and Bar* (Boston: The Boston History Company, 1894), p. 240. Hereafter cited as *History of the Bench and Bar.*

Washington D.C.
July 22nd 1861

My Dear Jennie:

We are so constantly on the alert here that I have but time to say a few words to you and to acknowledge yours of the 20th inst. which I have just received together with papers I wrote to you yesterday. We are in our camp yet—may not be here long—can't tell—all excitement.

The first black contraband I capture I will box up and send home to little Julia.[38]

I do not know what to say about Mrs. O'Donnell's proposition to furnish Lizzie with a soldier—I want her to state more particularly as to whether she prefers one with both legs etc. After she sends me a more particular description of the kind of a retired soldier she wants, I will consider the subject.

Darling, I am well—strong—and in good spirits—our whole regiment is in great glee at the prospect of being allowed to participate in the fight. My own opinion is we will only be used as a reinforcement in case of a temporary repulse by the enemy.

By the papers which you sent I see that Col. [Robert] Cowdin of the 1st Mass. Regmt. is unjustly attacked.[39] It is said here that yesterday in the battle near Manassas Junction he proved himself a man of splendid courage.[40] These attacks upon soldiers in the field are wretched.

I have heard nothing new to-day about the fight yesterday— There are rumors enough but unreliable. The fact is the soldiers here get more news from Boston and N. Y. papers than from any

---

[38] Contrabands were escaped slaves who took refuge behind Union lines; often, they followed the army and acted as servants to willing officers. For more information, see James M. McPherson, *Battle Cry of Freedom* (New York: Oxford University Press, 1988), pp. 350–58.

[39] Colonel Cowdin's horse was shot from beneath him during the battle. His brigade commander Joseph Hooker recommended him for promotion for gallant service during the Peninsula Campaign; he received it on September 26, 1862, to brigadier general of volunteers. Warner, *Generals in Blue*, p. 96.

[40] The First Massachusetts went up in support of the Twelfth New York, but the New Yorkers withdrew, exposing Colonel Cowdin's left, and seven companies had to lie down to avoid murderous Rebel fire. Davis, *Bull Run*, p. 120.

other source. We are not allowed out of camp and no one allowed in unless on pass from Gen. Scott.[41]

So you see you will be posted on our progress before we know where we are.

Fitzgerald just came into my tent full of news.

Good bye love
Guiney

Washington, D.C.
July 24th 1861

My Dear Wife:

Your dear letter of the 21st inst. is at my side. It was almost as welcome as your own dear face would be to my eyes. It is so gratifying to me to receive these frequent letters from you that my heart is full—and my eyes are not always otherwise. How I like to hear from you and my little pet! Nothing on earth could give me more true satisfaction. Continue, Darling, to thus show your remembrance of me, and I will continue in the full and ever present thought that my life is not my own, but that however imperiled, my duty is to preserve it, if I can do so with honor, for your dear sake and that of our cherished, loved little one.

You long to be with me, you say; Dear, and O! how truly I might say do I yearn to be with you in that peace and happiness of which we have so often spoken, and of which I now so often think. Yet, I fear to speak too much of these imagined future times lest the thought of them would bring over me an unbecoming sadness. I must postpone the anticipation of these pleasures to a time nearer to the welcome realization on these beautiful moonlight evenings when our band plays so sweetly the airs of "Home Sweet Home" and others of equal power to touch an absent one, how

---

[41] A veteran of the War of 1812, Major General Winfield Scott went on as commanding general to lead United States forces to victory during the Mexican-American War. Early in the Civil War he acted as nominal general-in-chief of the U.S. Army, although his age and poor health prevented more active service. He soon retired, but survived to see Union forces victorious. Warner, *Generals in Blue*, pp. 429–30.

my mind turns to you and walks with you and revels in the communion of our plighted love. And I see my little one and kiss her until she wonders and then weeps at one who loves her beyond measure, and yet whom she cannot know. But Darling I cannot pursue these thoughts. Nevertheless, I must say a word to you of a domestic nature. Now, perhaps, is the time to say it. Knowing you as I do, it seems to me unnecessary to offer any advice to you. You have truer instincts and better judgment than I ever did or ever will possess. Yet, you will not blame me if in the face of those circumstances which surround me, and which will continue to surround me for some time, I suggest to you that if we should never meet again, you have for my sake, as well for her own, a strict, pious, and never ceasing watch over our little Julia—Her prayers—her education—her piety—her associations. If I should fall upon these Southern plains, if I had a moment for reflection, that moment would be embittered at the thought of my careless life, but in whatever pain, how I would smile at the thought of my pious intelligent little angel clasping her hands in prayer for me when I am gone. But this is predicated on fear, Jennie, yet I have no fear of not returning. But I have had a sort of vague apprehension that my chances might not be magical and that I might say with propriety what I have said. But enough of this.

The Great Battle

I suppose you have heard of it—all about it. It is the common theme here and we all listen with avidity to accounts and incidents of it as given by the straggling soldiers who have returned from the scene of the disaster—from all I can learn the fight was lost by us through downright cowardice on the part of some of our troops. The officers deserve most censure—they were not to be found even at the beginning of the fight—they hid behind trees and ran etc. more particularly in those regiments from country districts. This, of course, started the men. I could give you many amusing details but I will do so when I get home.

The N. Y. 69th [Colonel Corcoran's and Major Meagher's regiment] is praised by everybody here. They fought most bravely—they charged against the enemy's lines repeatedly and at every point swept the rebels before them. I told you in my last how they shouted for us. When [Colonel George] Clark's [Eleventh] Mass.

Regmt. went into the field the men of the 69th mistook it for ours because they wear the same sort of hat.[42] How they cheered the Mass Ninth but lo! in a few minutes the felt hats ran—and then the 69th <u>knew</u> we were <u>not</u> there. The N. Y. 79th fought well. Cowdin's [First] <u>Mass.</u> did nobly. Ellsworth's Zouaves [Eleventh New York] fought desperately—when they struck the rebels they would shout "Revenge for Ellsworth," and down went the rebels.[43] Col. Corcoran was wounded but concealed the fact from his men as long as he could. Finally he was lost in the conflict and it is not known whether he is dead or taken prisoner. Meagher's horse was shot under him—but himself is unhurt.

Although I cannot promise to write to you every day—yet I will do so often as <u>possible</u>. We are under orders and do not know the moment we will be summoned away—not allowed to leave camp. I get lots of Boston news papers. Who is the kind friend who sends them all?

God Bless You
Guiney

---

[42] A Dorchester militia officer, George Clark, Jr. was instrumental in raising the Eleventh Massachusetts Volunteer Infantry and became its first colonel. He resigned October 11, 1861. *Massachusetts Soldiers, Sailors,* 1: 737.

[43] The Eleventh Massachusetts engaged in a swaying battle over several Northern cannon, but were forced back by the Rebels. The Seventy-ninth New York, a Scottish regiment, rushed up Henry Hill, only to be devastated by two volleys of Confederate fire. After the Highlanders' Colonel James Cameron, brother of Secretary of War Simon Cameron, fell mortally wounded, the men withdrew. Meanwhile, the Eleventh New York advanced from Matthews Hill after 2:00 p.m., and the Southerners waited to let loose destructive volleys into the Zouaves' ranks. The demoralized men retreated behind the cover of a battery, but a Confederate attack later swept through the area and captured the cannon. For the actions of the Sixty-ninth New York and the First Massachusetts, see footnotes for the letters of July 21 and July 22, respectively. Colonel Elmer Ellsworth died from a gunshot wound inflicted when he attempted to remove a secessionist banner from atop the Marshall House in Alexandria on May 24. As Ellsworth descended the stairwell with the flag in his hands, the owner of the hotel, James Jackson, inflicted the mortal wound. Immediately, a Federal private shot and killed Jackson. The death of the gallant, young Ellsworth shocked both the nation and the Lincoln family, who knew him personally, and inspired much patriotism across the North. His body lay in state in the White House, and funeral services were held in the East Room. Timothy Regan, while visiting Alexandria on pass, even made a point to see the Marshall House where the young officer was shot. Regan diary, October 15, 1861. Davis, *Bull Run,* pp. 205–206, 209, 212, 216, 218. E. B. Long, *The Civil War Day by Day* (Garden City: Doubleday & Company, Inc., 1971), p. 78.

On July 24 a courier from Brigadier General Mansfield informed Colonel Cass that the Ninth Massachusetts, along with the Twenty-second, Thirty-fifth, and Thirty-ninth New York, were to take two days' provisions and forty rounds of ammunition and cross the Long Bridge to Arlington in northern Virginia to report to Brigadier General Irvin McDowell.[44] The regiment had not yet received its blue uniforms and traveled through Washington in its original gray hats and coats. According to one correspondent, some watching ladies waved their handkerchiefs to the soldiers as the green Irish flag caught the breeze. Upon reaching the muddy "Sacred Soil" of Virginia, several nearby regiments cheered for the Irish regiment as it passed along the road. The Ninth stopped for the night upon reaching Arlington Mansion, the former residence of Confederate General Robert E. Lee recently confiscated by the Union government.[45]

Virginia
July 26, 1861

My Dear Jennie:

This is the first moment at which I could send you a word since our advance into Virginia.

We are situated on the Southwesterly side of the Potomac river about a mile beyond Fort Corcoran. There is no Regiment camped outside of us—we are on an advanced Post. Still, Darling, you will direct your letters to me as before with the slight addition which I suggested to you in a former letter.

I have just now had a change of underclothing which refreshes me very much. So just now I feel pretty well. We started from our old campground on last Wednesday and marched over the Potomac to [Brigadier] General McDowell's Headquarters in this state about 12 miles inland. We had no tents with us and we all slept on the ground without covering. When I awoke in the morn-

---

[44] Brigadier General Irvin McDowell, Federal commander at First Bull Run, was relegated to lead a corps. Following the Union loss at Second Bull Run, he was placed in unimportant commands for the duration of the war. Warner, *Generals in Blue*, p. 298.

[45] Although high in rank in the Confederate army, General Robert E. Lee had not yet achieved the reputation for which he was destined; he would take command of the Army of Northern Virginia in June 1862. *The Pilot*, August 10, 1861. Macnamara, *Ninth Regiment*, pp. 42–44.

ing my hair was all wet with the heavy dew which invariably falls here in the night. I had a pillow however, and what do you think it was? It was the grave of a little daughter of the present Rebel General Lee, on whose land we slept. I need not tell you my reflections while awake. The next day we were ordered off to another point at a distance of five miles. Arriving at the new place we were obliged to sleep on the grass again with no variation in the comforts, but to-day our tents arrived and we have just finished putting them up—It is now eleven o'clock at night. The Regiment are sleeping on their guns to-night as we know not the moment we may be summoned to meet the enemy. My Darling, as it is so late, you will pardon me for writing so briefly. Write to me often. We have all been living for last three days on hard bread and warm water, but a friend has just come in with a lunch for me. I have good reason for not saying anything about our staff officers. I do not wish to say how much of these privations might be obviated by a proper exertion on their part. I do not wish to say either how reckless of our welfare those are who ought to be our most watchful protectors. If we live, there will be something said hereafter. This is <u>exclusively</u> intended for your ear.

We have received no pay yet, simply, in my opinion, because our Colonel does not ask for it—he does not care a cent, he has money enough himself. But good night and God Bless You Darling.

Guiney

The regiment remained at Arlington Heights near Fort Corcoran until it broke camp to occupy a forward position on September 28. Pioneers cleared a hillside to provide space for a campground and field where the men engaged in early morning drills and two-hour battalion drills each afternoon, both with special emphasis on double-quick marching.[46] *Colonel Cass wanted to ensure his unit's discipline and training, constantly honing it to become a sharp fighting instrument. A Boston* Herald *war correspondent observed at this time that "Guiney's Company (D) is in a fine state of discipline and that the Captain is highly popular."*[47]

---

[46] Macnamara, *Ninth Regiment*, pp. 46, 49.
[47] Article signed "Nonpareil," Boston *Herald*, August 4, 1861.

Meanwhile the Ninth's chaplain, Father Thomas Scully, attended to the regiment's spiritual needs and the Irishmen eventually constructed a small altar on which their chaplain could celebrate Mass. In the evenings, some participated in spiritual readings held in selected tents.[48]

Arlington Heights near
Washington, D.C.
July 31st 1861

My Dear Jennie:

Yesterday your letter of the twenty sixth inst. came to our camp but I did not receive it until late last night, having been down in the forest with my company throwing up some defences about three miles from here. Of course I was delighted when I saw your handwriting upon the envelope, but on reading it, I was taken somewhat by surprise at the expression of your desire that I should return home. It did seem to me that your sentiment in this particular was more impassioned than well-considered; but, on reflection, I have become suspicious that you are right. Perhaps the letter which I sent to you encouraged the idea of my return home. I do not now remember one word of what I then said, as everything here is done under some degree of excitement, and in a hurry. My illness, too, has had something to do with your desire to have me at home. I know it has. But that has passed. I am well now. <u>That</u> was only the usual process of becoming acclimated in Virginia. I never felt better in my life (in health) than I do at the present time. So, Dear, I pray you give no entertainment to any fears for my general health.

I wish to say to you, Jennie, that although I do not for a moment think of going home now, yet that my presence here is conditional and circumstantial and not by any means a fixed thing, for instance, if the officers of this regiment should continue to be treated like prisoners in a chain-gang by the Colonel—if oaths and insults are to be the standard of his official intercourse with his officers—if ignorance and the ugliest arrogance are to be

---

[48] Father Scully from Arlington Heights, Aug. 12, 1861, in *The Pilot*, August 24, 1861.

flourished in the faces of those who are sensitive enough to feel—if these things continue—I say I will resign my commission. Of course, he never troubles me, neither does he Fitzgerald. Yet, how painful it is to be obliged to associate with, and mind you, to pay honors to, one like Colonel Cass who has grown worse with the progress of his days. Then the Lieut. Colonel [Rowell] is an ex-Boston-Policeman and no more of a genial companion, I assure you. Then there are several unprincipled fellows here who are sort of pimps for Cass and Rowell, and in fact everything here is calculated, and to some extent, designed, to embitter our days in camp. Were it not for two or three considerations, to me this state of things would be unbearable. One reason I need not commit to paper you, perhaps, will readily imagine it. We talked of it together—then—the cause in which we are enlisted is truly a good and grand one—one that will entitle those who labor in the achievement of its success to the gratitude and remembrance of the present, as well as of unborn generations—one that of itself compensates by its sublimity and goodness for all which may be sacrificed in its defense. Then again there is the friendship of many officers which serves to modify the hardships of the hour. These considerations, I say, delay and may continue to postpone, my return home. But the thought occurs to me, what do these reasons amount to when opposed by the wishes and welfare of my wife whom at the taper-lit and sacred altar I vowed to love, cherish, and protect? They amount to little, Jennie. Yet Dear, this is what I would impress upon you—That these very ends—your ultimate wishes and welfare will be best promoted by my retention of my commission for some time yet. Then, it is true, there is the danger of losing life in this contest. But that is one of the hazards of the times and I feel that fate will not do her worst upon me.

About going to your Brother John's, I would say that I have no choice as to the locality in which you may put yourself—wherever you are there is my home. My heart is entirely free from all bias as to whither you may go. There are only two places in the world to which I turn with the eye of affection—where you are—no matter where it is—and my native home. But then not in a personal point of view, but as matter of interest to us, I think the step may be a good one. The West cannot be worse than the east for one of my age, race and creed. I think well of it Dear on the whole. If you go out there perhaps two months will be the extent of our separation. But Jennie, where will you get the money to go with? I will not be able to send any for several weeks yet, perhaps not for one month to come! Capt. Fitzgerald says he will send his family out to St. Pauls, if I go out there, and start business when he leaves the army.

Captains Plunkett and Gallagher have both resigned and want to go home, but the Col. is persecuting them and detaining them here to have them tried by a <u>court martial</u> for some imaginary offense.[49] It is mere revenge on his part although they are not blameless. Unless we are attacked here, there will be no fighting until Sept. If I had more room and time I would talk with you more. I received papers. I must close. No, I guess I will go and raise another sheet of paper—

Dear Jennie—I suppose you have heard enough about the Battle of Bull Run. I think I gave you my opinion of it. The Yankees feel sore over it. The 79th New-York and the 69th—one Scotch and the other Irish, did the best fighting. Many of the <u>natives</u> ran and no mistake.[50] I will tell you a good joke. Our Regmt. was set to work doing a job which they did not well understand. An Army officer (native) rode up, and addressing Capt. Fitzgerald said— "It is strange that when your countrymen undertake to do anything they do it wrong." "There is one thing about it," says the Capt. in reply, "<u>They</u> <u>stand</u> <u>their</u> <u>ground</u> <u>in</u> <u>a</u> fight—<u>they</u> <u>don't</u> <u>run.</u>" This hit a sore spot—and he immediately, and in high dudgeon and in peals of Irish laughter, spurred up his horse and left.

There was an alarm here the other day, we were informed that the Rebels were advancing upon Washington and coming in our direction. We turned out in line of battle—and as soon as we had completed the formation of the line Father Scully came over to me and made a very appropriate address to my company, after which we all made an act of contrition, bent on one knee, and received absolution from him. He then went to all the other companies with the same result. His coming to my command <u>first</u> was gratifying to me, more especially as he and I had not been for some time on the best of terms. The cause of the little estrange-

---

[49] Captain James Gallagher stayed in the service until resigning on July 9, 1862. Captain Christopher Plunkett left earlier, resigning on August 7, 1861. He re-enlisted on August 14, 1862, following Colonel Cass's death. *Massachusetts Soldiers, Sailors*, 1: 620, 630.

[50] The term "natives" refers to American-born soldiers.

ment was a very trifle and entirely owing to the peculiarities of his and my dispositions. It is not worth mentioning. It's all forgotten by him now—and I forgive. But, about the rebels! Well, they didn't come and we returned to our camp with a feeling of disappointment, flying colors, and with curses on the rascals for having fooled us so often.

There are some things in this letter (and your good sense will tell you the parts to which I refer) which it is for my welfare that you keep them to yourself. I tell you Jennie, revenge on the part of the Colonel upon his officers is easily obtained here; and if he knew that I told so much truth about him, it would cost me some pain of mind. My Lieuts. are now doing some better. My company are very much devoted to me.

And now Dear Jennie, farewell, until I write again; And may the angel spirit of our first-born whisper to you of the hope and affection which my thoughts this moment twine around you, and return then to me in this forest, and so far away, to tell me you are well, and happy, and full of cheer and hope![51]

Guiney

Arlington Heights near
Washington, D.C.
August 1st/61

My Dear:

I have had no opportunity of sending the letter enclosed with this one until today and last night when I received yours of the 28th inst. I was rather glad than otherwise that I had not sent it off as this delay gives me an opportunity of sending with it a few words more as well as the small sum of forty dollars which I herein transmit. We were paid yesterday for 20 days service in June. Our July pay will not be given to us for some time. I would like to send you more, Dear, if it were possible but I was obliged to borrow some money here which I feel bound to pay now. If you receive the 40 dollars write me word immediately to that effect. If you do

---

[51] The Guiney's first-born, a son, died in infancy.

not receive it let me know, also, and I will send on the Express company's receipt to which you will oblige them to pay over.

I have just learned that Plunkett's and Gallagher's difficulty has been temporarily settled. The Colonel managed it so that their resignations were not accepted. They can't go home. This satisfies Cass and he has dropped his <u>Court Martial</u> against them.

My Dear, you will be particularly careful in reference to what I have said about Colonel Cass. He is very vindictive, aye, revengeful. And if he set out to do so, he could give me a great deal of trouble. I do not intend to say anymore about him to anybody. If you would like to know how he acts and appears to us, I wish to refer you to that volume of Moore's works on the table near you in which you will find his character delineated in that of <u>Makanna the Veiled Prophet</u>, but without his intelligence.[52]

I am very sorry for those rumors about Capt. Fitzgerald in Salem as told to you by our friend [Henry F.] Fallon.[53] The malicious scoundrels! He is one of the noblest of men and the columnies can do him no harm in the end. What a wretched element this low malice is in human nature, and how strongly developed it is in the composition of many Irishmen!

I have not received those looked for and precious pictures of you and my little pet. [Quartermaster John] Moran has not arrived here.[54] He is a sort of loafer who calculates to live at the public expense and do nothing to compensate the government. I suppose he is either in New York or Washington having one of his vulgar sprees. My opinion is that if our government is worsted in this struggle, the defeat will be owing in no small degree to the barroom idleness and criminal neglect of duty of such men as he. If the soldiers who went to fight at Bull Run had been properly cared for, fed, and refreshed as they ought to have been after a steady march of twenty miles in a hot sun and in the night dew without shelter, the Rebels would not have cause to rejoice in victory. The government ought to hang every man who assumes a

---

[52] An Irish romantic poet who died in 1852, Thomas Moore published a four-part series titled *Lalla Rookh* in 1817. Mokanna, a Mohammedan imposter, is a main character of the first part.

[53] Henry W. Fallon was a fellow lawyer, admitted to the bar in 1858. Davis, *History of the Bench and Bar*, p. 638.

[54] Quartermaster John Moran was discharged by Special Order of the War Department on November 26, 1861. *Massachusetts Soldiers, Sailors*, 1: 617.

duty of military character at the present juncture and who shirks its performance.

My Dear: I do not wish to write for any news paper as, if I did so, I would certainly tell the truth and consequently injure my own prospects. Those who do write from this camp are mere puppets in the hands of two or three—the Colonel is one of them—I know the fact that these correspondents record not a word which is not substantially dictated by the Colonel or Lieut. Colonel. These men are both ignorant and of course are highly delighted with any mention of their names in the papers—and mind you, it will displease them very much to mention anybody else. And if I should write for the public without submitting my composition to the Grand Bashad of the camp, I would get myself into trouble. I cannot praise—it will not pay to condemn. I can't be a slave. Some men here depend more upon news-papers than upon good deeds to make them heroes. I will not be a tool in their hands; neither will I be a tool to injure myself. Tell my friend Dr. March my reasons for not writing for press.

I am well, Dear, there is no present danger of a battle here. I hope Mr. Mulrey will recover.

> Farewell wife
> Guiney

> Arlington
> Aug. 7th 1861

My Dear Jennie:

I was in Washington yesterday on official business and took advantage of a spare moment to have an ambrotype taken and which I sent to you per Adam's Express. When in the city I saw Ex-Mayor [Theodore] Otis of Roxbury, and I also met John McElroy Jr. of Roxbury on Pennsylvania Avenue.[55] They both promised to call and see you on their return and to tell you how well I was. On my return to camp I found a letter from you and some papers.

My Dear, I am surprised that you do not receive my letters more

---

[55] Theodore Otis served as mayor of Roxbury (1859–1860) and worked with Guiney when he represented Ward 3 on the Common Council in 1860. *Catalogue of City Councils*, pp. 210–11.

promptly than you do. I write often, although at irregular intervals. I am always sure to write as soon as I receive yours; but then I am sometimes absent when your letters come and this causes a delay. And again the mail communication with the city is sometimes interrupted. I think you will receive all my letters, and I think I receive all yours. My Dear, I receive lots of papers from you every week, in fact every day or two. I sent you a little money; did you get it? Have you made up your mind yet as to where you will spend our <u>separation</u> months? Let me know of your minutest thought on this subject, so interesting to me.

In reference to what that young fellow said in his letter to his friends I must say in justice that his story is entirely false. There is no such thing as "Starvation" or "exhaustion" here. I assure you Jennie, our suffering is more <u>intellectual</u> than physical. I refer you to one of my late letters for further particulars. Does he say <u>anything</u> about ill-treatment on my part? There are many men here who complain of all sorts of imaginary wrongs. They are lazy, and a nuisance in any army. Everything which they are asked to do, they consider an oppression upon them. Then they are so malicious there is no end to what they will say. They see everything in a different light from that in which a person of experience and intelligence does. Then again we have about two hundred here who seem to be ambitious only to eat, sleep, loaf, and get all they can generally. They think a soldier should never be called on to do duty, to march a long distance or to sleep out-doors. I look at it in a different light. It ought to be known by these young brats who grumble so much that privations in war are unavoidable sometimes.

My Dear, I am tired writing so much of fact to you, to whom I should rather speak of my hope and love. I will say no more about others at present and, Dear, I must close with that ever recurring feeling which utters "God Bless You Darling."

Your Husband

On August 4 the Ninth Massachusetts was brigaded with the Fourteenth Massachusetts, Forty-first New York, Fourth Michigan, Hamilton's Battery E of the Third U.S. Artillery, and Company I of the Second U.S. Cavalry, all under Brigadier General William T. Sherman's command.

In this letter, Guiney reveals his low estimation of Sherman, headquartered at nearby Fort Corcoran.[56]

Arlington Heights, Va.
August 8th 1861

My Dear Jennie:

The last letter which I received from you informed me that you would write another and a longer one to me the next day. Now Dear, if you did so I would have had it two days ago. I thought it would come in to-day's mail, but it did not. O! I have a great mind to scold you for exciting my anticipation and then disappointing me. If I were at home now, how I would pout, swing my shoulders nervously, sit down on a chair and get up again, go out in the yard, pull hard on my cigar, come in again looking grim, take a secret peep at you to see if you were laughing at my nonsense; and then, if you were, how I would take hold of you and twitch you round to me, and break the little cloud with an amazingly long kiss! But I will not say a word to you for probably I will get the letter tomorrow or next day, and it will be full of dear words and good thoughts and then, if I had said anything cross to you in this, how sorry I would be, Darling! I always look ahead, you see, more especially where my Dear precious wife is in the long waving distance.

Since I wrote to you last, I had a fortunate opportunity to visit Washington. I went on last Monday and while I had a few moments to spare I stepped into a Saloon and had an ambrotype taken and I sent on to you by Adam's Express. I thought it quite accurate except the face and head which are rather indistinct, on account of having it taken full size. I met Hon. Theodore Otis there (in the city) and also John McElroy Jr. of Roxbury. They both promised to call and see you on return home. Our place of

---

[56] *The War of the Rebellion: A Compilation of the Official Records of the Union and Confederate Armies*, 128 vols. (Washington, D.C.: Government Printing Office, 1880–1901), vol. 51: 434. Hereafter cited as OR. William T. Sherman fought under Major General Ulysses S. Grant at Shiloh and Vicksburg, and later directed the Federal armies of the Western theater in the capture of Atlanta and in what is now known as Sherman's March to the Sea. He aspired to command of the United States Army after the war. Warner, *Generals in Blue*, pp. 443–44.

encampment has not been changed since I wrote to you before; but we are <u>Brigaded</u> under [Brigadier] General Sherman now and we know not how soon our location may be changed. He is the same Sherman of whom Meagher, in last week's <u>Irish American</u>, speaks so scathingly. Unless, on further acquaintance I change my mind in regard to him, I will continue to agree with Mr. Meagher in saying that Sherman "is a rude and ignorant Martinet." But what need I care for these fellows, they hardly ever interfere with me or anything which concerns me. Fitzgerald, also is another whom they will not trouble. They are wise enough to know that either or both of us could make an essential contribution to that storm which might be at anytime agitated to their public distinction.

I see that in last Sunday's Herald (Boston) I am slightly noticed by the correspondent of that paper in this camp.[57] This is surprising as I am not of those who court favors from newspaper writers in camp, as I regard them as flunkeys and panderers.

Last night the cavalry company which is attached to our Brigade met with a severe repulse near the Chain Bridge, on the Potomac. As usual, the repulse was the result of a blunder. We are frequently turned out here to meet the enemy in the night time, but he never comes near enough to give us battle. Everybody here is in good health and our hospital is emptier than that of any regiment in the Army of the Potomac. This shows that our men are neither <u>starved</u> nor <u>exhausted</u>.

I understand that our Brigade is looked to as being the fighting Brigade of the Army here and the next Battle fought in Eastern Virginia will find our Regiment, I think, in the Smoke of the field; yet, as <u>McClellan</u> is to command, I apprehend no such loss of life, no such miserable blundering as occurred at Bull Run.

The weather is extremely hot here in day time but in the night it is so lovely here that I am constantly reminded of my native home. Who knows but you and I would settle down in Virginia yet?

Guiney

---

[57] The article asserted that "Guiney's Company (D) is in a fine state of discipline and that the Captain is highly popular." "Nonpareil," Boston *Herald*, August 4, 1861.

Arlington Heights, D.C.
August 8th 1861

My Dear Jennie:

I write you this to inform you as hastily as possible that I have just been delighted with that visit from you and little Pet. Moran arrived last night.

You look to me, Dear, as good as ever, but with a deeply saddened expression. Why is this Dear? Do you not hear me asking you to be of good cheer? O! that expression. Darling, let me feel assured that in the future the thoughts which I fancy, I see in your Dear face, will be banished from your mind; and that you look upon my position here with pride instead of sorrow. Let me, Jennie, determine the time of my going home. I will go when I can do so with honor and when our circumstances will justify me, ever mindful, as I will be, of the Dear ones and duties at home. But your views, Dear, are always welcome to me. I only ask you, Dear, not to be impatient.

How our little Darling has changed! I would not know her. She is so fat. She has the face, head, and expression of a statesman. As true as I live, she resembles Lewis Cass the late Secretary of State under Buchanan.[58] All officers are laughing about her. I wish I had her here the little Darling. I know she would cry before I would let her alone.

My Dear, the next visit you pay me, I wish you would leave off your bonnet as I do not want anything in the way when I wish to kiss you. No news today. All well. Farewell, Dear; I expect a letter from you soon.

Your husband

Arlington Heights
Virginia Aug 9th 1861

My Dear Jennie:

Your two letters—one of the 5th inst. and the other of the 6th inst. arrived here yesterday. The one dated 5th inst. was sent by

---

[58] A former brigadier general during the War of 1812, governor of Michigan

some one of that inevitable and irritating series of great and little blunders which seems to pervade all departments of the government, to the encampment of the 11th Regmt. M. V., and was brought to me by one of my men who was over there by accident. However, the reception of a line from you at any time sweetens the bitterness of delay. I do not think that it is possible for you to realize the delight with which I receive your dear letters. They are so welcome, so good—so like my dear Jennie, that when I read them I feel myself in your presence, communing with you in that little domestic ecstasy which so often seemed to surround us when I was at home. I know that my dear little darling keeps you busy most of the time, but still, I trust you will continue to write to me often.

There is no news here of any special importance. The same routine is repeated every day and night—men all sleep with guns by their sides, and their equipments on. We rise at day-break and retire at 9 o'clock in the evening. We are <u>alarmed</u> (as the military phrase is) almost every night. The Rebels are getting very bold— they frequently dash down near us, but retire on finding us ready. One of our picket guard shot one of them yesterday evening. We are to be moved two miles farther into Virginia towards Falls Church, where it is intended that our whole Brigade will encamp under General Sherman. But we do not know the moment all this will be changed since in the middle of this whirl-wind of excitement, conclusions cannot be come to by the previous thought, but must be determined rather by this swift current of events which is upon and around us. All I can say is that the present <u>intention</u> is that our encampment shall be changed. Whether it is changed or not, any address will be the same as heretofore until I notify you to change it.

All the men and officers are well, with one exception. Plunkett complains of illness. The fact is he wants to go home some way or other. I know, from the first, he had no sufficient steadiness of purpose, and I felt that he would leave as soon as the feathers and

---

Territory, secretary of war under President Andrew Jackson, Michigan senator and supporter of popular sovereignty as a way for states to resolve whether they would or would not allow slavery, Lewis Cass served as secretary of state in President Buchanan's cabinet. He was an unsuccessful Democratic candidate in the 1848 presidential election, having been defeated by Zachary Taylor. Johnson and Malone, eds., *Dictionary of American Biography*, 3: 562–64.

novelty were worn off. Our Adjutant whose name is [George W.] Perkins has gone home to Boston.[59] Bull Run is an excellent exterminator of all those who are, or have been, in the army, and who do not wish to risk a permanent separation from the tinkling goblets and gushing fountains of the Tremont and the Revere. The shadow of a fight has scared them; and I think it is well for the government, as well as for us all, that their timidity ripened so soon in the hot sun of Virginia.

As these resignations are getting frequent, they are eliciting much comment, not without some reason, as the men who are resigning are those who have never been within range of a hostile gun. For my part, I think it too soon altogether to return home. Yet, no man would love to be at home more than I, if honor would permit. By the way, Jennie, did you not say something to me about a young Baxter who was said to have been killed at Bull Run? I learn that he is now in Washington, wounded but recovering.

My Dear, word has this moment come to camp to send out one hundred men about two miles, and I suppose there is some trouble. The matter cannot be serious. The drum is rolling, and I cannot stay in my tent but just so long enough to say to you how dearly I cherish you and little pet.

Your Husband

Arlington Heights,
Aug. 15, 1861

My Dear Jennie:

I was awake just now by a boy with a letter from you of the 13th inst. Capt. Gallagher has arrived and brought along that Box so agreeably full of the reminiscences of home. I shared some of the contents with my brother officers who expressed their satisfaction by giving cheers for Mrs. Guiney. The doughnuts and cakes were so suggestive of home—of days gone by—that I did not wonder they made such an impression. Upon my word Jennie, the cake made a <u>sensation</u> here. We had a good time over the box. My

---

[59] Forty-seven-year-old Adjutant George W. Perkins was a Boston cooper, discharged by resignation on August 4, 1861. *Massachusetts Soldiers, Sailors*, 1: 617.

select company devoured all but the bacon which I have hung up for mastication on the road. Thank you, Dear, for such proofs of your thoughtfulness.

I am quite rested now . . . [letter incomplete]

The Ninth busied itself with construction of a small fort to the southwest of Arlington, built under the direction of Captain B. S. Alexander of the United States Corps of Engineers. Erected of earth and stockade and surrounded by wooden abatis, it mounted five cannon and had bombproof shelters for its magazine and garrison. Upon completion, Captain James Gallagher and the 82 men of Company A occupied the position. In this letter, Guiney angrily relates that Colonel Cass would most likely name it after himself. In fact, the work was named Fort Ramsay, to the annoyance of the Irishmen who had hoped to name the fort as they wished, as other regiments had been allowed to do. But on November 16 Major General McClellan changed the name to Fort Cass in General Order No. 45, a move which bolstered morale in the regiment.

The Ninth had other excitement during this time, receiving a visit by Major Thomas F. Meagher on August 17. On the 19th, McClellan reviewed the division in the presence of President Lincoln and Major General Winfield Scott; McClellan rode between the ranks of the Massachusetts regiment. The next day, the quartermaster issued the United States regulation uniform to the Irishmen, and they proudly donned the Federal blues for the first time. Also, Colonel Cass accepted a United States flag entrusted to the regiment by the boys of Eliot School in Boston.[60]

Arlington Heights, Va.
Aug. 20th 1861

My Dear Jennie:

I received your last letter several days ago and I assure you that this is the first and only opportunity since I received it which I have had to write even a word to you. In fact my ideas are dull now. I have just awoke from a few hours sleep—the first I have had for 48 hours and nearly the first for 72 hours. You scarcely

---

[60] *The Pilot*, October 12, 1861; October 19, 1861. Regan diary, August 17, 19, 20, 21. Macnamara, *Ninth Regiment*, p. 50.

can imagine how we are employed here—we have so many duties to perform—so many calls to meet—Perhaps I told you before that we are engaged in building a fort. It is now almost completed and doubtless, the irrepressible vanity of our commander will christen it Fort Cass. Our picket guard has been doubled since I wrote to you before and every thing here—the preparations, the precaution, the increased activity indicates the fear of an immediate attack upon our position, preliminary to a grand attempt to take Washington. If this is not the result of the present apparent lull, more than me will be very much disappointed. I came in from the outpost of our Picket guard last night; and, this time, Fitzgerald was not with me. I was the only captain on that duty. I had two Lieutenants with me belonging to other companies. A most severe rainstorm has raged here for the last six days, and I assure you that in the midst of it, it was no joke to wade knee deep in mud in the corn fields of Virginia or to rest occasionally on a platform of rails which I had taken from a fence. Yet I stand all this first rate. All I want is, when I come home to camp, a change of underclothing, a good cup of tea, and a few hours sound sleep—all of which I have on such occasions. Besides, as a general thing in fine weather, I would rather be off in the fields and forests than to remain in a monotonous camp. But there I have splendid air—plenty of exercise and there is a sort of romance in it which, to some extent, fascinates me. The country is novel. The farming class with whom I come in contact are good people, but as ignorant and gullible as primitive simplicity could make them. Their houses are built of logs—one room and a little attic aired by a hole not originally made in, but broken through the humble and ancient walls. I saw a school house—such a Harvard as it is! I walked in; no one in it. It would make a decent hen coop in hard times. The only extravagance I noticed about it was a very seedy coat of red paint on the outside. Well an old farmer showed me the parish church, and upon my word, as plain and square as a sugar box. It was small, too, and no ornament—no paint, nothing about it except a rig which looked to me like a large worn-out bird cage on the centre of the square roof, and which, I suppose, was put there to remind parishioners that a steeple ought to be purchased and put up. You may think I ridicule; but this is the truest description which I can give. The land here is excellent—the crops are fine looking. The people are prisoners, hemmed in on one side by rebels and on the other by our troops, they cannot pass either line.

The regiment is well—in good spirits—the boys have just received their uniforms. It was high time. The old rags were worn out. Plunkett has left here—to go home. He received his discharge yesterday. Pay no attention to anything he says about matters and things out here. He is not a competent judge. He never had a heart in the movement. He liked parade and title but no fight. After all, many of us will miss Chris Plunkett. He was noisy and jolly. Fitzgerald and I will resign when we can do so with honor. Unless something turns up to change our minds, and if we live, we would rather remain until the war is ended, but if it continues more than three months longer we have said to each other that we would resign and go home to our families in about two or three months. However, Dear, we must be controlled in these matters, as well as in everything else, by time and circumstances. The war may terminate in a day. It may be transmitted to unborn generations.

My Dear, I wish you to remain in the East, at present, unless the prospect in the West is good beyond a doubt. Still, my eyes are ever looking to the West when I am thinking of our future. Of course, you will let me know what news from Brother John.

The papers which you send I receive regularly. Send me this weeks' Irish American. I would like to see local news of Roxbury. The Norfolk Co. Journal will do for one. The Boston Journal is quite a treat. Of course, I do not ask you to continue to send all these. We can buy the New York papers here once in a while.

Yes, poor brave [Brigadier General Nathaniel] Lyon is gone! may he be honored by the American people, as he deserved to be. I fear he will not. What singular stroke of fate is it which, in every engagement, falls heavily devoted heads of our best and bravest commanders. Ellsworth, Lyon, Ward and Cameron![61] They died with eternal honor, in the halo of a cause bright and

---

[61] For Colonel Elmer Ellsworth's death, see footnote 43. Brigadier General Nathaniel Lyon died while rallying his troops during the Federal defeat at Wilson's Creek, Missouri on August 10. Commander James Ward of the Potomac flotilla perished in the skirmish at Matthias' Point on June 27, and Colonel James Cameron of the Seventy-ninth New York died of mortal wounds received at Bull Run on July 21. Davis, *Bull Run*, p. 253. Long, *The Civil War Day by Day*, pp. 78, 108. Macnamara, *Ninth Regiment*, pp. 27–28. Patrick R. Guiney to Jennie Guiney, Washington, D.C., July 2, 1861.

grand as the Sun. Who will think of them in a few years? Perhaps no one, but those "Dear ones at home"—at <u>home</u>—where the noble and the good are ever remembered in tears and blessings.

My Dear, perhaps in the course of a few weeks I might get leave of absence to go home, if I desired it, providing we remain in our present camp and no onward movement contemplated or no attack made. I have not intimated to any one that I thought of such a thing. I have not made up my mind to apply for leave of absence at any time and the reason is the long distance and the large expense—say $50—too much for me to expend under our present circumstances, even for the boon of seeing you, Dear, and my little child. It may be better to stay here and save the money. Yet I thought of it and of course I tell you, on that point, simply what is in my mind for the moment.

The medical authorities are discharging some of our men because they are not sound and able bodied. We are right glad to get rid of them. They have done nothing—eaten more, and grumbled more, than better men. I suppose they will tell horrible tales when they get to Boston. Their views must be valuable to the public, and comprehensive indeed.

Our friend Meagher paid us a visit here last week—he looks hearty as ever. We gave him an enthusiastic reception. He remained here 5 hours. He seemed delighted to see so many of his old friends. Mrs. Colonel Cass and Mrs. Cornelius Doherty are here on a visit.[62] This life in camp may do well enough for a day or two for ladies, but after that O! my, how ruffled the dresses, no closet to put them in—no mirror—no toilet table—no bed fit for a Christian, no sofa, lounge or cain-bottom chair—"how could I live here." This I suppose they talk as I understand they are going back soon. We expect no more pay until some time in Sept. next.

Now dear, good bye and believe me ever

Your devoted husband
Patrick R. Guiney

---

[62] Of the four men named Cornelius Doherty in *Massachusetts Soldiers, Sailors, and Marines in the Civil War,* none seems likely to have been the husband of the woman mentioned here. However, a city directory lists a Cornelius Doherty representing Ward 1 on the Boston Common Council in 1860; perhaps he was her husband. *The Boston Directory . . . For the Year Commencing July 1, 1860* (Boston: Adams, Sampson & Company, 1860), p. 521. *Massachusetts Soldiers, Sailors,* 3: 260, 4: 163, 805, 7: 161.

Arlington Heights, Va.
Aug. 21st 1861

My Dear Jennie:

I have this moment received your Journal and Herald containing much entertaining information. But that little scroll on the margin of the Herald caused my ideas to wake up, I assure you. I ask myself whether I had omitted a single opportunity of writing to you; and in looking back over the varied duties which I have been called upon to perform within the last ten days I hold myself not guilty of neglecting to write to my Darling. This is the usual tendency of my mind. No matter how wrong I might be, you know, I always held myself piously sufficient in all things. Don't you remember my failing? Well, perhaps, Dear, I ought to have written to you, so that you might have received it on Saturday evening. How gladly, Darling, I would anticipate even your smallest desire, if I were not tossed about so much in this sea of excitement! Indeed, I hardly remember anything disconnected with my immediate duties, from one day to the other. I wrote to several, I think, the same day on which I wrote to our Dear and kind friend Miss Crespy. Now, I do not remember who they are. I mistrust that I sent you a few lines the same day. But if I did not, pardon one whom you have often pardoned before—

My dear, dear, Jennie, news has just reached here that an attack has been made upon our forces a few miles below here—at the Chain Bridge, it may turn out to be a false report, or the matter may be simply a slight skirmish. No matter which it is that I must close this conversation with you, which I did intend should not be so brief. A battle will soon be fought here, if it has not already commenced.

Good bye love and may God protect you and my child. May Mary [Guiney has made a cross after Mary's name] ever blessed, to whom I have often appealed but never in vain, watch over you both. "To Arms" is ringing through the camp.

Patrick R. Guiney

On August 28, Brigadier General William T. Sherman went to a new assignment in the Department of the Cumberland, and Brigadier General

Fitz John Porter assumed command of the brigade.[63] *Soon afterward,*
Porter received promotion to command the division, and Brigadier General
George Webb Morell took over the brigade, consisting of the Ninth Massa-
chusetts, Colonel Dwight A. Woodbury's Fourth Michigan, Colonel James
McQuade's Fourteenth New York, and the Sixty-second Pennsylvania
under Colonel Samuel W. Black.[64] *Meanwhile, the Irishmen participated*
in minor skirmishing in the vicinity of Bailey's Cross Roads.[65]

Arlington Heights, Va.
August 29th 1861

My Dear Jennie:

I have read your sweet little note of the twenty sixth inst., and I
assure you I am satisfied fully and heartily that you never neglect
opportunities to send me word how you are, which is all the news
from home about which I have a never ceasing anxiety. You know
how impatient one situated as I am, in a far off and strange land,
is about a matter so dearly concerning him as the welfare of a
loved wife and a child who is more than loved, if there is any
feeling in the heart more intense than this. Dear, I need not say
any more to you about this.

The aspect of affairs here is that a move onward, or a speedy
attack upon our lines by the enemy, is soon to be made. If we are
only let alone for a few days until we get our pay, I shall be more

---

[63] OR, vol. 51: 461. A West Pointer, Fitz John Porter distinguished himself in
the Mexican War and returned to his alma mater to teach artillery. The outbreak
of the Civil War prompted his rapid promotion, and he formed a devoted and
loyal friendship with Major General McClellan. Porter eventually attained corps
command and served with the Army of the Potomac until his and McClellan's
removal in November 1862. Afterward, he faced a politically charged court martial that found him guilty of insubordination and retreat at Second Manassas
and dismissed him from the army. Sixteen years later, a board exonerated him,
and Porter was vindicated of guilt. Warner, *Generals in Blue*, pp. 378–80.

[64] First in his West Point class of 1835, George W. Morell served in the Mexican
War and practiced law. During the Civil War, he attained leadership of Fitz John
Porter's division when that officer received corps command in May 1862. Promoted to major general, Morell's testimony during Porter's court martial proved
unhelpful to those seeking Porter's downfall, and he was relegated to minor
commands until mustered out of service. Warner, *Generals in Blue*, pp. 330–31.

[65] *The Pilot*, September 21, 1861. Long, *The Civil War Day by Day*, p. 112.

satisfied. If we were ordered toward Richmond before getting paid, I fear you might want some money before the government could scarcely find us to pay our salaries. If nothing of an extraordinary character occurs, we will be paid next week. The rebels are getting savvy. They have kept us awake and on the move for the last 48 hours. They frequently run up from the vicinity of "Falls Church" and, planting some pieces of artillery on some hills near the picket lines of our troops, give us some lead. They watch us, and when they find us (officers) resorting any house to get our meals, they wreak their wretched vengeance upon the poor inhabitants by firing at the suspected houses. A house in which I had dinner when out on picket a few days ago was fired at and the barn standing in the yard was smashed to pieces by a shell. You may wonder why it is that we do not follow them. The reason is our general will not allow it, at present. It is raining here very much. Up to our knees in corn-fields. We get drenched in going through the woods. I have pleasant evenings in camp. Many officers come to see me in my Arabian hut. I might give you the most disgusting chapter in the history of commanders by telling you what was said and done yesterday when we were called into line to meet a supposed attack of the enemy. I forbear to say anymore now. All communication with Washington was suspended yesterday, we had no mail until today. Do not be surprised if you do not receive letters regularly.

PRG

Arlington Heights, Va.
Sept. 1st 1861

My Dear Jennie:
   Your letter of the twenty ninth inst. was duly received by me this morning. This is Sunday. Everything about me seems holy and subdued, as if fanned and shaded with the wings of angels. Even the little rustic cross which marks our canvas Cathedral, is as full of hallowed significance to us, to-day, as if it were well chiseled, and glistening on a Calvary of Marble. The legions who are upon these hills seem unusually quiet. No firing of cannon or musketry is heard. No alarms are given. Is there a meaning in

this? I suppose none but that which my own impression attaches to it. At any rate, your words—your sweet words—possess a power which, as it would seem, I did not feel before. We are ordered to be in readiness to advance at a moments notice. Either, it is believed, we will be attacked here soon or it is determined to press on towards Richmond. This state of things causes me to reflect upon my home—to think of my loved ones. I have a stronger sense—a more active appreciation, of what I have done in the past, and what I risk in the future, than was plain to me before. You ask me, Dear, to come home. This time, it is harder than ever to say "I cannot at present." Yet Dear, I must say it. If any consideration would induce me to return, you never again would be obliged, or have an opportunity to repeat your affectionate request. I would not leave now. It would seem to me disgraceful to do so in the face of the enemy. This impassion would go with me through life. Perhaps this is imaginary, but whatever it is, it is real to me. It is said that public opinion has undergone a change since we left Massachusetts. I do not wonder. This is not the first time. I expected as much from the beginning. The sordid misers who are not accumulating in these novel times, and the craven Democrats who rot in office and starve out of it, are trying all over the country to get up an opposition to the government. Yes there is another class, Jennie; natural carpers who possess neither capacity to think nor hearts to feel for their country in this great hour of her career. These are spread out in all parties. Many of them were torch-carriers for Mr. Lincoln last fall. O! for a tongue to curse them. It makes no difference to me. The cause is to me the same as it was when I left Boston. Not a hue of it is changed. I care not who becomes corrupt, the cause is pure. Well, Dear, to close on this subject, I will say that any change of public opinion, any military tyranny which is bearable, any trials which I can endure, will never cause me to resign my commission. Honor and the welfare of my wife and child must accompany that act, and nothing else but these. I speak of a purely voluntary resignation. Circumstance may arise which, according to military rule, might render the holding of my commission disgraceful. If they do arise, I go home at that time whenever it is. Tyranny I can stand, but a studied insult will make a civilian of me if ever given. Then Darling, I have thought to myself that I would resign after seeing service. However, I will not be positive as to time. By the way, a friend of mine who is a Lawyer in Boston, advises me to "Remain in the army" for life. This would be well enough in Peace when you and Julia could be with me; but, in war, it is too much of a sacrifice for me, to make such an arrangement as that suggested.

Capt. Fitzgerald has resigned.[66] He sent in his resignation several days ago. He will go home in a few days.

Sept. 4th 1861

On writing the above I was suddenly summoned to take charge of a detachment of ninety men and to go out with them about three miles near enemy's lines. I have been there ever since. Every moment I expected to be disturbed. In the night Rebel rockets intended for signals were thrown up and cannon were heard booming on all sides. This was intended, I suppose, to draw us on farther, but the attempt failed. However the Rebels are pressing up towards us wonderfully. And if a fight does not occur within six days, I shall consider myself mistaken. I told you about sleeping on the grass with a three cornered rail for a pillow. I should not say "sleeping" for we never sleep here. The most one can do here is to enjoy a precarious doze. The Regiment is all well. Assistant Surgeon [Patrick A.] O'Connell has resigned.[67] Some two or three other officers talk of it. I would not be surprised to find the Colonel himself going home soon. I have no authority for saying this. It is one of my impressions which are not easily accounted for. The reason assigned by the officers who have resigned is the bearing and conduct of Colonel Cass. They are the best judges, as to themselves. As for me I am not disappointed in him. I saw what kind of man he was at the start. I have found him as I thought I would. Others took him for more than what he was, and now feel sore. I hardly ever take men for more than what they are, and consequently, I save myself many perplexities which afflict others from an opposite course. When I resign, it will not

---

[66] Captain Fitzgerald's resignation was accepted to date from September 3, 1861. *Massachusetts Soldiers, Sailors*, 1: 652.

[67] Assistant Surgeon Patrick A. O'Connell resigned and received his discharge on September 12, 1861. Thereafter, he joined the Twenty-eighth Massachusetts Volunteer Infantry, where he was commissioned surgeon on October 25, 1861. O'Connell was captured by the Confederates at Second Manassas on August 30, 1862; he eventually was released and discharged from the army to date June 7, 1863. 1: 617, 3: 190.

be from either fear or hatred of any man, but rather because I
want to be with my family. Until this takes place, Jennie, bear up
gallantly. I will be with you yet. Capt. Fitzgerald resigned before
we received orders to be in readiness to march against the enemy,
and therefore his honor is unstained and bright as ever. If I had
received your letter before the reception of these orders, my
thoughts might have taken a different course. There is but one
course now for me to pursue; to hold on a while longer. I think I
will see you soon whether I resign or not. Have you heard from
your brother John? If so, what is the prospect out West? I am
expecting to be paid from day to day. When I do get paid, I will
send on to you. By the way, is the city subsidy continued?[68] My
company hereafter is to be the "Color company" of the Regiment.[69] So the stars and stripes and the green flag of Ireland will
fling their shadows over me in the Battle field, if I should ever see
any. How are all my good friends? Lizzie, Mrs. O'Donnell, Mr.
and Mrs. Campbell, Mr. and Mrs. Mulrey, Mrs. Merrill, Miss
Crespy, are they all well?

Mrs. Cass and Mrs. Scanlan [wife of First Lieutenant Michael
Scanlan of Company A] are here but are going back.[70] This is no
place for them; Mrs. Nugent came to Washington lately.[71] She did
not visit camp. She had a travelling companion with her all the
way stopping at Philadelphia. If her husband had a harder head,
what pain his wife would cause him. He is a butt for everyone, on
her account. But why should I speak of this to you? What the
frivolous may do can be of no concern to those who, like you and
me, live in a little world of our own with a purpose to make life a
blessing and death not a curse. I receive papers from you regularly. Dear, kiss little pet on forehead—on both cheeks and on
the lips for me.

P. R. G.

---

[68] See footnote 10 of this chapter.

[69] The color company bore responsibility for carrying and protecting the regimental flags—an honorable, if dangerous, duty.

[70] Guiney consistently misspelled this name as "Scanlin" throughout the letters. A Boston trader, Lieutenant Michael Scanlan received a commission as
captain dated January 28, 1862, and he resigned as captain of Company B on
October 15, 1862. *Massachusetts Soldiers, Sailors*, 1: 624.

[71] Wife of Lieutenant Richard P. Nugent, a Boston printer before the war
began. Commissioned first lieutenant dated January 28, 1862, he was killed in
action at Gaines' Mill on June 27, 1863. *Massachusetts Soldiers, Sailors*, 1: 673.

P.S. I wish, Darling, if you can, you would make me a new "fatigue" suit. The one you sent has done good service but is worn out. The sky blue is good color if you can get some that won't fade. Make it thick <u>for</u> <u>winter</u>. Put Captains (cheap) shoulder bars on the jacket—put some green into the trimmings somewhere. Send out by Adam's Express or some other reliable conveyance. At the same time send me out some good brandy, as we cannot get it here. It's a first rate drink after exposure. It is preventative of fever and ague—put in to the box a few of Savells Cigars for smoking at "Home Dreams." Do not attempt this until I send you money.

Good bye again
P. R. G.

The following letter is on stationary used for the August 29 and September 5 letters; furthermore, just as the fragment breaks off, he seems to be ready to refer to the fatigue suit which he wrote his wife about the day before. This letter is from September 5, 1861.

. . . The weather is very wet here. It rains almost incessantly. Perhaps this is the reason why we have not made a decisive move yet. My tent keeps out the rain very well, and unpleasant as the day is outside, it affords me a welcome opportunity to write this to you. When I am [in] camp, I have a pleasant time of it. I seem to be welcome in every officers' quarters; and this is a great pleasure. The men, too, seem to think much of me. When I want anything done they do it without a murmur. I sometimes, when passing them, hear some one make to remark, "Be Jabers! The Ribils will have hard work to touch him, while I'm alive." This is flattering to me. Other officers are continually in hot water. Mrs. Cass visited my <u>mansion</u> last evening. She saw those red drawers which you sent me, and likes them very much. She says she must have a pair like them. They are just about <u>her</u> <u>size</u>, I should think. The fact is these "Red Drawers" have become so popular in Camp that everybody wants to borrow them, to sleep in. They are so nice that the contrast between them and the little stiff crochet-bed made of branches of trees and oak leaves, is painful. I believe I said something to you yesterday about making me a . . . [letter discontinues at this point]

Arlington Heights, Va.
Sept 5th 1861

My Dear Jennie:

I wrote to you this morning and immediately after putting my letter into the rude little Post office which we have here, I received your letter of the 24th August. What does this mean? I had your letter of the 2nd of Sept. before I received yours of the 24th ultimo. These confounded officials blunder so that I am really vexed with them.

Taking advantage of the leisure of which I spoke this morning, I hasten to say a word or two in reply to yours of the 24th ultimo. This discrepancy in the receipt of your letters will explain to you some remark which I made in the letter which I wrote this morning. By all means, my dear, visit our friends in Portland. They are so kind that I am heartily anxious you should go. I say any more, I want to read again your jewel of a letter.

Adieu,
PRG

The first part of this letter is missing, including the date. However, several references in it indicate that it was written shortly after Brigadier General William S. Rosecrans's victory at Carnifax Ferry on September 10.[72]

. . . not careful enough and venture too far and are taken prisoners by the enemy. We have lost three in this way.

---

[72] Although the letter could conceivably date to the Federal victory at Rich Mountain on July 11–13, it seems unlikely. At that time, Major General McClellan commanded the West Virginia military district and most of the acclaim for the victory, although it was largely due to Brigadier General Rosecrans's efforts. Therefore, it seems Guiney would probably have referred to McClellan, not Rosecrans, if he was discussing Rich Mountain. Furthermore, in mid-July the Ninth Massachusetts was located in Washington, where it did not experience much skirmishing. Guiney mentions such activity as well as the Chain Bridge, lending credibility to the interpretation that the letter was written while at Arlington. An alternative date for the letter, that it was written in January 1863 and refers to Rosecrans and the battle of Stones River, is even less likely. At that time the Ninth was in winter quarters at Falmouth, Virginia, nowhere near Washington or the Chain Bridge. Long, *The Civil War Day by Day*, pp. 93, 116, 302–307.

Last night was an exciting one here. The rebels drove in our Picket Guard and evinced a disposition to advance upon us. Our Regiment was out all night and camped on the grass. As the shades of the evening fell and the moon and stars began to beautify the scene, the eye could discover in the distance a row of rebel fire-balloons evidently intended to pass for stars. It was no use. We immediately knew what they were. We know too much of astronomy to be duped in that way. At the same time we could discern black columns of smoke gradually rising up in the still air. I never will forget the majesty and meaning of that sight. The rebels had advanced towards and burned the dwelling of those who were suspected of hostility to them. A wagon rushed by us loaded with women and children weeping and wounded. We felt certain that the great battle would be fought here to-day but for some cause or other we are again in our camp. I wish I could stop to describe everything to you as it was. Perhaps these things are not pleasing to you. But there is scarcely anything else out here to talk about. However, as I write this the cannons all along our line of defence from Chain Bridge to Alexandria are booming in honor of Rozencrans [*sic*] and his gallant Army who have just gained a great victory. Our turn will come soon.

My Dear, I feel oppressed with the kindness of your words. I know not how to be sufficiently grateful. I hope that suit will arrive here in time for service. I will warrant you will sew in an Agnus Dei in the jacket. I found one in the other.

We expect to be paid next Tuesday. I receive papers from you regularly—and marginal notes. Do not expect to hear from [me] now so often as heretofore. Write to me often, if only to tell that yourself and my other little Darling are well.

PRG

At this point, the Federals sought to clear the area of northern Virginia near Washington from Rebel forces. The Ninth broke camp on September 28 and marched toward Munson's Hill seven miles away, evacuated by the Confederates earlier that day. Upon reaching the hill that chilly night, the picket line of the Ninth Massachusetts and that of another Federal regiment mistakenly fired into each other. At dawn the next day, a six-gun battery nearly fired on the regiment, under the impression that it was a

Southern unit. Superior officers had failed to properly coordinate the advance and prevent such "friendly fire" accidents from occurring. The Irishmen proceeded to the right of Falls Church near the Leesburg Turnpike, deploying skirmishers against Confederates in the distance.[73]

Virginia
Oct. 1st 1861

My Dear Jennie:

I received a letter from you yesterday. It was so welcome away out here in the woods. It would be anywhere Jennie. But as we have left our camp, and advanced to vicinity of Falls Church, I scarcely hoped to hear from home again for some time. I am afraid your letters will not reach me until after the Battle, when, I suppose, we will again settle down. We left camp last Saturday. The enemy retired before us like so many hares—Evacuated Munson's Hill, Falls Church etc. We are in possession of them all. It is expected that we will make <u>gradual</u> advances upon Richmond. Three men of the California Regiment [Seventy-first Pennsylvania] were killed—several wounded. Our Regiment is fortunate— "No one hurt." The Rebels left every point against which we were sent, without waiting for a fight. Well, we will catch up with them soon. Their bloody red Banner of Rebellion will pale before the Green, as sure as heaven. We may fall, but we will die or live victorious—or die trying to be. Yesterday I went to Falls Church Village across a dense wood with a small scouting party. Adjutant [William] Strachen was with us.[74] He is a brave, dashing soldier. Rebels not there. We stopped New York soldiers from burning houses. Did some good in this way. No tents; we sleep on the grass. All healthy. Whole army advancing. I will write when possible. Con-

---

[73] *The Pilot*, October 19, 1861. Macnamara, *Ninth Regiment*, pp. 57–59. Long, *The Civil War Day by Day*, p. 122.

[74] Adjutant William Strachen was an East Boston glass finisher or last maker, and he was commissioned adjutant on August 26, 1861. He was dismissed from the service by a general order on February 25, 1862 and re-enlisted in the Ninth Massachusetts on August 18, 1862. Promoted to sergeant major to date from September 26, 1862, Strachen was discharged for disability on February 14, 1863. He later served in the Fourth Massachusetts Heavy Artillery Regiment. *Massachusetts Soldiers, Sailors*, 1: 617, 661.

tinue to write. Your letters may reach me. Father Scully and Major [Robert] Peard send respects to you.[75]

My Dear, stop in Roxbury, prepare for winter. Kisses to little pet. Love to my dear friends—to them all. Pray for me without fear, Darling, cherished wife.

God bless you,
Patrick R. Guiney

Willard's Hotel
Washington, D.C.
Oct. 7th 1861

My Dear Jennie:

I received yours of the 4th inst., last evening. I believe that I received one a day or two ago, but I did not answer it. Also, I am in constant receipt of papers from you. My Dear, how much I would like to write to you every day, you are so good to me, so kind and watchful and loving. But I cannot. If I give myself up to thinking of you and my little pet even for an hour, an impression is made upon me and I feel less fitted for my duties as a soldier. Thoughts of home unnerve me. This is my composition. Thought leans heavily upon me—work is nothing. If I know you are well—I am satisfied—you darling, must be content with this knowledge of me. I am well and strong and my constitution promises that I will remain so. Every hour now is so full of meaning to our Army and cause that my thoughts are necessarily bent towards the battle field. If I am spared, how happy you and I will be. The pain of absence will be the source of renewed pleasure when we meet again. Even if I should forget to write to you as often as I ought, pray for and bless me still. Whatever I do, love me and teach our little one to love me. This is all I ask. I know it is so. I know it ever will be so. God bless you my Jennie, I wish I had an age to speak to you, but I must close. I am here on business with Secretary of

---

[75] Major Robert Peard was a forty-nine-year-old Milford manufacturer and received his commission as lieutenant colonel to date October 24, 1861. He died of illness at the brigade hospital on January 27, 1862. *Massachusetts Soldiers, Sailors*, 1: 617.

War [Simon Cameron].[76] I must go to camp at Falls Church—10 miles, or 12. Have you seen Father Scully? He is a good friend to me. I am now <u>acting</u> <u>Major</u> of the Regiment.[77] I am going ahead you see. Mrs. Peard is in camp. Rebels still dodging us. All well. Love to Lizzie. Farewell Dear, I will write soon again.

P. R. G.

In mid-October, the Ninth occupied Minor's Hill, an eminence immediately outside the western corner of the District of Columbia rising 454 feet above tide-water level. The regiment set up its winter quarters, and a detachment of 60 men under Lieutenant William W. Doherty at Fort Cass received orders to rejoin the regiment when the Thirteenth New York was detailed to occupy the forts in this sector. Although the nights were cold, the troops remained in good spirits, bolstered in part by music provided by the regimental band at night.[78]

On October 20 several officers of the Thirty-third Pennsylvania visited the Ninth Massachusetts, during which Colonel Cass, Guiney, and Lieutenant John W. Mahan delivered brief speeches.[79] On the 21st a Federal force crossed the Potomac River at Leesburg near Ball's Bluff but the Confederates repulsed the attack. The battle turned into a Union massacre as many troops drowned while trying to escape the hot Rebel fire. A total of 921 Federals were lost at Ball's Bluff, over 700 of them missing and pre-

---

[76] In 1845, Pennsylvanian Simon Cameron won the United States Senate seat vacated by James Buchanan, who resigned to enter President Polk's cabinet. He lost re-election bids in 1849 and 1855 but, after throwing in his lot with the new Republican party, was able to return to that body in 1857. Despite allegations of prior scandal, Cameron's supporters mounted such a strong campaign on his behalf that Lincoln gave him the War Department. While there, Cameron displayed his inefficient and corrupt manner of conducting business, and had to be replaced shortly afterward. Johnson and Malone, eds., *Dictionary of American Biography*, 3: 437–39.

[77] Lieutenant Colonel Rowell was sick and recuperating in Washington; therefore, Peard acted as lieutenant colonel, and Guiney as major. Lieutenant John H. Rafferty commanded Company D at this time. *The Pilot*, October 19, 1861; October 26, 1861.

[78] *The Pilot*, October 26, 1861. *Official Military Atlas of the Civil War*, Plate 7. Minor's Hill is sometimes also spelled Miner's Hill.

[79] A Boston counsellor, Lieutenant John W. Mahan became captain on October 25, 1861, and received his commission as major to date from March 30, 1863. He received a brevet promotion to lieutenant colonel to date March 13, 1865. *Massachusetts Soldiers, Sailors*, 1: 635.

sumably drowned. One of the dead was Oregon Senator Edward D. Baker,
a friend of Lincoln serving in the army as a colonel. The Irish Ninth was
held in readiness to march in support of the beleaguered Union troops,
and slept on its arms that night.[80]

Miner's Hill Va.
Oct. 22 1861

My Dear Jennie:

I am in possession of your letter of the 18th inst. papers, also, duly received. With what pleasure, Jennie, I reflect upon your ever gushing kindness to me, and how happily I sit in my little tent and think of you and read over and over again your affectionate words. Perhaps some would be sad if circumstanced as I am—so far away and a cherished wife and child at home. But, no, I am not affected in that way. My thoughts make me joyful and content. My heart could not be satisfied and my life would be a bleak and painful one, if I had not even one to love me, to think of me and to speak my name in the holy accents of prayer. Having you, Darling, to do all this, I feel blessed and happy. My life amid the coarse vicissitudes of camp is passed away without a tinge of sorrow; and, Dear, I know it is a great pleasure to your woman's ear to know that you make me so happy. If I have never spoken to you of that grey early morn when you and I were together at the sacred altar, it is not because I do not think of it. I do often. It is the only one which impressed its scenes and hues upon me. I remember it well. That day shall ever be the welcome anniversary of a great gift to me. Bless you Darling if I had you near me now, how fondly would I press you to my heart. Now, Jennie, while writing the above I was quite serious, but upon my word I am laughing now. What am I laughing at? I'll tell you: those evenings when we were in that parlor and I trying to read the "Reveries of a Bachelor" under circumstances extremely adverse to a proper appreciation of his supposed felicity. Well, Dear, my mind has come back again from its ramble into our <u>young</u> days. What of our present and future? I have such unlimited confidence in your good judgment that it seems to me to be superfluous to advise

---

[80] *The Pilot,* November 9, 1861.

you; and since you informed me that you were comfortable for the winter, my anxiety for you is not so painful as it was. I am glad you made up your mind to visit our kind friends in Portland. I feel sure that you will enjoy it. All the fear I have is that my little Julia will be sea-sick on the boat. She is so fat and so full of life it would be a pity to have her ill. But I suppose it is all over by this time and the little Darling is as lively as ever. Remember me kindly to the family. I hope to get a letter from you as soon as you can after arrival in Portland.

As to myself, I have already told you how I am. I am enjoying the confidence and esteem of my fellow officers and soldiers— there is a welcome for me in every tent. Good health, too, is my fortune. Everyone out here says that I am the happiest looking man imaginable. This is the secret of it, Jennie: My home beams upon me and encircles me with a halo which is ever bright. O! may God permit us to be happy together again.

Our situation is unchanged since my last. Expecting to move every day. We were not in the fight at Leesburg last night. The prospect is that in the course of a few weeks, I will be Major of the Regmt. I am not commissioned as such, but I am doing the duties of Major. Father Scully is here. I made him describe yourself and Julia to me. I am in want of nothing love. I fear the comforter would encumber me on the march. Unless you have sent it before this, Dear, do not send it at all. When we go into Winter Quarters, I will inform you and then you can send me a few things. I am in a hurry, love, with that likeness of yours. I had two pictures taken but, O! my conscience, they were shockingly bad. The artist was rather spiritual, I suspect, and therefore, made a ghost of me. I would send you one but I am afraid it would frighten the child. So I will not send it. My Dear, it is getting late and I must close this without telling you one half of what I intend to when we meet again.

P. R. G.

P.S. Excuse the envelope I cannot find any other. I hate these daubed ones.

P. R. G.

This was a time of further training for the men of the Irish Ninth. Three times a week the brigade drilled in battalion formation, often under the eye of spectators such as other generals and, once, the governor of New Hampshire. Meanwhile, Rowell received a discharge on October 23 and was replaced as lieutenant colonel by Peard; Guiney received promotion to major dated October 24. Sergeant Michael Finnerty wrote for The Pilot *that "No better selection could be made. Major Guiney, well known to your Roxbury neighbors as a promising member of the Suffolk bar, has done much for the honor of the regiment, and is certainly more entitled to recognition than any outsider can possibly be."*[81]

There were a few events to break the monotony of camp life for the soldiers of the Irish Ninth. Major General McClellan reviewed the entire division near Hall's Hill on November 9, and as the twelve regiments of infantry and twelve companies of cavalry passed by their commanding general, peals of cheering filled the air.[82] *On November 20 the brigade marched toward Bailey's Cross Roads. Here, McClellan organized a great review of troops, and over fifty thousand infantry and ten thousand cavalry assembled for President Lincoln, Secretary of State William Seward, and Secretary of War Simon Cameron, as well as a number of senators and congressmen. The President rode up and down the lines with McClellan, and then the troops conducted a grand review parade which took four hours to complete. Although the Ninth had three hundred men detached on picket duty, it presented a figure of strength, and as the Irishmen passed before Lincoln, its green flag fluttered in the breeze.*[83]

Guiney might have missed the grand parade at Bailey's Cross Roads, however. On November 12, he received a leave of absence to visit Boston on regimental business and seems to have left around the time of the review. While in Boston, an abscess formed on Guiney's right groin, confining him to his room for several days. Enclosing a signed medical certificate, Guiney requested an extension of leave until December 15, and presumably received it.[84]

---

[81] Commonwealth of Massachusetts Certificate of Service, United States Army Adjutant General's Office, Boston, August 8, 1935, in Dinand Library Rare Book Room, College of the Holy Cross. *The Pilot*, November 30, 1861.

[82] *The Pilot*, November 30, 1861.

[83] *The Pilot*, December 14, 1861. Macnamara, *Ninth Regiment*, pp. 63–64.

[84] Patrick R. Guiney to Brigadier General George Morell, Miner's Hill, Virginia, November 12, 1861; Patrick R. Guiney to Brigadier General Seth Williams, A.A.G., Roxbury, Massachusetts, November 29, 1861; Medical certificate, dated November 29, [1861]; all located in Patrick R. Guiney Military Service Record, National Archives, Washington, D.C.

In December, upon Christmas' approach, the soldiers decorated their camp with evergreen and ivy, and tents were adorned with crosses and green wreaths. Christmas Day dawned clear and bright as the regiment crowded at the first High Mass celebrated by Fr. Scully in the new chapel tent; several officers and visiting ladies later sung Vespers. According to his letter, Guiney attended the Christmas banquet furnished by a Washington caterer, which lasted long into the night. A number of division officers and their wives joined in the food, music, dancing, speeches, and poetry of the occasion—among them, Brigadier General Fitz John Porter's staff, Brigadier General George Morell and his staff, Colonel Woodbury of the Fourth Michigan and his wife, Colonel McQuade of the Fourteenth New York, Colonel Lansing of the Seventeenth New York, Colonel Black of the Sixty-second Pennsylvania, and Colonel Cass, his wife, and the other officers of the Ninth. Among the many toasts that evening, Guiney offered one to honor Major General McClellan.[85]

Miner's Hill
December 27 /61

My Dear Jennie:

I received your note sent by Col. Cass. My health is the same as it was when I wrote to you last. My lameness is gone, but when I get chilly I find myself incapable of much exertion. However, I am indulging the hope of feeling entirely well in a week or so. How are you love? How is our little pet? Tasso was never haunted by the face and form of his Laura to such an extent as I am by that little prattling heart.[86] Well, although it makes me sad, the vision is ever welcome. I wish it were not a sin to ask a bond of our good Heavenly Father for the safety of you both. Indeed, Jennie, this thought has often recurred to me that to love and be loved is as fraught with pain as with pleasure. Think of the anxieties which it induces. What little regard fate has for our wishes. What a mystery life seems to me out here amid these strange

---

[85] *The Pilot*, January 11, 1862. Regan diary, December 23, 1861. Macnamara, *Ninth Regiment*, pp. 65–66. Macnamara, *Bivouac*, p. 75.

[86] Torquato Tasso (1544–1595) was one of the most influential poets of the Italian Renaissance. Author of satire, epic, and tragedy, he died before being crowned as poet laureate in Rome. Johann von Goethe later wrote a drama entitled *Torquato Tasso*.

scenes; but it is no use to moralize. Experience and reason teach this maxim to us all: "Live well—cheerfully, submit—and be as happy as you can."

I would have you with me Darling but for our Julia. I am satisfied that she could not live in camp. Even if you were in Washington, it would be perhaps only once a month that I could see you, and then only by the reluctant assent of my superior officers. Then, Darling, I am fully impressed that our army will be advanced in January.

We had a grand banquet Christmas Night. Gen. Morell and a host of Colonels were here. They all confessed that they were Irish—Blarney, but true of some of them. The general "went in" on the dancing.

Mrs. Cass and Mrs. Doherty are going home in a few days. I will miss Mrs. Cass very much—she seems to us indispensable. How is Lizzie?

                                                            PRG

1862: "We are <u>now</u> engaged in <u>war</u>. <u>The holidays are over</u>."

Washington
Jan 10th 62

My Dear Jennie

I came in town last night so as to get money from our paymaster to send to you. The Regmt. has not been paid, and unless I came in I thought that possibly we might be sent off without being paid. I could not bear to go off knowing that you and Loolie were in want.[1] I enclose one hundred twenty dollars. You must buy furs and everything you want to make yourself and Loolie perfectly comfortable. I must return to camp immediately. Do not be displeased, Darling, if I do not write to you. Events are culminating in a crisis now at hand. We are preparing night and day. I spent last evening with Gen. Shields at Herndon House.[2] I am quite well and strong.

Farewell Dear
P. R. G.

Miner's Hill, Va.
Jan. 20, 1862

My Dear Jennie:

I am in possession of three letters from you which I received since I wrote my last to you. I cannot give any reason for allowing your favors to thus accumulate without acknowledgement, except this that, for the time being, my thoughts are indivisible. I cannot

---

[1] "Loolie" refers to Louise, Guiney's daughter.

[2] James Shields was born in County Tyrone, Ireland. In 1826 he arrived in New York Harbor and settled in Illinois. A veteran of the Mexican War, in which he served as a brigadier general of Illinois volunteers, Shields went on to serve as United States senator from Illinois from 1849 to 1855 and from Minnesota in 1858. He did much to stimulate Irish immigration into Minnesota, organizing towns with such names as Shieldsville, Erin, and Kilkenny. During the Civil War, he confronted and was defeated by "Stonewall" Jackson in the Shenandoah Valley campaign of 1862 and eventually resigned; his skill as a military leader was never what many Irish made it out to be. After the war, Shields re-entered the political arena and briefly represented Missouri in the United States Senate. Johnson and Malone, eds., *Dictionary of American Biography*, 17: 106–107.

command a detachment of men on a scouting expedition towards Vienna, or a large Picket Guard posted close to the enemy's lines, do duty as "Brigade Officer of the Day" or, in fact, do any military duty without having my whole thought centered upon and occupied with the particular thing which I am about. It is only, my Dear, when I am off duty, (which seldom happens now as Lt. Col. Peard is not well) that I can write to you. Still, Darling, I know that I have not written to you as often as I might. But then I know it's all right. You may get vexed at me, but I defy you, Jennie, to keep vexed with me. I know you can't. So you see, Jennie, I presume upon your good heart and kindness to forgive me, no matter how negligent I may be. I must be always myself—I never can act the character of somebody else. I am not to blame for the manner in which the Lord made me. Negligence is but a development of myself. You ought to like this quality, Darling, because it is me all out. It is no use talking any more upon what I have not done. I feel your forgiveness. I know you would kiss me if you could.

My Dear, I did think of "that day" in January; and I was all alone too in my little tent. I had a quiet day-dream of days gone by—and you and little Loolie. I was sad, Darling. Sadness is sweet to me. But O! Jennie, how heart-wishes are denied—what sport is made with love, and hope, and purpose, by Fate—that irresistible power which commands "Onward, Onward!", "Look neither behind nor to the Right nor Left, but onward!", and so we go through life to the end—to the grave—to another and to a nobler life.

My Dear: I could not help laughing at the idea of our having money in Bank. I begin to feel more important than usual—I am sorry that we are not in a position to increase the amount much. My horse and equipments cost me a great deal. I got cheated in the horse too. Congress is going to reduce our pay.[3] Why? I know not. We cannot save anything scarcely. The wretched humbugs in

---

[3] Congress engaged in efforts to reduce the expenses of the government, and hoped to cut four million dollars from the cost of the army roll. The New York *Herald* reported that John Sherman, Senator from Ohio and brother of William T. Sherman, proposed a bill prohibiting brevet pay except for services performed appropriate to the rank, and contemplating a general reduction of the pay of all officers' grades from one-fifth to one-third their prior amount. *Herald*, January 14, 1862; January 18, 1862.

Congress must have hobbies and therefore pitch in to the Army. Just the very thing they ought to let alone, at present, or cherish and encourage it. The attention of these nervous, weak-eyed political brokers is more upon the dollar than upon the country. They wish to replenish the Treasury by bleeding the officers of the Army. I wish I had a Congressional Battalion of them under me for the usual three days on picket in the snow and slosh and cold and danger. O! my, how delighted they would be! And then I would send them back to <u>reduce</u> our pay. They never thought of doing it while there was nothing for soldiers to do, and the Army was filled with traitors. Now that friends to the country are in the Army and hardships are to be endured and dangers to be encountered, the politicians must reduce the pay of officers so as to save money to the Government. Why do they not reduce their own pay? Oh! no.

In my last, I spoke to you about an "Advance." <u>Our</u> Regiment has not moved yet. Perhaps will not for some time. Contradictory orders are still the order of the day. I enclose you twenty dollars— all I can afford—as a contribution to your fund. Who knows to what proportions this little commencement will swell? I will endeavor to save all I can.

My health is good—rugged as ever I was.

This is Sunday and I am glad to be able to spend part of it with you. How is Loolie?

Mrs. Nugent [wife of Lieutenant Richard P. Nugent] is in camp.

So James is married! Well, well!

Good bye Dear and kiss Loolie for me.

P. R. G.

P.S. Remember me to your brother John, your Father, Sisters Mary and Lizzie. There is some talk here of our being sent into an "Irish Division" under [Brigadier] General Shields. Some talk also about Col. Cass being made Brigadier.[4] If these changes take place, I will aim for a high mark—and hit it too.

P. R. G.

---

[4] This was desired by many Irish serving in the army, especially those in the Ninth. John W. Mahan, now captain of Guiney's old Company D, wrote a letter to *The Pilot* on February 20 calling for such a division to be formed under Brigadier General Shields's command, and the promotion of Colonel Cass to brigadier general. *The Pilot*, March 8, 1862.

Jan. 23rd 1862

My Ever Dear Jennie:

Owing to the mud Blockade, we are still in our old camp. The "Sacred Soil" is in a most profane condition. Did you ever notice a fly endeavoring to walk through a dish of molasses? If you did, you can form some idea of our abortive attempts to wade! So here we are all ready and only waiting for the sun, to use a vulgar expression, to "Dry up." In the meantime I will write to you every day or so. I cannot tell where we are going to. Some say that we are going back to Annapolis, there to embark for some point on the Southern coast. I hope not. We want to go up to that Bugbear Manassas where only we can redeem the character so wretchedly flung away at Bull Run. But McClellan will decide where we are to distinguish ourselves.

I send pictures of McClellan, Davis, and Beauregard.[5] God forgive me for naming them together! In McClellan you will notice the dauntless and dashing soldier—in Davis the cold blood and great intellect—in Beauregard the stern commander. I hope little Loolie will call none of them Da Da except McClellan.

The Colonel, myself and most of the officers have sent the greater part of our baggage into Washington. I will never wear a white shirt until after the "Ninth" is immortalized. But, oh! the Mud.

The sun is setting beautifully this evening—promising well for tomorrow. We came near having a duel fought today between Capts. Gallagher and Mahan. They were blood to the eyes! Settled by myself and another friend. Who wouldn't be an Irishman?

---

[5] Jefferson Davis, who served as an officer in the Mexican War, was a West Point graduate, a Mississippi planter, and a spokesman for the Southern way of life. He represented Mississippi in the United States Senate, served as secretary of war under President Franklin Pierce, and was the Confederacy's only president. Pierre G. T. Beauregard graduated from West Point and participated in the Mexican War. As a Confederate general he opened the Southern bombardment on Fort Sumter which began the Civil War. He later led the Confederate army at First Manassas, played a key role at the battle of Shiloh in Tennessee, and commanded the defense of Charleston. He was also important in defending the Southern approaches to Richmond in 1864. Johnson and Malone, eds., *Dictionary of American Biography*, 5: 123–31. Ezra J. Warner, *Generals in Gray: Lives of the Confederate Commanders* (Baton Rouge: Louisiana State University Press, 1959), pp. 22–23.

My Dear, I will write to you as often as possible until we leave, and then whenever I can.

Ever

P. R. G.

On January 27 Lieutenant Colonel Robert Peard died after complaining for some time of headaches. Found unconscious in his tent earlier that day, he passed away at the hospital two hours later. On the 29th, Companies A, B, C, D, G, and H escorted his body to Alexandria while the regimental band played the "Dead March in Saul." From Alexandria, several officers from the Ninth Massachusetts and Irish Brigade accompanied the remains to Washington, where Adam's Express took charge to deliver it back to Massachusetts.[6] Guiney replaced him as lieutenant colonel on January 28, although the promotion was not officially known until February 16.[7] Correspondent Michael Finnerty expressed in an article to The Pilot *that, while the men and officers would miss the pleasant Peard, Guiney was "in every way qualified to take the place of an upright, honorable and patriotic Irishman."[8]*

Miner's Hill, Va.
Jan. 30, 1862

My Dear Jennie:

Yesterday we escorted the remains of Lt. Col. Peard to the Depot at Falls Church and put them on board the cars for Alexandria from whence they were sent by steam boat to Washington. The funeral was a splendid one and was attended by the Regiment as well as all the Colonels, Lt. Colonels, Majors, and various other officers in our Division as well as by [Brigadier] General Morell and staff. The officers of the "Irish Brigade" (Meagher's) met the cortege at Alexandria. The Colonel and all the Captains accompanied the remains to Washington. As the Colonel went, I could not

---

[6] "Dublin" in *The Pilot*, February 15, 1862. *Irish American*, February 8, 1862. Macnamara, *Ninth Regiment*, p. 66.

[7] Guiney's Commonwealth of Massachusetts Certificate of Service, United States Army Adjutant General's Office, Boston, August 8, 1935.

[8] *The Pilot*, March 15, 1862.

go farther than Falls Church, and took command of the Regmt. home to camp. Poor <u>Peard</u>! He was a good hearted man and a lover of his native land. He died a lonesome death and a very dreary one. O, God save me from such a death; if I am not to die at home, give me a death amid the smoke, roar and glory of the Battle Field. He died on last Monday at noon in our Brigade Hospital. His disease was Hemorrhage of the brain. I pity his wife and his numerous young family. But they shall not be forgotten nor allowed to want while the officers of the Ninth are <u>able</u> to remember.[9]

Probably, I will be appointed Lt. Colonel. I do not know who is to be Major. There are many aspirants and as Colonel Cass cannot please them all, there will be a loud but harmless rumpus among the disappointed ones. I love to rise in Rank, Jennie, but it makes me sad to rise on the grave of an old friend. Yet, as fortune invited me, and has been heretofore so lavishly kind in my rapid advancement, I do feel like taking her favors as they come!

When I went in to Washington to send a <u>telegram</u> to Mrs. Peard, I met Dr. March of Roxbury. I was glad to see him. Today Mr. Huston and a friend of his dined with me.[10] Mr. Huston is so warmly patriotic that I enjoyed his visit very much. I regret that our camp was so muddy. He could not see it to advantage. I wonder how he got through the "Sacred Soil" to Washington?

I have received three letters from you within two days, one by politeness of Mr. H. This was very pleasant, as I had not received one for a week before. My Dear, your kind and wife-like advice will not be lost upon me. How delighted I am to be assured by you that my little pet still remembers me. Bless her!

I am glad that the subsidy from the city has been discontinued. I felt like a pauper while I was getting it. Thank heaven I do not need it now. My salary is and <u>will be</u> large enough for you and me while I live and remain in the army. If I should fall <u>in battle</u>, if I am correctly informed, <u>you</u> would be entitled to half my present pay during widowhood—beg your pardon, Jennie, I meant to

---

[9] The Ninth did not forget; in June 1862 the regiment sent $234 to Lieutenant Colonel Peard's widow for her support and that of her children. *The Pilot,* July 12, 1862.

[10] A William R. Huston served on the Roxbury Board of Alderman (1862–1863), and it is probable that this is the man Guiney refers to in this letter. *Catalogue of City Councils,* p. 212.

say—life. So darling, we have nothing to fear as to money matters. Do not put away <u>one</u> <u>cent</u> <u>of</u> <u>what</u> <u>I</u> <u>send</u> <u>you</u> <u>so</u> <u>long</u> <u>as</u> <u>you</u> <u>can</u> <u>use</u> <u>it</u>.

The Colonel now kindly allows me to use the horse formerly used by Lt. Col. Peard. The Col. owns the horse so that <u>now</u> I have a good one and a <u>fast</u> <u>runner</u>. I hope he will break his neck if he ever runs well on a Bull Run Retreat.

Do you remember the little watch which you gave me? It was sent out to me by some one from Boston. Does not fortune smile upon me? As I am going on Picket tomorrow, it will be several days before I will be able to write to you. You must write to me, though, for your letter will be sent out to me on picket. I enjoy myself first rate out near the rebels. Their proximity makes things lively. I will return to camp Sunday evening—"If nothing happens" as the boys say.

But what of the "Advance?" I do not know. We are stuck in the mud yet. I think McClellan sends out these orders simply to shake us up. We are already Mack.

Remember me to all friends—you know them—and kiss my little pet for me.

Ever yours
P. R. Guiney

Camp 9th Mass.
Miner's Hill Va.
Feb 10 /62

My Dear Jennie:

I must confess that I have been negligent. I have yours of the 31st Jan. and 2d inst. and yet up to present, no answer from me. Well Dear, indulge my misfortune for such it seems. I have not written for some ten days and yet I can offer no reason for my neglect during such a period. God knows me, and I wish you could judge me as he does—by the heart. I am in such a reach of ideas of my future—in such dreams of "Days to Come"—in the way of such a multitude of little and important duties of a military character, that I even pass over the hope of my Soul—which is the welfare of yourself and little pet—to attend to them, to think, to act—to the end that my life may not be inglorious, but good, uncommon, perhaps noble! It is in such mental fancies that I forget to write to you and everybody else. My Darling, when we were married—nay, since I was born it was thus my mind was bent. This characteristic is your husband as well as I am—blame but do not condemn. But Jennie do not follow my example in this neglect—you are a woman and loved wife, whatever I may seem.

Here we are yet, sunk deep in the mud of Miner's Hill. O! sun, deliver us! I want this war finished in June next, if not sooner. I wish General McClellan's wife or some other influential person would tell or coax the General to Advance the Army.

As to that watch, Dear, I want it. Send on the Gourd. To show you how "immense" I am, as Mr. Huston says, I send on a likeness taken in camp in full military costume. I feel sure of being Lt. Col. I will not want clothes til spring. I will see about Bullet Proof Vest.[11] I received a letter from your Brother John.

Believe me Dear
Ever Yours

P.S. Enclosed I send $20 more soon.

—P. R. G.

Miner's Hill, Virginia
Feb. 12, 1862

My Dear Jennie:

I wrote to you yesterday, but I am so conscious of having omitted for so many days previous to that to write to you, that I feel like writing to you every hour for a week. This evening I received two letters from you. They conveyed to me sweet news which always delights me—about the welfare, progress, and tricks of my little pet. She is so bothered by mistaken Da das and pictures that while I laugh about her I pity her sincerely. And you say she pouts,

---

[11] Several firms manufactured metal vests that were supposed to deflect bullets, often with less than successful results. For more information, see Wayne Austerman's "Armor for the Soldier," in *Civil War Times Illustrated* (Vol. 26 No. 9) January 1988, pp. 34–37.

too! I guess she is older than we think for—she must have been peeping at us from the stars long before she was born.

By all means dear come on to see me as soon as you can. I need not say to you, of course, that your coming on will be determined by the ability of Loolie to do without your care. That is I mean just what you say yourself. Come on at <u>that</u> <u>time</u>. A trip out here will do you good—I will be delighted—and Loolie will not suffer so much as if you were with her. Let me know several days before you come. I feel sure that camp life would not be pleasant to you now, and I would not enjoy seeing you in Mud-misery. Mrs. Cass and the rest of the ladies wear great big military boots and over-coats. But "Come in the springtime."

Yet, Darling, while I fondly dwell upon your visit to me I cannot think that by the time you are able to come we will be in this vicinity. Our staying here so long is fast becoming "The Great Mystery of the Century." But wherever I am, come! Come, Jennie, to see me when you can.

Mrs. Cass is not going home until <u>the</u> <u>day</u> <u>after</u> <u>tomorrow</u>, as she says, meaning to never go home.

Mrs. Nugent is here yet—she is beginning to be disgusted with the roughness of Camps and Soldiers. I think everybody ought to admire her more—she would stay longer with us, but "She's going home." To crown all she says <u>somebody</u> stole 150 dollars out of Dick's pocket when both were asleep in the tent. Dick lost the money sure. Who stole Dick's money? I guess—<u>somebody</u>. But say nothing. <u>It</u> <u>is</u> <u>all</u> <u>in</u> <u>the</u> <u>family</u>.

Yes love, I shall soon want suit of clothes, sky blue pants with dark blue felt coat of same color as my present one rigged for Lieutenant Colonel of Infantry. I understand my <u>new</u> <u>commission</u> is in Washington—still address me as Major until I receive it. I cannot wear a bullet proof vest under my present coat—too small. Bullet Proofs are looked upon as indicating timidity, if not cow-ardice. Don't think I will have one anyhow.

Ever
P. R. G.

On February 14 the Irishmen participated in a reconnaissance, march-ing at daybreak through Falls Church to the small town of Vienna. Here

*they repaired a half mile of railroad connecting Alexandria and Leesburg,
torn up by Southern troops the previous September. While working, some
of the troops joked, "Irishmen first built it, and again destroyed it; of
course it must be Irishmen who will have to fix it again."*[12]

*On February 16 Brigadier Generals Porter and Meagher attended Colo-
nel Cass's address to newly commissioned Lieutenant Colonel Guiney,
Major Hanley, and Captain John C. Willey. With the regiment in dress
parade, Cass remarked on the importance of duty, discipline, and drill in
his brief speech.*[13]

Miner's Hill Va.
Feb. 16 1862

My Dear Jennie:

I am in possession of yours of the 14th inst. Ever so much
obliged for your kind forgiveness. Thus may it ever be with us—
considerate and generous to each other.

I received the Gourd. It is just the thing. There is a watch
pocket in my pants—I got an old tailor to put it in. I have come
to this conclusion, Dear, that I will have my clothes in Washington. In Washington, they make military clothes in <u>exact</u> conformity to Army Regulations. This is what I want. I want a nice suit to
wear on particular occasions. I know Dear, you would get them at
home if you were obliged to sit up at night to procure them; but
I do not wish to trouble you and the expense, you know, is not to
be considered as against the adaptation of a necessary uniform.

Last Thursday the "Ninth" along with about 3000 other troops
went out to hunt up a fight, but our general is very <u>prudent</u> etc.,
and owing to his masterly <u>strategy</u> <u>to</u> <u>preserve</u> <u>the</u> <u>Peace</u>, we were
not accommodated by the enemy.[14] If we had a different General
our story would be more glorious.

When are you coming? Let me know <u>precisely</u>—I want to meet

---

[12] *The Pilot*, March 15. Macnamara, *Ninth Regiment*, p. 67.

[13] *The Pilot*, March 8, 1862. Regan diary, February 16, 1862. A turnkey from
East Cambridge, John C. Willey started out as a second lieutenant. Promoted
first lieutenant to date October 3, 1861, his commission as captain was dated to
January 28, 1862. Captain Willey was dismissed from the service February 7,
1863. *Massachusetts Soldiers, Sailors*, 1: 680.

[14] From remarks in his February 18, 1862 letter, it seems Guiney is referring to
Brigadier General George Morell.

you in Washington. Let me know the very hour at which you intend to start. I wish you would start the 1st of March, but come sooner if you like.

I sent Daguerreotype by Adam's Express—I suppose you have got it by this time. I am Lt. Colonel of the Ninth, my commission is dated 28th of January.

Ever yours
P. R. G.

Not only Guiney felt this to be a satisfying period; the entire Union felt heartened as its troops experienced victory at Forts Henry and Donelson in Tennessee and on Roanoke Island, North Carolina. As the news was read out to the Ninth, drawn up in a hollow square, cheer after cheer filled the air. Despite the rain and mud, a member of Company A felt inspired to step forward and sing "The Star Spangled Banner."[15]

Miner's Hill, Va.
Feb. 18th 1862

My Dear Jennie:

Yours of the 13th inst. is before me. We are all well in camp. Capt. Hanley is Major—Hanley is a young widower, and is courting a niece of Colonel Cass—it is a family arrangement you see. This is, of course, private. I am glad Hanley has got the appointment—he is a good fellow. He is about my age perhaps a year older. He was formerly Plunkett's 1st Lieutenant. I enclose an account of our late "Reconnaissance" from the New York Herald. It does not do us justice—we did the skirmishing—we repaired the Rail Road—we first entered Vienna—we took up a bold position in a dense wood and behind a fence—we offered to commence a battle, but our prudent commander Brig. Gen. Morell—would not allow it. The reporter would not even do Colonel Cass the justice to spell his name correctly.[16] The ladies whom

---

[15] *The Pilot*, March 15, 1862. Long, *The Civil War Day by Day*, pp. 167–68, 171.

[16] The New York *Herald* spelled Cass's name as "Carr," and states that, while the cavalry and a company of the Forty-forth New York did all the skirmishing, the Fourth Michigan and Ninth Massachusetts guarded the railroad. Second

we left in camp were all weeping and praying all day. Poor blessed creatures! Are returned to them smiling and bloodless. You may send that <u>last</u> picture of mine to sister Mary. Do not send any to Lewiston. Father Scully has been sick for a long time—he had typhoid fever—he is now well. He does not remain in camp but is stopping at a Mr. Burke's House out near our picket lines. The family is a Catholic one—very good people. He comes in every Sunday to say Mass for us. He has frequently desired to be remembered to you, but I forgot to do so. My Dear, when are you coming? Have you got any money to come with? I am all out. If you wait until about 6th March I can send you some. But if you have got any, <u>use</u> <u>it</u> and come as soon as you can get ready. You had better sleep on the <u>ground</u> for some few nights before you come—so that you can appreciate fully the soft luxuriousness of my couch.

I am going to Washington tomorrow. Tell me, Dear, when you are coming. As usual I am impatient. But, Oh! Jennie <u>prepare</u> <u>for</u> <u>mud</u>. We are connected by telegraph with Washington, and consequently, get all the news from General McClellan immediately on its reception at War Department. We are in vociferous glee over late victories [i.e., Forts Henry and Donelson, and Roanoke Island].

P. R. G.

Miner's Hill, Virginia
Feb. 20, 1862

My Dear Jennie:

As I will not be able to write to you for several days to come, I thought I would drop you these words so that you might understand the reason. We are going on picket and will not come back to camp until next Sunday afternoon. In the meantime if any letter comes here for me it will be sent out.

Lieutenant Michael Finnerty, *The Pilot*'s correspondent with the Ninth, later criticized the *Herald* for ignoring the Irishmen's contribution during the May 27, 1862 battle at Hanover Court House. Finnerty believed the cause to be bias against the regiment's ethnicity. *Herald*, February 17, 1862. *The Pilot*, June 14, 1862.

Somebody in camp has given me an overwhelming puff in the Irish American.[17] I send it enclosed.

The travelling is improved much since I wrote to you last. The mud is degenerating. It was a nasty mud—not even "respectable" enough, as Byron says, "to perish" in. However, it is prudent that we should not chant the Requiem for old king-mud yet, as a single rain storm would resuscitate the dirty old fellow.

My Dear Jennie, when are you coming? Please tell me. But be sure and come precisely when you say you will. Do not miss the train. Can you not come on with Capt. Scanlan? The road is long and lonesome without company. How is my little Dear? How is sister Lizzie? Remember me to my friends, family, Mulrey, Mrs. C and Miss Crespy—in fact, to all hands!

Yours,
P. R. G.

Miner's Hill Va.
March 3d 1862

My Dear Jennie:

It is some time since I wrote to you. I think I received two of yours since I wrote to you last. Certainly I received one. I thought you would be out here before this date and was somewhat disappointed when I received your last letter postponing your promised visit so long. However, tonight I feel thankful that you did not come and principally because my personal relations with Colonel Cass are now very much changed. Since I became Lt. Colonel, of course I have never been necessarily in closer intimacy with him, and, he and I having very different views as [to] many subjects connected with the Regiment, this close relation only

---

[17] This refers to a letter from a member of the Ninth Massachusetts published in the *Irish American*, dated February 14, 1862 and signed "Erin." He wrote, "The vacancy created by his [Major Peard's] death has been filled by . . . Major Patrick R. Guiney, an officer who, by his gentlemanly deportment and many social qualities, has won the confidence and respect of all the officers and men." The letter was published in the February 22, 1862 edition of the newspaper, which suggests that Guiney either had an advance copy of the letter, or the date refers to the last day of the week of the particular issue. *Irish American*, February 22, 1862.

served to give rise to unpleasant difference. I think I will soon resign and go home. He seems to me unbearable. So, for the present, Dear, you will not think of visiting me. I will let you know when affairs take a different turn. The particular circumstance which occurred between us was that I discharged a soldier from the Guard house who was put in there without cause by his blockhead and malignant captain. I was in command at the time, Col. Cass being absent. When Colonel returned he countermanded my order and put the man in prison again. This was a censure on me. The secret of his course is that the captain, who is an ex-policeman from Cambridge, is a favorite of his—a sort of Regimental pimp.[18] The soldier has been tried by regimental Court Martial since and acquitted.

I have not received any money yet. I may receive it in a few days. The pay of Lt. Col. is $180 but I have to pay expenses of self and horse out of that. The expenses out here are immense. I have to pay the usual expense or misfortune of having a tide of friends and visitors. I will save all I can and send it to you. I will write to you again day after tomorrow.

Your Husband

On March 5, the Ninth roused from their camp to repair a section of railroad near Vienna, destroyed by Confederate raiders the previous autumn. After fixing several miles of track, a locomotive with flat-cars came out to return the men to their camp. The Rebels soon swept in and damaged the section, and the Irishmen went to repair it again on March 7. The next day, they continued fixing and guarding the railroad until relieved by the Third Vermont.[19]

The same day, March 8, President Lincoln issued General War Order No. 2, organizing the Army of the Potomac into four corps. Brigadier General George Morell's Brigade, in Brigadier General Fitz John Porter's division, was assigned to Brigadier General Samuel P. Heintzelman's III Corps.[20]

---

[18] This is probably Captain John C. Willey, a turnkey with residence in East Cambridge recently promoted with Guiney. Willey remained problematic after Guiney assumed command of the regiment. Massachusetts Soldiers, Sailors, 1: 680.

[19] Regan diary, March 5, 7, 8, 1862.

[20] OR, vol. 5: 18, 20. A West Pointer, Samuel Heintzelman proved to be a

Miner's Hill, Va.
March 9th 1862

My Dear Jennie:

I have yours of the 6th inst. The trouble of which I spoke in my last is not ended although much modified. The Colonel never forgets, and will not even forgive when he knows he is wrong. He is sometimes strangely generous and at other times selfish and unjust. No act of mine could merit his permanent or spasmodic wrath, yet he <u>attempted</u> to shower it upon me. But he finds that I am not an easy victim. I attribute his conduct to two or three combined causes. He does not seem to be governed by any <u>fixed</u> principles in life, and his nature is crossed in the grain. I am, although I say it myself, popular not only with our own officers and men but also with those with whom we have from time to time come in contact. He does not possess this good fortune to such an extent. I think the difference causes the difficulty. Then again, although in an exclusively military point of vein I think he is fitted for it, I do not exert myself over much to have him promoted to Brigadier Generalship. This may seem strange, as his promotion would make me Colonel of the Ninth. Heretofore, I have been advanced because I deserved it, and I never will advance in my position hereafter at any price. However, Jennie, I may be giving this little matter undue prominence and doing Colonel Cass injustice. A great deal of my anxiety may arise from my own sensitiveness and imagination. He has, so far, done nothing <u>decidedly</u> offensive to me, but he has been severe in his exactions of duty. Last Wednesday we went out close to the rebel lines and were out all night and the next day—we were sure of a fight. He ordered me with two companies to his front about two miles beyond Vienna. I went and the rebels only exchanged shots with my cavalry, but did not molest the infantry. I had no orders to attack and did not, but kept the rebels from destroying a Rail Road. If the fight went on I would have got it hot and heavy with my small force and so far away from means of support. Then in the night when we withdrew into Vienna, he sent me out again to command

---

personally brave officer, but of mediocre competence. After the Second Manassas campaign, he was relegated to relatively minor commands. Warner, *Generals in Blue*, pp. 227–28.

a picket guard. I dare say that in the battle field, too, I will be sent, nay <u>ordered</u> to dangerous points. It is not <u>this</u> I object to but his spirit which seems to prompt him. But I will <u>go</u>, and under all circumstances, exult in opportunities for glory. I think my course at Vienna astonished him—he saw I was not vexed, but rather pleased and I guess in a week or two he will give me up as a victim and treat me better. He is much more agreeable to-day. These remarks also, my dear, will give you the reason why I did not write sooner and as I promised. After coming here I went in to Washing[ton], endeavoring to get any pay so as to send you some money but I failed to succeed. Our paymaster has gone down to pay [Brigadier General Ambrose E.] Burnside's men and we will not get any money until near the last of this month if we do then.[21] You must do the best you can do.

I visited the "Irish Brigade" to-day and dined with General Meagher and lady in their tent—about ten miles from here. He was very cordial to me, and Mrs. Meagher is not only beautiful and entertaining but good. Colonel Cass and General Meagher are not so friendly as at a former period so that my visit to him has a <u>local</u> significance.

My Darling I was just going to talk to you and Loolie but infer all. Think of me kindly Jennie. An order to move at Daylight has just come. It is now 12 o'clock at night.

Farewell sweet wife—may Heaven protect you and bless the child of our love with beauty, intellect and virtue. May God give us speedy victory and our wives and children again.

Patrick Robt. Guiney
Lt. Col. 9th

P.S. As there are no postage stamps in camp—I am obliged to endorse this a "soldiers' letter" on which you must pay 3 cents in

---

[21] At this time, Ambrose Burnside was employed in an expedition against the North Carolina coast, where he met with great success. A West Pointer, Burnside returned to the Army of the Potomac to lead his IX Corps against the Confederate right flank at Antietam, charging over what is now known as "Burnside's Bridge." He later reluctantly accepted command of the army after McClellan's removal, and led the troops in the Federal debacle of Fredericksburg. After spending a period of time in the Western theater, Burnside returned to lead his IX Corps in Lieutenant General Ulysses S. Grant's 1864 drive to Richmond and the siege of Petersburg, and later served as governor and senator from his home state, Rhode Island. Warner, *Generals in Blue*, pp. 57–58.

Roxbury. The movement is <u>general</u>—probably toward Manassas. We'll squelch the Rebels sure.

PRG

On March 10, the Ninth broke camp at 4:00 a.m., received three days rations, and proceeded with their brigade to Fairfax Court House. The difficult march, conducted in the rain along muddy roads cut up by the artillery and cavalry preceding the foot soldiers, tired the men. Upon reaching Fairfax, the cavalry went ahead to investigate the Rebel works at Centreville, only to find them abandoned. Some of the military stores there still smoldered, having been burned by withdrawing Southerners only the day before.[22]

Fairfax C. H., Va.
March 11, 1862

My Dear Jennie:

I gladly embrace this opportunity to say a word to you. Yesterday at daybreak we left our old camp and came up here, as we thought to engage the enemy. <u>But they fled</u>. We are within a few hours march of Manassas. One Regmt. of our division went up last night and took possession of their works at Bull-Run—This Regmt was the 44th N. Y.—Ellsworth Avengers. The intention was that this Regmt. should commence the Battle and that the rest of the forces should go up immediately after and carry on and finish. But the Rebels had fled even from Bull Run and Manassas. They (the Rebels) have burned and blown up everything destroyable between Bull Run and Richmond. What are they up to? is the question here. McClellan is here with us. Tomorrow we will move again, whether towards Richmond or not we do not know.

The roads were in a very bad condition but the men stood the long march like heroes. There are only a few inhabitants here and they are very poor.

Our Regmt. is quartered out in the field. I am lying on my face

---

[22] *The Pilot*, April 26, 1862. Regan diary, March 10, 1862. Macnamara, *Ninth Regiment*, pp. 71–72.

and hands while I write this. The Earth is a fine centre-table—very firm, but awkward.

I will write again to you first opportunity, write to me as usual to Washington.

The nights are cold but we all stand it well. I am rugged as a maple stump. How is Loolie?

Yours
P. R. G.

While at Fairfax Court House, the regiment received a distinguished guest: Boston's Bishop John Bernard Fitzpatrick, who had been visiting Washington. Colonel Cass put the Ninth through a series of maneuvers and formed the men into a hollow square with Fitzpatrick in the middle. After meeting the officers of the regiment, the bishop addressed the men.[23]

Fairfax Va.
March 13 /62

My Dear Jennie:

I send you a word in acknowledgment of yours of the 9th inst. I received it last night. It afforded me great pleasure to hear from you way out here. My right hand was slightly injured yesterday and it is painful for me to write. Besides my trunk portfolio and all I had except what is on my back I was obliged to leave behind me in camp. It is so with all the officers, and it's a great favor to get a piece of paper to write a word upon. Therefore, my Darling, I cannot write much to you. Probably we will go on towards Richmond within 48 hours. We are delayed here for want of provisions. It is too bad that we were not able to pursue the enemy the 1st day of his retreat. We got inside his works just as he left. McClellan ought to have provided for every contingency. I _fear_ his reputation is damaged by this affair. However we expect to meet our enemies somewhere very soon. That difficulty is settled for the present.

P. R. G.

---

[23] O'Connor, *Fitzpatrick's Boston*, pp. 202–203.

*After remaining at Fairfax for six days, the regiment received orders to
report to Cloud's Mill, near Alexandria. Leaving at five in the morning
of March 15, the troops endured a torrential rain and resulting floods, in
which "Boots, army overcoats, uniform, hats, all failed to be proof against
the continuous storm."*[24]

March 19, 1862

My Dear Jennie:

I have received a letter from you three days ago. Having just
arrived from Fairfax after a most fatiguing march and being
drenched to the skin, I did not answer you immediately. We are
now encamped about ten miles from our old camp ground, and
three miles outside of Alexandria. No baggage is allowed to us
and but very few tents. We are <u>now</u> engaged in <u>war</u>. The <u>holidays</u>
<u>are over</u>.

It was expected that our Division would be off on an expedition
along the Southern Coast immediately after we returned from the
direction of Manassas, but for want of transportships we have
been delayed here. The ships are coming up the river today and
we are momentarily expecting orders to embark. I have no idea of
our destination. Unless a singular change takes place in present
arrangements, this, perhaps, will be the last which I will be able
to write to you from this vicinity.

The whole Army of the Potomac are disappointed in not having
a battle at Bull Run. To fight there and win had been the day-
thought and night-dream of every soldier for months. Our army
is so splendidly fit for victory it is really a pity that we were obliged
to come away from that cursed field defeated in the purpose of
our Advance. But still I do not wish to join the unarmed but mer-
ciless battalions of fault-finders who cry out against McClellan for
this. Yet I am by no means an admirer of his. I think, in the ordinary sense, he is a good officer, abounding in popular qualities
which endear him to those who know him personally—but a great
<u>Military</u> Leader he is not. He has the Science of War but he seems
to me to be without the great comprehensive genius so essential
to its successful conduct. I think a good general should have pro-

---

[24] *The Pilot*, April 26, 1862. Regan diary, March 15, 1862.

vided in advance for the contingency of a rebel retreat. Instead of which we were obliged to stay at Fairfax and Manassas for want of provisions and means of transportation. I have heard it said however that this state of things was brought about by the treachery of some government employees to prevent us from pursuing the rebels. But no matter whose fault it was that we did not go on. I have come to this very wise and laborious conclusion: that such a fracture in the system of war-strategy looks badly, even at a distance. I suppose we are going now down on some of those rivers leading up to Norfolk or Richmond, and when we get to a landing, I'll wage my existence there will be something wanting. I, for one, rely on the gallantry of our troops and not upon the genius of our generals for victory. But it's no use talking about this war arrangement. I guess it will soon come out right. How are you Darling and my little idol?

Yesterday evening I went in to Washington and endeavored to get some pay but it was no use. I failed even to get a dollar. My anxiety for your welfare Dear is great. I am so happy when I think that my wife and child are comfortable; and when I have the least reason to think that you may be in want I am troubled day and night until I am assured that you are well provided for. But I have tried to get some money to send to you and I have failed. I am very sorry Darling. You <u>must</u> <u>use</u> <u>that</u> <u>hundred</u> <u>dollars</u>. Do not borrow <u>from</u> <u>anybody</u> so long as you have any of our own. Do not dear for our future love. All will be well with us if I live. But speaking of my journey to Washington, I must say that it was not without a result. As it was expected that we would embark this morning early, the Colonel ordered me to be here at sun-rise in the morning. I had only an hour and a half to come twelve miles, and I was bound to be here according to appointment. I put my old horse to his full-speed and lo! he plunged into a tremendous mud hole, fell and flung me about thirty feet ahead on dry land. I laid on my back for a few minutes reflecting on the probabilities as to whether I was hurt or not, and I finally concluded that I was not created to die in Virginia. My knee is injured some and is quite sore tonight but the injury is not serious and I will be well in a day or two. This is the second accident which has occurred to me within ten days. I was in hope that the old steed was dead. When I went back to the mud-hole I found that he was buried in the mud and I could not help laughing when I thought how kind he was to save me the trouble of digging his grave. But old Bucephalus was simply in a trance. A few spirited kicks brought him to. I got here before sun-rise.

Capt. Scanlan has arrived but his baggage has not been brought up yet.[25] The camp-ladies have gone home. The Colonel is quite good natured tonight—he just came into my tent and presented me with the pictures I enclose to you. My love it is now 12 o'clock at night, and as of old, about this time, I say to you "Good night Darling."

P. R. G.

Major General McClellan intended to attack Richmond and the Confederate army under General Joseph E. Johnston by transferring the Army of the Potomac to the Virginia Peninsula and advancing from there, using steamers to ship his men down the Chesapeake Bay. On March 21, the Ninth Massachusetts boarded a large, comfortable vessel, the State of Maine. *The next day Captain Cauldon had the regiment's green Irish flag hauled to the main truck amid the proud shouts and cheers of hundreds of men. Morale ran high in the army, and Timothy Regan wrote, "It is a beautiful sight to see this fleet of splendid steamboats crowded with soldiers, bands playing, and colors flying, the men shouting and calling to each other from one boat to another. . . . this is the grandest excursion I ever saw, or expect to see." On March 23 the* State of Maine *entered Hampton Roads and the Irishmen disembarked at the wharf near Fort Monroe. From here the regiment proceeded to the town of Hampton, burnt to the ground by withdrawing Southerners, and set up camp two miles outside its remains. In the evening the men enjoyed music provided by the regimental band for several hours while they smoked, talked, and relaxed on their blankets near a large campfire. The next day, Brigadier General Fitz John Porter's division advanced several miles to make room for other Federals still landing.*[26]

---

[25] Captain Michael Scanlan had been on recruiting duty and had brought a number of new enlistees to the Ninth. Regan diary, March 17, 1862.

[26] Regan diary, March 22, 23, 1862. *The Pilot,* April 26, 1862. Macnamara, *Ninth Regiment,* pp. 74–75. Macnamara, *Bivouac,* pp. 78–79.

Bethel Va.
March 25 /62

My Dear Jennie:

I send you this to inform you of my whereabouts. We are situated about ten miles above Fort Munroe, Va. in the direction of Yorktown, where, probably, our first battle will be fought. We came down the Potomac in steamboats last Sunday. We are now experiencing the severest privations incidental to an active campaign—ever moving to-night in one place, next night in another. The officers find it hard work to procure food—the government takes care of the men. I went 4 miles this morning to get breakfast—venerable pork! We marched through the town of Hampton burned by the rebels in the early stages of the war. It <u>was</u> a charming place! Now how black and desolate! It would make you weep to pass amid its ruins.

The climate here is much pleasanter than it was in North-Eastern Virginia. The houses are either burned or deserted in this neighborhood.

Our stay here will be short. The government will make quick moves and push the rebels to the wall. Yorktown is well fortified, but not well enough to withstand the assault of truth and Union-steel.

Darling, it will be impossible for me to communicate often with you. It is said the [word deleted—perhaps "government" or "army"] detain or open all letters. I know not that this will ever reach you. If you reply God knows where I will be at the time. Direct to Fort Munroe Va. for me. Keep up good spirits Dear and kiss my little pet for me every night.

Good bye love
Yours ever
P. R. Guiney

The regiment marched to Big Bethel on March 27, ready to confront Southerners reportedly fortifying there; upon approaching, the Rebels offered no resistance and the Ninth pursued them with no effect. Later, the Irishmen went back to enjoy a dinner prepared by the Southerners before their surprise, in addition to Federal rations. The Massachusetts men re-

mained here for several days on routine duty. On the picket line, Guiney received five black females into his lines and eloquently proclaimed, "In the name of old Ireland and Massachusetts, I set you free." [27]

Near Bethel Va.
March 30, 1862

My Dear Jennie:

I wrote to you once since our arrival here but I do not know that you have received it as at that time our mail arrangements were in an imperfect condition. I am well, but in common with all others, I am <u>enjoying</u> hardships of which we never, until now, even dreamed. In fine weather we can do very well but now that the weather is very stormy, living here is at least novel. Last night when I retired I constructed my resting place, (cannot call it a bed) on a raft so as to float off easily but in the morning I found myself mysteriously in the same locality. I am very impatient to hear from you. You must use any money you can control—<u>Do</u> <u>not</u> <u>borrow, remember</u>—if you can help it. It will be a long time before we get paid. Troops are gathering here fast. McClellan will be here in a day or two. The dust will fly in Richmond ere long. The rebels fled from Big-Bethel two days ago when we went up there—our troops shot three of them. Poor fellows! Perhaps they left those who love them at home—but adieu. Direct to <u>Fort</u> <u>Mun-</u><u>roe</u>, Va.

P. R. Guiney

Near Hampton, Va.
April 2nd 1862

My Dear Jennie:

On last evening I was delighted to receive from your hands two letters—one containing this paper. How thoughtful you are of me, Dear. The letters which I received from you were directed to Washington and this causes me to think that my letters from this

---

[27] *The Pilot*, April 26, 1862. Macnamara, *Ninth Regiment*, pp. 78–79.

vicinity have not, or had not up to the time of your writing, reached you. The surest way to direct letters to me now is to "Fort Monroe, Va." We are not at the Fort but it is the nearest Military Depot.

I dare not indulge the hope of our being here more than a few days more. But if I am alive in June next I will either go to see you or you must be with me.

Colonel Cass is excessively cross—out of sorts with everybody— vindictive—vulgar—malicious. When he is pleased he is quite a different man, but the Government have not made him a "Briga- dier General" and therein is the cause. Well, perhaps after all, disappointment in a matter on which the best of men had set his heart would operate upon him much in the same manner, if not to the same extent. But however it may be the men are punished more than usual and the officers are being hauled over the red- hot coals of his unappeasable wrath in a manner that would de- light the eyes of a Prince of Dahomy.[28] He talks of going home— pretends to be disgusted with the Regmt. etc., but probably he will not resign until after a battle. Of course his steel vest [i.e., a bulletproof vest] will save his life. I think he would dislike to see me Colonel of this Regmt. and that may delay his resignation some time.

Although I say these things to you I would not say them to any other living person. Still what I say of him is true. But heretofore he has done me many kindnesses. Gratitude will forever prevent one from doing him any injury and I would not even tell the truth of him if I were not sure that it would do him no harm. Never speak of this to any person nor show this letter; everything consid- ered I ought to be a friend of his. What does Mrs. Cass and her sister say?

President Lincoln and General McClellan have just arrived here and I suppose we will be off soon.

The stamps which you sent me I gave away to poor soldiers at Fairfax. Pardon me Jennie, for giving away your presents—I could

---

[28] Existing from the seventeenth century until colonization by France in the nineteenth, Dahomy was a West African state in the region of modern Benin, and a major source of the slave trade. Richard S. Dunn, *Sugar and Slaves: The Rise of the Planter Class in the English West Indies, 1624–1713* (New York: W. W. Norton & Company, 1972), p. 235.

not help it. Who is that German of whom you speak? Can it be old Valcers? If it is—he will want to borrow some money of you, sure. Many a five-cent-piece I lent him. Father Scully is well and living in a little tent that would scarcely shelter a primitive hermit. I wish I had the power I would not allow a priest to live in such a manner when I could better him—but I have nothing to say of course in such a matter. Farewell my Jennie and believe me,

Ever yours
Husband

April 3 1862

I have a moment to say to you that this probably will be the last time at which I will be able to write to you until we make a new lodgement somewhere in Virginia. I wrote you yesterday evening and just after I sealed the letter I received one from you directed to "Fort Munroe." It gave me great happiness to read it. Your description of Loolie is very pleasing Dear and I long to see her and you so much. I kiss you both tonight. I will write again if I can but I fear I will not have time. Farewell Love. Tell Mr. Huston that victory is sure to flash upon our flag.

Ever yours
Ptr. Robt. Guiney

April 3d 1862

My Dear Jennie:
I wrote to you this morning but as it was not then certain that we would go on farther I now inform you that we will positively "march on" tomorrow morning at day break. The rebels may give us battle tomorrow or perhaps they will retreat and delay the fight a day or two. They must fight somewhere between here and Richmond or give up the rebellious ghost. Direct my future letters to Washington. They will be sent to me from thence wherever I am.

We are in good spirits. You will hear from me again as soon as we rest. God bless you love and Loolie.

                                                        Guiney

I went to Communion last Saturday morning. This will be pleasant news for you—a good precaution for me.

                                                        PRG

On April 4, the Ninth broke camp and, with three days cooked rations in the troops' haversacks, made for Yorktown. The regiment bivouacked for the night in a cornfield enclosed by woods near Cockletown. The next day, the Federal siege of Yorktown began, and the Ninth participated in skirmishing before the Southern fortifications. Upon nearing the works, a salvo of artillery shells burst above the regiment, and the Irishmen occupied a woods toward their left. Two companies deployed as skirmishers and advanced to within 300 yards of the Southern cannon when Rebel fire forced their retreat with no casualties. Brigadier General George Morell and his staff joined Colonel Cass and Guiney under fire as they surveyed the enemy, and soon, the Fifth Massachusetts Battery under Captain George D. Allen rode into position to engage the Confederates. The Ninth waited in support sixty yards behind Allen's cannon, and Federal artillery fire joined the superb marksmanship of the elite First United States Sharpshooter regiment, under Colonel Hiram Berdan, to silence several of the opposing guns. Later, a rumor spread that the Rebels were preparing to charge the Fifth Massachusetts Battery and the Ninth readied itself to defend the guns, but the attack never materialized. Allen's battery, the Sixty-second Pennsylvania to the Ninth's left, and the Twenty-second Massachusetts sustained some casualties from the skirmishing, but the Ninth came out unscathed.

That night the men slept on their arms. On the evening of April 6, 200 troops of the Ninth engaged in throwing up a line of embankments in advance of their present position. On April 7 Colonel Cass and Guiney went forward to reconnoiter, and were greeted with the hot lead of a dozen bullets whizzing by them.[29]

---

[29] *The Pilot*, May 3, 1862. OR, vol. 11 part 1: 298–99. Regan diary, April 5, 1862. Macnamara, *Ninth Regiment*, pp. 79–80. Macnamara, *Bivouac*, pp. 81–82. Long, *The Civil War Day by Day*, pp. 193–94.

Under the Guns of
the Batteries Defending
Yorktown, Va.
April 8 /62

My Dear Jennie:

We came up here last Saturday morning and the enemy opened fire upon us from their batteries. Our artillery replied to them and during the whole day an incessant fire of shell was kept up. Berdan's Sharpshooters went up to three of the enemy's batteries and by concealing themselves in the thickets shot over one hundred of the rebels while they were loading the cannons. I do not know the exact number of our killed so far because our line of battle is so extensive. I <u>know</u> that we lost eight killed and perhaps twenty wounded—none of them from our Regiment. Sunday by a tacit arrangement the fighting was suspended on both sides. Monday morning, fighting was renewed—but during the whole was of a trivial character. We occupy the nearest position to the batteries. We are down in a very deep ravine. The enemy's shell[s] break over us. We go out at night and throw up entrenchments for the artillery. The battle has not become severe yet but it may at any moment. Myself and Colonel Cass went almost up to one of the rebel batteries to take a view of it when a volley of rifles was fired at us, but we escaped unhurt. McClellan is here—but his higher officers say that he is detained from ordering a general assault upon the batteries by the detention at Manassas of McDowell's Corps de Armee. It is said here that the politicians at Washington caused this delay because they wish to see McClellan defeated here.[30] God help the set of men who for a personal prejudice would sacrifice this army and jeopardize the nation. The whole Confederate army in Virginia seems to have been concentrated here. The rebels have a large force. Their batteries are truly formidable. Fort Donaldson's [Fort Donelson in Tennessee] defences were mere shams compared with the elaborate works defending this place.

---

[30] In reality, Major General Irvin McDowell's men were retained near the Federal capital to protect it against attack. The brilliant Shenandoah campaign conducted by Confederate Major General "Stonewall" Jackson resulted in the defeat of several Northern forces and prompted Lincoln's concern for the safety of Washington. McPherson, *Battle Cry of Freedom*, pp. 457–60.

This morning (now 8 o'clock) a shot has not been fired—it is raining severely. We do not know the moment a <u>general</u> assault will be ordered upon the batteries. When that order is given—although thousands should be met with a leaden-death storm, we will be victorious still for this army is unconquerable! The rebel bands play the Marseillaise hymn morning and evening in their forts—they seem to be enthusiastic too.[31] More troops are coming to our support daily. The losses sustained by us thus far seem to be confined to our artillery and to some Regiments on our left—also Pennsylvania 62d lost one killed and 2 wounded—this regiment is with us. This may reach you or not, I send it under protection of fortune. Farewell my Dear wife and believe me.

Ever Your Husband
PRG

P.S. Kiss Loolie for me.
I received your letter of March 4th.

Near Yorktown
April 8th 1862
10 o'clock P.M.

My Dear Jennie:

This evening I received your very interesting letter of the 3rd inst. and although I write this acknowledgment of it, I merely hope that it will reach you sometime within a week or two. The mail is somewhat lazy and irregular. To-day the firing was very slight. The rebels do not seem inclined to press us into a decisive

---

[31] The Confederates adopted this anthem of the French Revolution for their own cause, and it was a favorite of many Southern bands. Clifford Dowdey recorded the lyrics to the Southern version:

> Sons of the South, Awake to glory,
> A thousand voices bid you rise. . .
> Your country every strong arm calling,
> To meet the hireling Northern band
> That comes to desolate the land . . .
> To arms! . . .

Clifford Dowdey, *Lee* (1965; reprint, Gettysburg: Stan Clark Military Books, 1991), p. 701.

engagement at once and our commander (McClellan) is evidently waiting for developments in the enemy's rear and flanks before making the assault in front general and final. However, both sides pass the interval in incessant skirmishing with occasional cannonading. The Ninth are the nearest Regiment to the enemy. There are two other Regiments on our right and various divisions on our left—thousands in our rear. I do not know the amount of troops. I think we have sufficient force. The enemy are said to have some seventy five thousand men or rather rebels without a cause to fight for or a principle to exult in. We understand from some deserters that there are some Irish troops inside the batteries and that the sight of our Green flag has made some commotion among them. I hope they will act as the Irish Battalion did in the Rebel service at Winchester—or better still come boldly over where they belong. But perhaps I ought not to expect so much, as many of them doubtless have families in the South.[32] Well, if the Green flag does not affect them and quiet their rebellious emotions—steel may. As I write there is a brisk skirmish going on in the field fronting us—It is raining hard and very dark. We are becoming familiar with the rebels and it is astonishing how much "To home" we feel here.

The Irish Brigade (Meagher's) is back of us about five miles. It came two days ago. O! how many incidents I could tell you Dear of these few days past—but O! how many more I may be able to tell you of the next few. I must close love. I only meant to say to you that I am well. I wrote you this morning.

Guiney

On April 10 corps commander Brigadier General Samuel P. Heintzelman ordered Brigadier General Fitz John Porter's Division to relocate south

---

[32] This refers to a doubtful anecdote that two Confederate companies of Irishmen refused to fire on fellow Irishmen bearing the Federal flag during fighting at Winchester. A poem called "The Irish Boys," written by a "C. M." and first published in the Philadelphia *Press*, commemorated the event and claimed:

> They saw the old and honored flag
> Bourne out upon the air
> And not a gun was raised against
> Its floating folds so fair!

Frank Moore, ed., *The Rebellion Record* 12 vols. (New York: G. P. Putnam, 1861–68), 5: 2 (in "Poetry and Incidents" section).

of Wormley's Creek, taking the troops out of range of the Southern cannon.
They remained here on the extreme right of the Union line throughout the
siege, engaged mostly in skirmish duty. On the evening of April 10, five
hundred men and twenty officers of the Ninth under Major Hanley served
on the picket line.[33]

> Near Yorktown, Va.
> April 12, /62

My Dear Jennie:

Your note of the 7th inst. came to me this morning, also a <u>Boston Journal</u> containing an extract from London Times with reference to the "Ninth." All of us think much of this compliment as it comes not only from a hostile but a very influential source.

One week ago we came up here to these batteries and as the rebels opened fire upon us we commenced the battle of Yorktown. In a straggling manner hostilities continue. As we are obliged to confine ourselves within the limits of our respective camps, I cannot give you any list of casualties. But this I know, that with our usual good fortune, no one in this Regmt. has been deprived of life or limb up to this time. I often hear it remarked that our numerous escapes from harm is attributable to the unceasing prayers which we all feel are offered up to Heaven for us by our "home angels." The fact is singular—the <u>cause</u> assigned may be true.

But, I have no doubt it is asked in the North, why is the Battle not fought and won by this time. I do not wonder that this question is asked. Even here we ask it. Well, what is the reason? Let me explain. I think when we were up in the vicinity of Bull Run I wrote to you and said something about a want of due preparation for a swift pursuit of the enemy. I thought then that <u>Genius</u> did not direct the Army of the Potomac. I think so now, and have more evidence of the fact. Here we are within speaking and seeing distance of the rebels and came here to fight and yet, Jennie, would you believe it, we are not prepared to give the enemy battle. It is said that one hundred thousand men are behind yon-

---

[33] OR, vol. 11, pt. 1: 311. *The Pilot*, May 3, 1862. Macnamara, *Ninth Regiment*, pp. 80–81.

der batteries with [President Jefferson] Davis and [General Joseph] Johnston and 500 pieces of artillery.[34] We have men enough—but the proper means of reducing the batteries we have not. Our Ordnance is not of sufficient caliber. This place must be taken by a <u>siege</u>. Where are the siege guns? About ten of them are five miles in our rear—no facilities for getting them up—and we are obliged to await their coming. When will they come? I know not. Today some feeble effort is being made to bring them on—but they should have come when we did, and the <u>Genius</u> which swept over the Alps in the mid-winter and carried the weight of a world upon her wings would have had them here, if she presided over us in our movements. I like McClellan but I hate delays. Perhaps I do not fully understand the circumstances with which our General has to contend. I hope not. Before this reaches you, however, the country may have cause to weep or exult. I hope the latter, I <u>believe</u> that when the battle is fought it will be well fought and gloriously won by our army. We would not retreat and we could not if we would, owing to the character of the country. <u>This</u> <u>army</u> <u>will</u> <u>either</u> <u>be</u> <u>annihilated</u> <u>or</u> <u>victorious.</u>

There is a rumor here that the "Merimac" [*sic*] went out and captured some transport ships in Hampton Rhoades yesterday.[35] Can this be? What is that soporific Secretary of the Navy doing?[36] Send the paper, love, so that I can see what the facts are. These disasters and delays cut me deeply.

"The Irish Brigade" have arrived here. I have not seen Meagher yet but I hope to soon.

---

[34] Only 34,000 Southerners, under Major General John B. Magruder, defended Yorktown at this time. However, "Prince John's" theatrics and information given by captured Rebel prisoners led McClellan to believe he faced a force of over one hundred thousand men. Stephen W. Sears, *To the Gates of Richmond: The Peninsula Campaign* (New York: Ticknor & Fields, 1992), pp. 43, 45.

[35] At six in the morning on April 11, the ironclad C.S.S. *Virginia* (often called its former, U.S. Navy name, *Merrimack*) steamed toward Hampton Roads with several other vessels to battle its counterpart, the U.S.S. *Monitor.* However, most of the Federal transport ships were under the protection of Ft. Monroe's cannon, and neither the *Virginia* nor *Monitor* engaged each other. Three transport ships were captured by Commander Joseph N. Barnes of the C.S.S. *Jamestown,* but decisive battle did not occur. William C. Davis, *Duel Between the First Ironclads* (Baton Rouge: Louisiana State University Press, 1975), pp. 148–49.

[36] Hailing from Connecticut, Gideon Welles played an important role in state politics and helped organize the Republican party in New England. He proved to be a capable administrator while in charge of the Navy Department during Lincoln's administration. Johnson and Malone, *Dictionary of American Biography,* 19: 629–32.

My Dear, how goes the world with you? I need not ask, though. I know how you are. I can see you every moment of the day. I am with you and by you. I see you walk and sit and play with Loolie. I can see a woman's goodness in your face and the wife and mother in your thoughts. No! Jennie, I need not ask. I know how you are—I seem a part of yourself. You are the same as ever in the mirror of my life.

Farewell Dear
Guiney

Camp Winfield Scott
near Yorktown Va.
April 18, 1862

My Dear Jennie:

Last evening I received your kind letters of the 12th and 13 inst. Letters from home, out here, are the most highly prized favors. Officers who let them go about with them in their hands holding them up and tantalizing the poor unfortunates whose downcast-looks indicate that they have received no "news from Home." Although I am not so demonstrative as some of my friends in this respect, I assure you, Dear, that your letters give me peculiar pleasure and in the case of your last deepens it with a shade of sadness on account of your illness. From what you say I cannot infer, however, that your illness is of a serious nature. I hope not, love, for Loolie's sake as well as for your own and mine, too, as I am sure to participate in your feelings if I know them. I trust this will find you well.

I told my colleagues Hanley and [Lieutenant John M.] Tobin of my good fortune in having the prayers of Miss Reed, along with your own, offered for my welfare.[37] I told them under such

---

[37] Lieutenant John M. Tobin was appointed adjutant on January 17, 1862, commissioned captain to date August 28, 1862, and was wounded at Spotsylvania on May 8, 1864. He received the Medal of Honor for his action at Malvern Hill on July 1, 1862, where he "Voluntarily took command of the 9th Mass. while adjutant, bravely fighting from 3 P.M. until dusk, rallying and reforming the regiment under fire; twice picked up the regimental flag, the color bearer having been shot down, and placed it in worthy hands." *Massachusetts Soldiers, Sailors,* 1: 662.

circumstances I felt invulnerable. Of course, I described Katy. As both of my friends will want "pious and pretty" wives when the war is over, I would suggest a previous marriage so that she may avoid too many invitations to surrender.

Our circumstances are substantially unchanged since I wrote to you last. We are having occasional encounters with the rebels. [Brigadier] General [William F. "Baldy"] Smith made an assault on one rebel battery—took it—(I am told) and lost 150 men— battery recaptured by the enemy—this happened about 1 mile from here.[38] McClellan is not ready yet. He may in <u>one hour</u>—I know not when. We expected the rebels to come out last night—we were under arms all night—Rebels didn't come as far as us—came part way—were driven back by picket Guard. Farewell Dear. I am in haste.

                                          Your Husband

                                          Near Yorktown, Va.
                                          April 25, 1862

My Dear Jennie:
    I have duly received two letters and lots of journals etc., since I wrote to you last. I would have written to you several times since but I have been quite unwell. I was out during one stormy night

---

[38] Brigadier General William "Baldy" Smith commanded the second division of the IV Corps at this time. On April 16, Major General McClellan ordered Smith to prevent the Confederates from improving their works at Dam No. 1 behind the Warwick River. Accordingly, Smith advanced his artillery and Brigadier General W. T. H. Brooks's Vermont Brigade to fire away at the Rebels from long range, with little effect. Four companies of the Third Vermont, 192 men, waded across the river, dispersed the Southern skirmishers, and fell into their vacated rifle pits. No support reinforced them, however, and a counterattack by Georgians and Louisianians pushed the Vermont boys back with 83 killed, wounded, or captured. The day ended with a total of 165 Federal casualties and nothing accomplished. Smith went on to lead VI Corps at Fredericksburg, but his stinging criticism of Burnside's actions at this battle led to his loss of corps command. He was sent out west, where he performed well at Missionary Ridge, and Lieutenant General Ulysses S. Grant brought him back to the eastern theater for the 1864 campaign. Before Petersburg in June, while the city was lightly defended, Smith let the chance to capture it slip by him and the war dragged on for nearly another year. Sears, *To the Gates of Richmond*, pp. 55–56. Warner, *Generals in Blue*, pp. 462–64.

with a party of men engaged in building a breastwork in front of one of the enemy batteries.[39] Early in the evening I was wet through to the skin and remained so until morning. I have often been wet as much and had not trouble but <u>this time</u> I was taken down. However, to-day I feel quite well. Father Scully has been very kind to me during my illness. I am quite restored—and am going on duty tomorrow.

We are progressing in our preparations for attack. McClellan evidently thinks highly of "our friend—the enemy." Our delay and elaborate precautions is a compliment paid in advance to the rebels. It was thought that the Bombardment of Yorktown would commence this morning—but I have heard nothing of it yet—If it were going on I would likely to <u>hear</u> of it. We have got a few wooden gun-boats here which keep us awake at night with their river pranks. They can't go up in the day time so they run up at night and shake up the rebels. Probably next Monday something will be done.

The extreme kindness of Colonel Cass will not permit me to rest until tomorrow. I have just received notice from him to go off again to-night. It is raining too. Be silent on the subject. I will <u>take care of myself</u> tonight. <u>He is very kind</u> but complaining is boyish—away with it.

> Ever [yours,
> Guiney]

> April 25, 1862

My Dear Jennie:

I dropped you a few lines this noon and closed somewhat hostilely. I sent a communication to the General about my illness and he <u>at once</u> gave me leave of absence from duty for 24 hours. I was so vexed at Colonel Cass for detailing me to go to-night that I feel much better now—my blood got warmed up I tell you. All is right now. I will not trouble anybody for favors after tonight.

My Dear, if I should be injured in the coming battle, you will

---

[39] The Regan diary also recorded that the Ninth continued in digging trenches, building embankments, and chopping timber at this time, usually under enemy fire. Regan diary, April 26, 1862.

not be able to visit me—so an order has been issued prohibiting relatives or friends from visiting camp and promising that the wounded shall be well cared for. So, Dear, in any case, do not attempt to come on here. I do not anticipate much loss of life as fighting will be done principally by artillery at long range. If rebels try to capture guns then we will have close fighting. I do not apprehend a battle (we are fighting all the time) for several days yet.

When the siege of Yorktown is ended I will give you all particulars. Both armies are at work day and night entrenching themselves. Kiss little Loolie for me.

P. R. Guiney

P.S. Remember me to Lizzie, Miss Crespy, Miss Reed, Miss Moran—Mrs. Merill (how I miss her cherry cordial), Mrs. Mulrey, also Mrs. Campbell—Mr. Campbell, Mr. Mulrey, etc.

PRG

For want of another envelope I must reopen morning letter to enclose this. Plenty of stationary ahead—in Richmond—will be there soon—some of us.

PRG

Camp Winfield Scott
May 1st 1862

My Dear Jennie:

I enclose only fifty dollars—only got a month's pay—left $400 in government hands. I would have drawn my whole pay if I thought I would have only 50 dols. left to send you. I was surprised to find the total of my expenses for last three months so much. I got trusted for necessaries all along. In future I intend to pay cash so I am keeping enough to live on till next pay.

The "siege" is progressing vigorously. We have got trenches, breastworks and batteries close up within musket range of the enemy. We work every night. The rebels keep up a constant resistance but we <u>Yankees</u> are too shrewd for them. The first thing a man does is to dig a hole in the ground for himself; he then sinks down and in this position works away. The enemy may arch the sky with bursting-bombs, over his head, and in the red thundering blaze he still works on in security. The rain is our worst enemy.

Last night myself and some others were observing the enemy behind a breastwork when the rebels brought four of their guns to bear upon the party. One shell went into our bank and there bursting covered us all over with dirt. We were sorry looking objects coming in to camp this morning—covered with an honorable but dirty—glory.

When our army opens upon the enemy <u>in earnest</u> Yorktown will be too hot for a human being to live in. The only fear is that the rebels will clear out too soon and all our labor will be in some degree lost. <u>This army expects to be in full possession of Richmond</u> before the month of May expires. We will have it in its full proportions or perhaps in ashes—but Richmond anyhow.

Remember me kindly to our friends. I am in constant receipt of the <u>Journal</u>. Adieu love,

P R Guiney

Send me a few stamps.

On the evening of May 3, Southern artillery fired its parting shots before General Johnston withdrew his entire force through Williamsburg toward Richmond. The siege ended without decisive result, as the Confederates evacuated before experiencing any major attack. Nonetheless, Major General McClellan deemed it a major success. The next day the Army of the Potomac entered Yorktown and began a pursuit of the Rebel army marked by several sharp engagements, such as at Williamsburg on May 5 and West Point on the 7th. The Confederate force, however, managed to escape capture or destruction. Meanwhile, Colonel Cass marched his men to the York River on May 12, where all enjoyed a refreshing swim.[40]

---

[40] Regan diary, May 12, 1862.

West Point Va.
May 12 1862

My Dear Jennie:

I am in receipt of your note of the seventh inst.

I constantly receive papers from you and the side notes are always read first I assure you.

We are stationed on the bank of the York river opposite West Point for how long I cannot say, probably only for a few days.

The enemy are between us and Richmond and doubtless will retreat to the Cotton States.[41] However so, battle may occur on the Chickahominy river.

Since the occupation of Yorktown our Division has been in what is called the Reserve so that we have taken no active part in either of the two battles which have been fought—one at Williamsburg and the other here.

The army is disappointed. The rebels should have been compelled to fight or surrender on this Peninsula. McClellan would, in my judgment, have accomplished this had he been sustained in his plan by Secretary [of War Edwin M.] Stanton.[42] But I think McClellan is not blameless. He should have assaulted Yorktown long before it was evacuated. I felt all along that the rebels could have been conquered there yet the way for a partial retreat would have remained open to the rebels without McDowell's Corps at West Point to cut them off. I think Secretary Stanton has committed the crime of the age in discouraging McClellan's plan.[43] The result is a long, weary and expensive pursuit. When will it end?

My dear you will be patient and hopeful. I am well—very well—and dreams of our future will come to me and lighten the burden of this soldiers life.

Ever yours
P R Guiney

---

[41] The Cotton States were the Deep South.

[42] Ohioan Edwin M. Stanton served as President Buchanan's attorney general and replaced Simon Cameron as secretary of war under President Lincoln. An efficient, if brusque, man, Stanton was not liked by McClellan, and vice versa. Johnson and Malone, *Dictionary of American Biography*, 17: 517–21.

[43] As mentioned in an earlier footnote, Major General Irvin McDowell's Corps was kept near Washington, since Confederate Major General "Stonewall" Jack-

On May 13, the Ninth conducted a twenty-mile march along dusty roads to bivouac at Cumberland Landing, a position only five miles from where they started—an example of blundered planning. A few days later they marched to White House Landing, further up the Peninsula east of Richmond.

Major General McClellan reorganized his army into four infantry corps of two divisions each, effective May 18. Brigadier General Porter took command of V Corps and Brigadier General Morell assumed leadership of the division, also assigned to V Corps; Colonel James McQuade of the Fourteenth New York took charge of the brigade as its ranking officer.[44]

> White House Landing on
> the Pamunkey river, Va.
> May 18th 1862

My Dear Jennie:

I have been made happy by the receipt of two of your letters since I wrote my last to you from West Point. Your promptness, <u>Dear</u>, is in striking contrast to my own negligence. I receive your <u>Journals</u> every day.

If you look at the maps published in the <u>New York Herald</u> you will see where we are camped. We came up yesterday from West Point. <u>Hard</u> <u>work</u>—<u>Bad</u> <u>roads</u>—<u>No</u> <u>Rebels</u>. The enemy are some few miles in advance of us between this place and Richmond. They may give us battle but my opinion is that the Rebels are determined to retreat to the Cotton States. Poor fellows! How tremendous is their delusion! How tenaciously they cling to the mad councils of their heartless leaders.

I think we will be in Richmond, fight or no fight, next month at farthest. We may be there next Monday. The Rebel soldiers are constantly coming to our lines and surrendering themselves. They are poorly clad and seem delighted to escape.

---

son's Valley campaign left President Lincoln and Secretary of War Stanton fearful for the capital's safety. McPherson, *Battle Cry of Freedom*, pp. 457–60.

[44] Regan diary, May 13, 1862. Macnamara, *Ninth Regiment*, p. 85. Macnamara recalled bivouacking at Columbia Landing, but he probably meant Cumberland Landing on the Pamunkey River, a bit southeast of White House Landing. Concerning Colonel James McQuade, he was of Irish descent and edited a newspaper in Utica, where most of his Fourteenth New York was recruited. William H. Powell, *The Fifth Army Corps* (New York: G. P. Putnam's Sons, 1896), pp. 10, 15.

We came near having a fight to-day with the 18th Mass. We had just arrived in this ground and in obedience to an order from our General the men pitched their tents on a piece of a field near the camp of the 18th and within their guard lines. Col. Barnes undertook to drive us off by force and we turned out the whole Regmt. to resist them.[45] The 18th did not obey the Colonel and hence bloodshed was obviated. The conduct of Col. Barnes was atrocious—and he is universally denounced here. What he undertook to do by force might have been accomplished by a few words with our General. We were simply obeying orders of our Comdg. Gen. and were not to blame.

But a word with you Jennie; How does it happen that my kind and gentle Jennie has become so ferocious all at once as to ask as a trophy the hair of the Dead Head of Jeff. Davis? Oh! Jennie— How cruel. We are quite conservative out here on such matters. We have got Jeff. anyhow and no one seems to care whether he is dead or alive. The Southern ladies are all, as far as I have been able to judge, vindictive. I did not expect to find Northern ladies reciprocating. But I suppose the ladies all round are mad about the war as it keeps those they love away. I will send you the hair if I get it.

My relations with Col. are more agreeable now—how long I know not. Kisses to Loolie and you.

P. R. Guiney

Camp at Tunstall's Station, Va.[46]
May 20 1862

My Dear Jennie:
Having received a Journal from you this morning endorsed with a wish to hear from me, I take this opportunity, although

[45] A West Point classmate of Robert E. Lee, James Barnes led the division at Gettysburg in the absence of its regular commander at that time, Brigadier General Charles Griffin. He attained the rank of major general of U.S. volunteers by brevet on March 13, 1865—the same day that Guiney received his brevet promotion to brigadier general. Warner, *Generals in Blue*, pp. 20–21.

[46] Slightly under five miles west of White House. Sears, *To the Gates of Richmond*, pp. 170–72.

half stolen from other less agreeable duties, to avail myself of the rude facilities which this place affords for sending a few words.

We are almost constantly on the march only waiting at a locality long enough to permit our supplies and ammunition to come up. Truly McClellan is "pushing the enemy to the wall." Although I did think the rebels would get away from us and retire to the Cotton States, now, however, it seems to me, in view of the rapidity of our Advance, the condition of things on the James River, and above all, the overwhelmingly crushing effect which the loss of Richmond would have upon the Southern people, that a battle great in its result and most bloody in its details will occur between the two large armies in Virginia. The rebel army is said to be much larger than ours, and, there is no doubt will fight desperately to save Richmond. But it matters not. Our army may be smaller than theirs and actuated by higher and less vindictive motives than those which govern our enemies in the battlefield, and yet I feel firm in the belief that we will conquer a highway to that reservoir of treason. "The Army of the Potomac" tramples on the hills of Virginia with all the pride and conscious power of a God upon Olympus. We cannot be beaten. I do not boast—I tell you this from my observation and knowledge of the army. I have seen its boldness, grandeur, and defiant front.

Our Division together with a Division of the Regular Army forms the Reserve—a position of great honor and accorded to us on account of our superior discipline and presumed ability to fight well.[47] "The Reserve" is never brought up at the commencement of a battle—only when those in front are tired or to carry a "forlorn hope." So you see, Jennie, a battle might take place and the Reserve not fire a shot.

The main body of the army is now ahead of us but tomorrow we move on again. The next move will bring us to beyond the Chickahominy. This part of Virginia is luxuriously beautiful. How strange it seems that men will war with each other amid such scenes and blessings where everything is radiant with beauty, goodness, peace, and love! O! Jennie, how much less ought we to hate our enemies and how much more ought we to love our God. Nature is a Divine protest against War. But the curse be upon

---

[47] This is Brigadier General George Sykes's division of U.S. Regulars. Warner, *Generals in Blue*, pp. 492–93.

those who provoke it—not upon those who battle for Right, Liberty and Natural existence.

Colonel Cass thinks of going home soon—he is not very well. Will write you again next <u>halt</u>. Love to Loolie.

PRG

Near Bottom's Bridge Va.[48]
May 22d /62

My Dear:

I have just arrived here after a fatiguing march. This place is within 12 miles of Richmond. Enemy still retreats. They may stand close to Richmond—at any rate we will <u>be</u> <u>there</u> in a few days. I want a letter from you. I miss my <u>Journals</u> the last two days.

I enclose some fragrant Virginia leaves—a <u>trophy</u> more congenial to you than anything else I can find. They were given to me by the only Virginia lady I met on the march—<u>she</u> <u>was</u> <u>black</u>.

Everything goes well with our army—we are in splendid spirits. My health is excellent. My love to Loolie and Lizzie.

Ever yours
PRG

P.S. I wrote this in the dark.[49]

PRG

On May 26 the regiment moved to Gaines' Mill, eight miles distant from Richmond, and received orders to be ready to move at morning's light. With eighty rounds of ammunition and two days' extra rations, the Ninth Massachusetts fell into line nine hundred strong early on May 27. Under a hot sun, the regiment conducted a muddy march (it had rained that morning) toward Hanover Court House. Since Cass felt ill, Guiney

---

[48] Bottom's Bridge, a dozen miles east of Richmond, had been burned by the Confederates. Sears, *To the Gates of Richmond*, p. 109.

[49] It shows—the handwriting on this letter is sloppy and choppier then usual.

commanded the Ninth, but the Colonel soon galloped up—he did not want to miss the possibility of his regiment's first large-scale fight, its baptism of fire. The entire Federal force under Brigadier General Porter's command, consisting of Brigadier General Morell's division, the Fifth and Sixth United States Cavalry regiments, the Twenty-fifth New York Infantry, Colonel Berdan's Sharpshooters, and three batteries, was to clear the area for a linkup with Major General McDowell's corps, protect the right flank of the Army of the Potomac, and destroy telegraph lines, some track of the Virginia Central Railroad, and a bridge in the vicinity. The cavalry rode in advance of the main body and reached the crossroads of Ashland and Hanover Court House Road to find Brigadier General Lawrence O'Bryan Branch's North Carolina brigade and the Forty-fifth Georgia there— around four thousand men. Captain Benson's battery of Horse Artillery and guns of a Second U.S. Artillery battery, supported by the Twenty-fifth New York and Berdan's Sharpshooters, held the Rebels at bay until Morell brought up the main body. Brigadier General John H. Martindale's brigade reinforced the line until Brigadier General Daniel Butterfield's regiments deployed and launched an advance that pushed the Confederates back toward Hanover Court House, taking a cannon and some prisoners.[50]

A Federal detachment went off to destroy railroad and telegraph lines near Peake's Station, while other forces pursued the Rebels. However, the Confederates worked their way around Porter's right, driving back the Twenty-fifth and Forty-fourth New York regiments and capturing a section of Captain Augustus P. Martin's Third Massachusetts Battery C, left to hold the crossroads. Porter sent Colonel James McQuade's brigade to reinforce the position, and the Ninth Massachusetts double-quicked in column of companies through a wheatfield and formed line of battle at the edge of a woods.

McQuade rode up to the Ninth's colonel and, standing in his stirrups, ordered, "Colonel Cass, the enemy has taken two pieces of Martin's battery, and I want the Ninth Massachusetts to retake them, which I know they can and will." Cass shouted to his troops, "Boys, remember what you have to do; forward, Ninth, double-quick." With a cheer the Irishmen rose and pressed through the cornfield, charged through a woods over fallen trees and ditches, and captured eighty Rebels while under enemy fire. The left of the regiment, under Major Hanley, came out of the dense woods before

---

[50] OR, vol. 11, pt. 1: 680–84. Macnamara, *Ninth Regiment*, pp. 88–81. Sears, *To the Gates of Richmond*, p. 114.

the right, as the terrain it covered was less rough. Guiney, in command of the right, halted to locate the rest of the regiment; under Guiney's orders Sergeant J. W. Macnamara took Company I to make connection with the left. Macnamara deployed his men at speaking distance until reaching the left wing, which had similarly halted. Reunited, the cheering regiment pitched into the Rebel left flank and caused their rout, and recaptured Martin's two cannon. Through the steep bank of a railroad cut, the Massachusetts troops continued on in pursuit until darkness brought a close to the battle.

The Sixty-second Pennsylvania of the Ninth's brigade participated in the charge. A close relationship existed between the two units. When one Pennsylvanian asked, "How will we take Richmond," another replied, "Why, the Sixty-second will fire, and the Ninth will charge!"[51]

The Ninth lost one man mortally wounded and eleven other casualties, while the Irish flag was pierced by eight buck-and-ball shots. The entire Federal force lost 355 killed, wounded or missing, as opposed to estimated Confederate casualties of 200 killed, 200 wounded, and 730 captured. Of these prisoners, around 150 were taken by the Irishmen. For this effort at Hanover Court House, Porter gave the regiment his thanks and the sobriquet "Fighting Ninth."[52]

On May 28, the Ninth helped bury the battlefield dead, mostly in mass graves, while several details searched for stragglers or further destroyed the Virginia Central Railroad. Private Michael Kane of Company E captured the colors of the Cleveland Guard, left on the ground. Hailing from Cleveland County, North Carolina, the Cleveland Guard was Company H of the Twenty-eighth North Carolina. The flag of red silk, with a white stripe in which "Cleveland Guards" was inscribed, was sent by Colonel Cass to the city of Boston and received at City Hall on June 3. On May 29, the Ninth returned to camp with its brigade and arrived back at Gaines' Mill at 2:00 a.m. on May 30.[53] *Despite the operation, Major General McClellan's hopes that Major General McDowell would join him were dashed. While he believed that McDowell's men were at Fredericksburg,*

[51] OR, vol. 11, pt. 1: 699–701, 704–707, 717–20. *The Pilot*, June 14, 1862. Macnamara, *Ninth Regiment*, 92–93. Macnamara, *Bivouac*, 91.

[52] OR, vol. 11, pt. 1: 685, 720. Regan diary, May 27, 1862. Macnamara, *Ninth Regiment*, p. 94.

[53] The company was also known as the "Cleveland Regulators." *The Pilot*, June 14, 1862. Macnamara, *Ninth Regiment*, pp. 96–98. Louis H. Manarin and Weymouth T. Jordan Jr., eds. *North Carolina Troops 1861–1865: A Roster*. 13 vols. (Raleigh: North Carolina Division of Archives and History, 1966–93), 8: 196.

President Lincoln had ordered the corps to return closer to Washington for the safety of the capital a few days earlier.[54]

Gaines' Mills, Va.
May 31st 1862

My Dear Jennie:

I received yours of the 25th inst. I am sorry darling that I was not thoughtful enough to anticipate your own and Loolie's wants. I send you $ 40.00 enclosed. I hope it will reach you. To send money from here is somewhat of a dangerous experiment—but I will risk it.

I suppose you have read ere this of the battle of Hanover. Our Division started from camp at day-break on the 27th inst. and after marching 20 miles over a bad road and in a rain storm, we met ten thousand of the enemy under [Brigadier] General Branch. They fought the right of our Division on the main road and then retired still keeping the highway. Our General pursued them and this was exactly what the enemy desired for while we were driving them along a part of the rebel force was concealed in the dense wood to our left where they quietly waited until we had nearly all passed. When the last Brigade were passing the enemy opened a tremendous fire upon our rear. This astonished the commanding generals. They supposed that they were driving all the rebels on the main road—but back we went—Infantry, Cavalry, lancers, and Artillery to the rear at double quick! When we arrived there Martindale's Brigade—the 2nd, had been driven from their position and three pieces of Martin's Battery were in possession of the enemy. The woods all round were swarmed with rebels. The Ninth was ordered to press their way through the wood, and O! such a wood!—to deliver their fire and then to charge and recapture the artillery. We met the rebels on the verge of the wood and whipped them out of it in no time—such quick work I never saw—the rebels made a stand in the open field—out our boys jumped and forming an excellent line of battle—Let a yell and rushed upon the rebellious hounds. The rebels fled for

---

[54] Macnamara, *Ninth Regiment*, p. 97. Sears, *To the Gates of Richmond*, p. 118.

some distance and then made a stand again. At this point we lost Sergeant [Daniel J.] Regan Co. G. Nine others were wounded—one taken prisoner—Again we pressed upon the enemy—captured one of their flags—and drove them in the most indescribable disorder.[55]

It is unnecessary for me to say that the Artillery was recaptured. This charge of ours turned dismal defeat into exultant victory—O! it was grand indeed. I would like to say that some other Regmts. did something towards our triumph but on my soul I cannot. True the 25th and 44th New York fought well and were beaten and 2nd Maine too fought well and was beaten, heroes all of them but the <u>Ninth</u> came against them like a fatality and swept them from the bloody field. I wish I had time to tell you all . . .[56]

[letter breaks off]

During the Battle of Seven Pines, Brigadier General Porter's V Corps remained north of the Chickahominy River while the fight raged south of it. On June 1, the Ninth marched with its brigade but, because of flooding and poor bridges, was unable to cross the swollen river and participate in the battle.[57] During the first day's fighting, May 31, Confederate General Joseph Johnston was wounded, and a few days later General Robert E. Lee assumed command of the Southern forces defending Richmond. In a few weeks they truly became his army, the Army of Northern Virginia, and Lee would lead it until war's end.

On the evening of June 7, Federal command decided that Brigadier General Daniel Woodbury's Engineer Brigade would construct a bridge over the Chickahominy River, around 300 yards above Sumner's Bridge and nearly opposite the Trent House. On the 8th, the Ninth Massachusetts moved near this position and, for the next week, helped guard and build Woodbury's Bridge and its corduroy road approaches. The weather was uncomfortably hot and the troops were sometimes waist-deep in muck and water. Daniel Macnamara recalled the men receiving a gill of whiskey at

---

[55] A shoemaker from Marlboro, Sergeant Daniel Regan was killed at Hanover Court House, May 27, 1862. *Massachusetts Soldiers, Sailors,* 1: 661.

[56] The Second Maine lost 32 casualties, and the Twenty-fifth and Forty-fourth New York lost 158 and 86, respectively. Brigadier General Martindale cited all three regiments for their service. OR, vol. 11, pt. 1: 685, 707.

[57] Regan diary, June 1, 1862. Macnamara, *Ninth Regiment,* p. 101.

noon each day to brace their spirits. The Twenty-second Massachusetts
relieved them from duty on the afternoon of June 12.[58]

Meanwhile, the regiment had not forgotten the dead Lieutenant Colonel
Robert Peard and on June 16, Guiney joined two other officers in signing
a letter to his widow, Hannah Peard, telling how the officers and some men
of the Ninth contributed $234 to help support Peard's wife and children.[59]

On June 19, 1862, the VI Corps crossed to the south side of the Chicka-
hominy; Porter's V Corps remained the only sizeable Union force north of
the river.

Near Richmond Va.
June 21 /62

My Dear Jennie:

I am in possession of your note of the 13th inst. I was fearful
that you would not receive the money which I sent on, there was
so much interruption about that time in the mails. I felt much
relieved to learn that all was right.

Our long delay on the Chickahominy is somewhat painful but
we all feel that <u>we</u> are the gainers by it. What was doubtful before
is brightening into sun-like certainty.

As you spoke after matter I will admit, Jennie, that I am in want
of a nice cloth jacket trimmed with green and copper or lead!
Something that will look well on a horseman when he is <u>dashing</u>
through Richmond. A <u>single</u> row of many small bright buttons
and to slope well around the neck. In fact Jennie, make it just as
you like. Also pantaloons light blue, dark blue stripe. Is there any
such thing as getting nice blue (light) shirts on which I could
occasionally pin or button an expensive paper collar? If not send
me red (not flannel). In fact throw in to the box just whatever
contribution you like. I am quite destitute of anything to put on
except my stiff and uncongenial uniform. I want something for
my careless moments when I am happy in my thoughts. You <u>know</u>
exactly what I want now, Jennie; fix them right off.

---

[58] Lieutenant Colonel B. S. Alexander to Brigadier General J. G. Barnard,
Camp near New Bridge, June 10, 1862; Alexander to Barnard, Camp Lincoln,
June 21, 1862, both in OR, vol. 51: 670–71, 688. Regan diary, June 12, 1862.
Macnamara, *Ninth Regiment*, p. 104.

[59] *The Pilot*, July 12, 1862.

Matters here (in the regiment I mean) are not all smooth, yet, perhaps not worth speaking of.

Father Scully is unwell but improving. The Colonel and Major [Hanley] are better. It's no use for me to get sick here, I would not be indulged, I would be obliged to write to the General so I guess I won't get sick—I'll be well, fat, and happy. I am so now. Good bye love and O! Darling I would like to shower upon you and my sweet little pet a cascade of kisses! I will sometime.

Ever Yours
P R Guiney

June 22nd 1862

My Dear Jennie:

I wrote you a short note last evening and spoke to you about some clothing etc. I said I would like a jacket with a single row of buttons. Come to think of it I would prefer a single breasted jacket with two rows of buttons, if such an arrangement be possible—the buttons should be small, bright, and numerous. The cloth may be any color you like. In fact I am not particular about having cloth—whatever material you please. Can you have some patriotic device on the breasts? Be quick Darling I would love to wear them in the fight now hourly expected. Send them per Adam's Express Co. to White House, Virginia.

Ever and Always Yours
PRG

Camp near Richmond, Va
June 24th 1862

My Dear Jennie:

Yours of June 19th received. Its contents gave me much pleasure, and also amused the major much when I read for him the killing little sayings of Loolie. The major, you understand, is a sensible young widower and can appreciate such things and therefore I read that part of your letter to him which related to our little pet.

Matters are remaining as before in this vicinity—we are in full sight of the enemy throwing up and arranging the means of attack and Defense—we are besieging the enemy's line. In fact, we are repeating the siege of Yorktown with simply a change of locality. We can rout them now I think with our artillery—but the rebels could, by falling back a mile closer to Richmond, get out of the range of our siege guns and this would necessitate a second and perhaps a third siege. This I think is the key to avoid more than the present siege and our delay. McClellan wishes to make short work of the enemy's present positions, to be well prepared for a swift pursuit clear up to Richmond where he intends to dash the brains of the rebellion out against the walls. I may be too hasty in assuming this, but things look so to me. Still it would not astonish me if the rebels, too, repeated the Siege of Yorktown on their part and evacuate. However this last is not expected—nothing indicates it, but, on the contrary, we see all round the red banners of Defiance.

We think some of having that cowardly Keenan brought back and shot for Desertion.[60] Capt. Willey is going home on Recruiting service. He is not the least service to the Regiment out here. He has not [done] duty (nor is he capable of it) for three months or more. But he may be of some use at home. He is the Colonel's particular friend. If he calls to see you treat him respectfully. He doesn't love me, but no matter.

If you like, Dear, you may send me some red flannel drawers (wide like that famous one) and shirts. Remember me to friends. Will you call upon Mr. Treanor and give him my respects? Send me his address.

PRG

---

[60] Of the four Keenans listed in *Massachusetts Soldiers, Sailors, and Marines in the Civil War*, it is hard to identify which one Guiney is referring to in this instance, as none are listed as having deserted or gone absent without leave at this time. Private Edward Keenan was killed at Spotsylvania on May 12, 1864; Private Michael Keenan was killed in action at Gaines' Mill on June 27, 1862; Private James Keenan was wounded at Gaines' Mill on June 27, 1862 and deserted in Maryland on June 29, 1863; and Wagoner John Keenan was discharged for disability to date February 21, 1863. *Massachusetts Soldiers, Sailors,* 1: 621, 628, 665, 671.

A series of battles known as the Seven Days began as General Lee tried
to relieve the Yankee threat to Richmond. The Ninth distinguished itself
in the fighting. Recently promoted Brigadier General Charles Griffin assumed command of the brigade in the afternoon of June 26. As he rode in
front of the Ninth Massachusetts, the Irishmen gave him three cheers,
followed by three more for Colonel Cass.[61] His first action as a general
officer came that day, as Lee ordered a concentrated assault on Brigadier
General Porter's men, hoping to overwhelm the isolated corps before Federal
reinforcements could cross the Chickahominy River. The Pennsylvania Reserve Division under Brigadier General George McCall remained at an
advanced position behind Beaver Dam Creek, with Brigadier Generals
John Reynolds's and Truman Seymour's brigades on the front line and
Brigadier General George Meade's regiments in reserve as a Confederate
assault force crossed the river.[62] Lee planned for Major General A. P.
Hill's division to cross at Meadow Bridge and clear the way for Major
Generals D. H. Hill's and James Longstreet's divisions to attack, while
Major General "Stonewall" Jackson arrived on the Federal right flank to
complete the destruction of Porter's solitary corps. However, when Jackson
failed to show up, only Hill went forward to attack.

The Rebels advanced around 3:00 in the afternoon, and McCall's reserve brigade came up while Brigadier General Morell's division advanced
to reinforce him. At 5:00 p.m. Brigadier General Martindale's brigade
and Captain Martin's battery took position on the Pennsylvanians' right,
while the Fourteenth New York and Fourth Michigan of Griffin's brigade
became hotly engaged aiding Reynolds. The Ninth Massachusetts, Sixty-
second Pennsylvania, and Captain William Weeden's battery remained in
reserve, although the Irishmen did relieve a regiment out of ammunition
and immediately began firing at the Rebels. With the Confederate repulse,
an artillery duel commenced which lasted until 9:00 that evening. The
Ninth lost only one killed and two wounded, and Porter's men lay on

---

[61] A West Pointer, Charles Griffin was an artillerist by training; even after receiving an infantry command he often paid close attention to the deployment
of nearby batteries. He eventually rose to command the V Corps in the closing
days of the war, commissioned a major general of volunteers on April 2, 1865.
Known for his sharp, tempestuous temper, Griffin was deemed by Colonel
Charles S. Wainwright to be "overbearing and supercilious." Nonetheless, he
was a good general officer who served the Army of the Potomac in nearly all its
major engagements. Charles S. Wainwright, *A Diary of Battle* Allen Nevins, ed.
(Gettysburg: Stan Clark Military Books, 1993), p. 167. *The Pilot*, July 26, 1862.
Warner, *Generals in Blue*, pp. 190–91.

[62] *The Pilot*, July 26, 1862. OR, vol. 11, pt. 2: 222, 312.

their arms under a cloudless, starry night sky. All told, eleven thousand Southerners unsuccessfully attacked fourteen thousand Federals, losing 1,475 troops to the Union's 361. Porter withdrew to the Gaines' Mill area a little before daybreak, having heard rumors that Major General "Stonewall" Jackson was in the vicinity of his right flank. A member of the Fourth Michigan asked, "We are not beaten, are we?" to which one of the Irishmen replied, "Faith, no! Don't niver b'lave you are whipt till you are whipt yourself! An' sure we are afther only drawing the ribels on." The Ninth Massachusetts reached their old camp around 7:00 a.m., June 27.[63]

Here the regiment ate an army breakfast and received sixty rounds of ammunition per man, then marched past the gristmill and pond toward New Cold Harbor, halting in line of battle with the brigade a mile from Gaines' Mill. In the forenoon, Griffin ordered Colonel Cass to backtrack toward Gaines' Mill and hold the bridge over which the Federals had just crossed the mill creek. Although the Ninth was not to make a stand here, only to harass and slow the Confederate crossing, Griffin informed Cass that two regiments would support him. They never came.[64]

Cass deployed Companies I and F as skirmishers and, rushing up on the double-quick, they immediately confronted Southern skirmishers of Brigadier General Maxcy Gregg's South Carolina brigade. Major Hanley reinforced his comrades with companies A and D and took advantage of the trees and terrain to stall the Confederate advance. As Gregg's brigade crossed, increasing Rebel numbers forced Hanley's stubborn withdrawal, and he rallied the men for one last volley before retreating to the main line. Company I lost all its officers during this engagement, and Timothy Regan reported a bullet passing through his canteen while he was drinking from it. A slug also smashed the stock of his rifle, but he replaced it from among several others available on the ground. The Fighting Ninth returned to its brigade under fire, their stance having been so effective that Griffin thought the Irishmen had received the promised two regiments of reinforcements. Porter himself later wrote, "At Gaines' Mill, Cass' gallant

---

[63] Regan diary, June 26, 1862. *The Pilot,* July 12, 1862; July 26, 1862. New York *Herald,* July 1, 1862. OR, vol. 11, pt. 2: 222–23, 271–72, 312. Macnamara, *Ninth Regiment,* pp. 111–12. Sears, *To the Gates of Richmond,* p. 208.

[64] Father Scully's chapel tent had to be abandoned at this time for lack of transport, probably fired to prevent its capture and use by the Confederates. *Annual Report of the Adjutant-General of the Commonwealth of Massachusetts . . . For the Year Ending December 31, 1862* (Boston: Wright & Potter, 1863), p. 120. New York *Herald,* July 15, 1862. Macnamara, *Ninth Regiment,* pp. 115–16. Macnamara, *Bivouac,* 96. Frank J. Flynn, *The Fighting Ninth for Fifty Years* (no date), p. 18.

Ninth Massachusetts Volunteers of Griffin's brigade obstinately resisted A. P. Hill's crossing, and were so successful in delaying his advance, after crossing, as to compel him to employ large bodies to force the regiment back to the main line . . . . This persistent and prolonged resistance gave to this battle one of its well-known names [Gaines' Mill].'[65]

Brigadier General Porter had formed his defensive line in a semi-circle, with Brigadier General Morell's division on the left, Captain Martin's Third Massachusetts battery in the center, Brigadier General Sykes' Regulars on the right, and Brigadier General McCall's Pennsylvanians in reserve behind Morell.[66] *Morell placed, from left to right, the brigades of Brigadier Generals Butterfield, Martindale, and Griffin; the Ninth held the division's extreme right to support Martin's guns, with the Sixty-second Pennsylvania on its right rear. Around noon the two regiments repulsed a Confederate charge against the napoleons.*[67]

At 2:00 the Rebels launched another attack, and as the brigades of Brigadier Generals Lawrence O' Bryan Branch and William Dorsey Pender attempted to capture Captain Martin's cannon, the Ninth Massachusetts, Sixty-second Pennsylvania, and double-charges of canister again repulsed the Rebels. During close fighting, the Pennsylvanians' Colonel Black fell dead. The Southerners charged and were repulsed several times, until the Ninth had used up its sixty rounds a man. At this point, Timothy Regan recalled, "we took the ammunition from the boxes of the dead and wounded and fired that also, and when we had charged the enemy and drove them three times, and had not a cartridge left we were relieved . . . to fill our cartridge boxes. We hardly had ammunition in our boxes when the regiment that had relieved us came running out of the woods with the enemy at their heels, and we were sent to take over our own place in the line of battle.'[68]

Brigadier General Porter's men fended off attacks all along the position while Brigadier General Henry Slocum's division of Brigadier General William Franklin's VI Corps reinforced the beleaguered V Corps; Brigadier

---

[65] *The Pilot,* July 26, 1862. Fitz John Porter, "The Battle of Gaines' Mill and its Preliminaries" in *Century Magazine* Vol. 30, No. 2 (June 1885), 318-19. Regan diary, June 27, 1862. Macnamara, *Ninth Regiment,* pp. 117–19. In Brigadier General Gregg's official report, he implied that other regiments were present, although only the Ninth Massachusetts was identified. The Ninth was alone throughout the engagement. OR, vol. 11 pt. 2: 854.

[66] OR, vol. 11, pt. 2: 224. Porter, "The Battle of Gaines' Mill," 315.

[67] OR, vol. 11, pt 2: 272–73. Macnamara, *Ninth Regiment,* pp. 119–20.

[68] Regan diary, June 27, 1862. OR, vol. 11, pt. 2: 313. Macnamara, *Ninth Regiment,* p. 122.

General John Newton's brigade took position behind Griffin's troops. A brief lull in the fight lasted until after 5:30, when Confederate Major Generals Longstreet, D. H. Hill, and Jackson led an all-out frontal assault on the tired Federals.[69]

This final attack pushed back Morell's left and center, and a similar Rebel charge caused Porter's right to buckle. The Federals had no option other than retreat. Meanwhile, Colonel Cass had become too sick to stand and, while resting upon a tree stump, relinquished command to Guiney. The Ninth formed the retreating column's rearguard. The tremendous pressure of the pursuing Confederates forced Guiney to take action to prevent the encircling and capture of his men. Ordering the color-bearers forward and calling the troops to "Follow your colors, men," Guiney formed line of battle and challenged the Rebel surge. With a loud cheer and the National and Irish colors proudly held aloft, the Fighting Ninth fired a volley and then charged the Rebels, driving them away with stubborn determination. In this way, Guiney bought enough time to withdraw a bit before having to repeat the procedure again—something the Ninth Massachusetts did nine times in all, with the Confederates often but sixty yards away. Ten colorbearers fell while holding the United States flag, while Sergeant "Jack" Barry of Company B, holding the Irish standard aloft, came out of the fray unscathed. Brigadier General Philip St. George Cooke of the cavalry saw and admired this gallant, unyielding resistance of the Ninth.[70]

Finally, Brigadier Generals Meagher and William French came upon the chaotic field and deployed their regiments to shield Porter's men, allowing them to reform and withdraw in safety. In the darkness, Meagher came up to the Ninth and mistook Guiney, in his shirtsleeves by this time, for Cass. Calling, "Hello, Cass, is this you?" Guiney replied, "Hello, General Meagher, is this the Irish Brigade? Thank God we are saved." Irish

---

[69] OR, vol. 11, pt. 2: 225. Macnamara, *Ninth Regiment*, pp. 123–25.

[70] OR, vol. 11, pt. 2: 42, 273. New York *Herald*, July 15, 1862. *The Pilot*, July 26, 1862. Macnamara, *Ninth Regiment*, pp. 126–27, 165. Macnamara, *Bivouac*, p. 99. Flynn, *The Fighting Ninth*, p. 20. Even the New York *Herald*, criticized by Guiney and Second Lieutenant Michael Finnerty for its accounts of the Ninth Massachusetts' participation in the actions at Vienna and Hanover Court House respectively, praised the Irish unit. It reported, "The Ninth Massachusetts regiment was the rear of the retreating column, which had just passed over a hill into a large plain. As the regiment were retreating over this hill they were hotly pressed by the rebels. To break and run was not for the men who had covered themselves with glory during the entire day." The *Herald* then provided an account of the Ninth's heroism, Guiney's call for the men to follow their colors, and the nine charges which he led.

Brigade historian D. P. Conyngham related that, during the Ninth's heroic stance, "Stonewall" Jackson saw its Irish flag and mistook the regiment for the entire Irish Brigade, ordering his reserves to remove "that d— brigade."[71] Later, a German correspondent following the Confederate army and writing for the Cologne Gazette recalled,

> While rows were mowed down by enemy bullets, nothing stopped their bravery. . . . it was man against man, an eye for an eye, bayonet for bayonet. The enemy brigade, M'Gaber [referring to Meagher and his Irish brigade], mostly Irishmen, showed heroic opposition. After heavy fighting our people began to retreat and all order and enthusiasm went for naught. They retreated in great disorder.[72]

The Ninth Massachusetts lost 249 men, 82 of them killed or mortally wounded, the highest loss of any regiment at Gaines' Mill. Father Scully was taken prisoner, ministering to the injured while Confederate forces advanced past him. As the Rebel guards grew drowsy that night, Scully managed to escape and return to the regiment. All told, the Confederates pitted 54,300 men in six divisions against Brigadier General Porter's 35,000, including reinforcements. The attackers lost 7,993 killed, wounded, and captured against Federal losses of 6,387, of which 2,829 were captured along with 22 cannon. At 2:00 a.m. on June 28, Porter marched his entire exhausted force across the Chickahominy—the Ninth filed over a road and bridge it had earlier helped to construct—and the men bivouacked at Trent Farm while the bridges across the river were destroyed.[73] The exertion of battle worsened a case of malaria that Guiney had contracted, and he fell extremely ill. Unable to move without help and confined to an ambulance, he was ordered home to recuperate.[74]

---

[71] OR, vol. 11, pt. 2: 226. D. P. Conyngham, *The Irish Brigade and Its Campaigns* Lawrence F. Kohl, ed. (1867; reprint, New York: Fordham University Press, 1994), p. 186. Macnamara, *Ninth Regiment*, pp. 128, 133. Flynn, *The Fighting Ninth*, p. 20.

[72] Cologne *Gazette*, November 25, 1862. Several months later, an unsigned letter from a member of the Ninth Massachusetts appeared in *The Pilot*, describing the recent maneuvers of the army. The author also assured that, "notwithstanding our late controversy on the statement of the Prussian officer regarding the fight at Gaines Mills [*sic*], as to whom,—the Irish Brigade or the 9th Mass—the laurels of that conquest belonged, we are in the best of humor with our brothers of the Brigade, and I am sure that the feeling is entirely reciprocal." *The Pilot*, February 7, 1863.

[73] *The Pilot*, August 2, 1862. OR, vol. 11 pt. 2: 274. Macnamara, *Ninth Regiment*, pp. 128, 166. Sears, *To the Gates of Richmond*, pp. 223, 248.

[74] Macnamara, *Ninth Regiment*, 155. Flynn, *The Fighting Ninth*, p. 22.

Later that day (June 28), McClellan began withdrawing toward the James River. Porter's men rested, and the Ninth received a mail delivery which caused several to shed tears upon hearing called out the names of men known to be slain. Finally, the V Corps began marching in the overpowering afternoon heat, passing through Savage Station to White Oak Swamp. At one point McClellan rode by the Ninth Massachusetts and as he surveyed the tattered National and Irish flags and the cheering, battle-scarred veterans, the commanding general smiled at the fighting regiment. Near the swamp, engineers constructed a road and bridge to facilitate the removal of Federal wagons and artillery, and a fatigue party of the Ninth joined those of other regiments in aiding them. Both Colonel Cass and Guiney remained ill and traveled with the regiment in ambulances.[75]

On June 29 Confederate pursuit resulted in a sharp engagement with the Federals at Savage's Station, while the Ninth Massachusetts moved to the junction of the Charles City and Quaker Roads and remained there all day. Father Scully was captured again at Savage's Station and sent to Richmond. He was allowed freedom in the city as long as he reported to the provost each day, but he had been unwell with fever. The Ninth's chaplain had probably contracted malaria and he remained unconscious or delirious for three weeks before being released and sent north. Scully eventually rejoined his regiment, but soon had to resign the chaplaincy due to his disability.[76]

The night of June 29 the regiment marched along muddy roads clogged with wagons, cannon, and men, to reach Malvern Hill in the late morning of the 30th. The day passed in skirmishing with the Confederates.[77]

On July 1 Lee designed to strike a blow against the Federals, planning a frontal assault against the strongly placed infantry and artillery crowning Malvern Hill. Brigadier General Morell's division held the Union left center supported by Brigadier General Sykes's Regulars and the Pennsylvania Reserves, with Brigadier General Griffin's brigade in the front line near Battery D, Fifth U.S. Artillery. The Fighting Ninth deployed between the Sixty-second Pennsylvania on its left and the Fourth Michigan on its right, and the men lay flat on the ground for over six hours in the swelter-

---

[75] *The Pilot*, August 2, 1862. OR, vol. 11 pt. 2: 274. Flynn, *The Fighting Ninth*, p. 21. Macnamara, *Ninth Regiment*, pp. 135–36.

[76] Macnamara, *Ninth Regiment*, pp. 137, 167, 429. Flynn, *The Fighting Ninth*, p. 21.

[77] Regan diary, June 30, 1862. Macnamara, *Ninth Regiment*, p. 137. Flynn, *The Fighting Ninth*, p. 21.

ing heat to avoid Confederate sharpshooter and artillery fire. Major General McClellan and Brigadier General Porter both rode up during this time and delivered brief, encouraging remarks to the men. In the late afternoon the Rebels advanced with a cheer and Griffin, a former artillerist engaged in inspecting the positions of the four Federal batteries in the area, rode to Cass, shouting, "Out Colonel Cass, get ready to charge; they are coming."[78]

Cass, still ill, had rested in the shade of a barn or tobacco dryhouse nearby, conserving his energy for the big battle ahead. Guiney remained incapacitated in an ambulance. The colonel roused himself, calling, "Up, Ninth, and at them." At a range of 150 yards the Federal artillery ripped large gaps in the Rebel ranks, but the gray tide swept forward nonetheless. When they closed to 60 yards the Ninth fired a volley and, with the Sixty-second Pennsylvania and Fourth Michigan, lunged at the Confederates, driving them back at bayonet point. The ground became covered with Southern dead and wounded. Colonel Woodbury of the Fourth Michigan fell dead while leading his troops in the valiant charge.[79]

A fresh force of Confederates came up, and the Twelfth and Forty-fourth New York and Eighty-third Pennsylvania regiments relieved Brigadier General Griffin's three regiments. During the Ninth's withdrawal, the right began to pull back, but the regiment's left did not hear the order, and a number of the Irishmen were captured in the confusion. Meanwhile, a bullet struck Colonel Cass' cheek, passed through the roof of his mouth, and knocked out six teeth before exiting near his ear, rendering him mortally wounded and unable to speak. Hanley took over until he was also borne from the field with a wounded arm, and command devolved upon Captain Timothy O' Leary.[80]

The Irish Brigade came up in relief, the second time during the Seven Days that the Ninth and Brigadier General Meagher's Brigade would be in such a situation. Upon seeing the brigade, the Massachusetts Irish

---

[78] OR, vol. 11, pt. 2: 274–75, 314. *The Pilot*, August 2, 1862. Flynn, *The Fighting Ninth*, p. 21. Macnamara, *Ninth Regiment*, p. 149.

[79] *The Pilot*, August 2, 1862. Regan diary, July 1, 1862. OR, vol. 11, pt. 2: 275–76, 314. Flynn, *The Fighting Ninth*, p. 22. Macnamara, *Ninth Regiment*, pp. 155–56.

[80] However, Lieutenant John M. Tobin received the Medal of Honor for his action at Malvern Hill on July 1, 1862, where he "voluntarily took command of the 9th Mass. while adjutant, bravely fighting from 3 P.M. until dusk, rallying and reforming the regiment under fire; twice picked up the regimental flag, the color bearer having been shot down, and placed it in worthy hands." *Massachusetts Soldiers, Sailors*, 1: 662. OR, vol. 11, pt. 2: 276, 314. *The Pilot*, July 12, 1862. Regan diary, July 1, 1862. Macnamara, *Ninth Regiment*, p. 159. Flynn, *The Fighting Ninth*, p. 23. Timothy Regan was one of those captured.

cheered their countrymen. By 9:00 that night the last shots were fired and it began to rain, adding to the sadness accompanying the aftermath of any bloody battle. The Rebels lost 5,650 men to the Federals' 3,007 in this failed assault. The Fighting Ninth had 166 casualties at Malvern Hill, making a total of 421 troops lost during the Seven Days.[81]

On July 2, the Ninth moved closer to Harrison's Landing and bivouacked nearby. The area teemed with the disheartening activities and scenes of a retreating army—stores piled on the banks, the movement of transport boats on the river, and ambulances filled with groaning wounded. On July 4, the Ninth's band played a concert for the men and Lincoln arrived that afternoon to review the Army of the Potomac. Captain O'Leary retained command of the regiment while Colonel Cass, Guiney, and Major Hanley were in Boston. The latter two recuperated, and when his strength improved, Guiney addressed a meeting in Roxbury to raise recruits; Cass, however, died of his battle wounds on July 12.[82]

Colonel Cass's funeral services were held at noon on July 16 at St. Mary's Church, led by Rev. J. Barrister, S.J., Mayor Wightman, the Boston City Council, Guiney, Major Hanley, and several other officers were present, while a massive crowd in and around the church joined in mourning. Inside, the front of the altar was draped in black, the candelabrum were covered with the American flag, and two ensigns and gold eagles with the mottoes "Union" and "We mourn his loss" hung before the choir.[83]

On July 26 Porter, now a major general, wrote to Massachusetts Governor John A. Andrew to assert his support for promoting Guiney to colonel and Hanley to lieutenant colonel of the Ninth, to date from the 26th with Andrew's approval. Two days earlier, Brigadier General Griffin had requested these promotions.[84] *However, as Colonel Cass had been forced to deal with conspirators and regimental intrigue while in command, so would Guiney.*[85] *In Guiney's absence a number of officers, led by Captain*

---

[81] *The Pilot*, August 2, 1862. OR, vol. 11, pt. 2: 276. Conyngham, *The Irish Brigade*, p. 213. Macnamara, *Ninth Regiment*, pp. 158–59, 162. Flynn, *The Fighting Ninth*, pp. 22–23. Sears, *To the Gates of Richmond*, p. 335.

[82] *The Pilot*, July 19, 1862. Macnamara, *Ninth Regiment*, pp. 170–74.

[83] *The Pilot*, July 26, 1862. Governor Andrew could not be present at the funeral, having prior commitments to attend the commencement of Harvard University. *The Pilot*, July 19, 1862.

[84] Charles Griffin to Captain J. Locke, A.A.G., July 24, 1862; Fitz John Porter to Governor John A. Andrew, Harrison's Landing, July 26, 1862. Both letters are in the Ninth Massachusetts File in the Executive Department Letters, Massachusetts State Archives, Boston, Massachusetts.

[85] Colonel Cass once wrote Guiney, stating, "The whole rest of conspirators are trying to bring charges against me. If it should prove so, I will want your

O'Leary, sought to prevent his promotion and penned a letter to Governor Andrew misrepresenting Guiney's actions while ill with malaria. When word of this reached Cass, he wrote Guiney a brief, scribbled letter from his deathbed which declared, "I am sorry to hear some one has tried to misrepresent you. . . . which is a lie whole and complete.'[86] *Nonetheless, the clique of officers sent the following letter.*[87]

Camp of the 9th Regt. Mass. Vol
Harrisons Landing
July 31, 1862

To His Excellency John A. Andrew
   Governor of Massachusetts

Your Excellency:

At a meeting of the Officers of this Regiment convened for the purpose of expressing their opinion of the fitness of Lieut. Colonel P. R. Guiney to fill the Colonelcy of this regiment left vacant by the death of our late gallant and lamented Colonel Cass, the following conclusion was unanimously arrived at.

That Lieut Col. P. R. Guiney's conduct at the battle of Gaines Mills has been much too highly extolled: that he was not seen by any of the Officers now present for two hours previous to the close of the engagement—Making his appearance just previous to the last stand made by the Regiment on the hill close to the hospital and which is so highly spoken of in Genl. Slocum's Official Report.

That about thirty six hours previous to the Battle of Malvern Hill Lieut. Col. Guiney was suddenly taken ill; he accompanied us close to the battle field in an ambulance and it was stated by those who saw him that he was much better able to take the field than Col. Cass, who nobly performing his duty, remained with us the night preceding the battle, and who, next morning, finding that

---

assistance in the defence." Thomas Cass to Patrick Guiney, Union Hill, December 4, 1861.

[86] Thomas Cass to Patrick Guiney, undated [July 1862].

[87] The original petition and a printed copy are located in the Ninth Massachusetts File in the Executive Department Letters, Massachusetts State Archives, Boston, Massachusetts and the Patrick R. Guiney Military Service Record, National Archives, Washington, D.C.

his little remaining strength was utterly failing him, sent an officer to Lieut. Col. Guiney, asking him for God's Sake to relieve him if only for two hours. Instead of doing which, however, he disappeared and was not heard of again until the arrival of the Regiment at Harrison's Landing after the battle, where he made his appearance for a few moments. Again for a considerable time nothing was heard of Lieut. Col. Guiney, and by direction of the General Commanding the Division, he was returned on the report "absent without leave." Only a few days ago has the Regiment received from the Adjutant General at Washington official notice of his having obtained a leave of absence. Previous to that we had heard of his addressing audiences in Boston while his Regiment was without a single Field and with very few line Officers, some companies being under the command of Sergeants.

We feel that Lieut. Col. Guiney while appealing to the patriotic people of our noble Old Bay State to fill up the ranks of this Regiment has been grossly neglecting his duty—instead of caring for the wants of the remnants who escaped from the Seven Days fighting has been making vapid speeches filled with spurious patriotism and accepting the thanks of a generous people to which he was very little entitled.

Therefore we conclude that the laurels which this Regiment has earned under its late gallant and heroic leader cannot be committed to the care of one who has so utterly neglected his duties. And we earnestly appeal to Your Excellency not to jeopardize the Honor of this Regiment or that of the Noble old state to which we belong by placing it in his hands.

> We have the honor to be Your
> Excellency's Obt. Servant

Timothy O'Leary—Capt. Comdg. 9th Regt. Mass
John M. Tobin—Adjt. 9th Mass Regt.
Thomas Mooney—Qu. Master
Thomas K. Roche 1st Lt. comdg. Co. H.
Michael W. Phalen   "   "   "   G
Archibald Simpson 2nd Lt.   "   "   G
Edward Timothy   "   "   "   "   K
Nicholas C Flaherty   "   "   "   D
Matthew Dacey   "   "   "   B

William A Phelan   "   "   "   A
William B. Maloney   "   "   "   E[88]

Meanwhile, Captain John C. Willey, in Boston on recruiting duty, joined the petitioners in opposing Guiney's promotion. On June 26 President Lincoln authorized the creation of the Army of Virginia, to be commanded by Major General John Pope. While in Boston, Guiney made a speech stating that the Federals would go to Richmond under Pope. Afterward, Captain Willey reported this to Major General McClellan, asserting that Guiney was "abusing his Genl," while reminding McClellan that "Col Cass was your friend, and the abuse this Guiney is a heaping upon you would be a dear thing to him if the Col could but speak." Captain Willey also accused Guiney of having "been drunk many times," an ironic charge since Guiney does not seem to have been much of a drinker.[89] In a later letter, Captain Willey wrote Major General Porter that Colonel Cass's

---

[88] Salem tailor Captain Timothy O'Leary received a wound on May 5, 1864 at the Wilderness (see footnote 119 in this chapter for more information). Quartermaster Thomas Mooney, a forty-six-year-old customhouse officer when the war began, died on March 29, 1863 of injuries received when he fell from his horse during a St. Patrick's Day race. Milford bootmaker Lieutenant Thomas K. Roche received his commission as captain dated July 8, 1862; he was dismissed from the service on September 30, 1863. A tanner from Salem, Michael Phalen mustered in as a sergeant; he was commissioned second lieutenant to date on September 7, 1861 and first lieutenant on January 28, 1862. He was appointed regimental adjutant on August 28, 1862. Phalen was wounded at Gaines' Mill on June 27, 1862, and again at Mine Run on November 30, 1863. Archibald Simpson was a Boston blindmaker and he was promoted to first lieutenant to date September 26, 1862; he was killed in action at Spotsylvania on May 12, 1864. Boston clerk Matthew Dacey mustered into the service as a sergeant and received promotion to second lieutenant on January 5, 1862; he resigned on October 14, 1862. While a law student, Nicholas C. Flaherty paused from his studies to join the Ninth Massachusetts with the rank of sergeant. He eventually reached the rank of first lieutenant on September 26, 1862, and was killed at the Wilderness on May 5, 1864. William A. Phelan mustered into the Ninth Massachusetts as a sergeant major and rose in rank to become a captain, his commission to date January 8, 1863; he was killed at the Wilderness on May 5, 1864. A Boston gas fitter, William B. Maloney, Jr. entered the service as a sergeant and attained the rank of first lieutenant to date September 26, 1862; he resigned on March 23, 1863. *Massachusetts Soldiers, Sailors, and Marines in the Civil War* gives no information on Lieutenant Edward Timothy. Lieutenant John M. Tobin has been discussed in an earlier footnote. *Massachusetts Soldiers, Sailors,* 1: 617, 622, 627, 640, 654, 655, 661, 667.

[89] Captain John C. Willey to Major General George B. McClellan, Boston, July 30, 1862; letter located in Patrick R. Guiney Military Service Record, National Archives, Washington, D.C.

widow wore a look of "Horror" on her face at the prospect of Guiney's promotion, and that "she . . . is almost crazy to think that her beloved husband's place is filled by such a miserable fellow as this Guiney. . . ." Captain Willey also claimed she ordered that, should Guiney wish to use Colonel Cass's mount, "to take the horse out and shoot him. . . ." In the same letter, Captain Willey supported Captain Timothy O'Leary's promotion to major, and concluded by stating, "I would prefer almost any punishment (even death) rather than disgrace myself by going back under this Guiney."[90]

The situation was complicated by the loss of Guiney's leave papers, referred to in the petition. Guiney left for Boston on July 3 with the necessary authorization, but when he requested an extension of his leave, he sent on the original leave of absence. Guiney received the extension but not his original leave papers, which seem to have been misplaced by the army bureaucracy. Lieutenant E. Waters, chief surgeon of Brigadier General Morell's division, recalled that he found Guiney "suffering from high fever" and gave him "a certification to the effect that his life was endangered by remaining under the then existing circumstances." Lieutenant Waters also remembered that the "certificate was written with pencil + no copy of it preserved, but I remember, distinctly, giving it."[91]

With all this going on, Major General Porter telegraphed Governor Andrew on August 4 to ask if Guiney's promotion might be deferred. In a second letter, Porter explained,

> I did this on the representations of an officer of the regiment which accused him of cowardice. Though the officers of his regiment had expressed a wish to have him promoted and his Brigade Commander had certified to his good conduct in action, and confirmed my impressions, I wished the appointment deferred (if you had decided to confirm the recommendation) till the matter could be investigated.
>
> I find much difficulty in extracting any evidence to confirm the accusation, but I wish justice done to the regiment and to him.

[90] Captain John C. Willey to Major General Fitz John Porter, Boston, August 10, 1862; letter located in Patrick R. Guiney Military Service Record, National Archives, Washington, D.C.

[91] Patrick R. Guiney to General [not identified], Roxbury, Massachusetts, July 21, 1862. Patrick R. Guiney to Major General Fitz John Porter, HeadQuarters Ninth Massachusetts, August 7, 1862; Lieutenant E. Waters to Captain F. T. Locke, Asst. Adj. Genl., HeadQuarters Griffin's Brigade, August 7, 1862; these letters are located in Patrick R. Guiney Military Service Record, National Archives, Washington, D.C.

I have ordered Colonel Guiney to return at once and shall confront him with his accusers and take the necessary steps to have a
fair trial in case there are grounds for the imputation.[92]

*However, Major General Porter was too late; Guiney's commission was
delivered to Guiney personally on August 1 and was "therefore irremedia-
ble by any action which it is possible for the Governor to take." Governor
Andrew, through his Military Secretary, expressed the hope that Guiney's
promotion was the correct choice, but that, if it was not, the Federal officers
would have to remedy the situation.[93]*

*On August 9 Captain O'Leary brought Guiney up on charges, claim-
ing that he had abandoned the Ninth during the battle of Gaines' Mill
and that during the final withdrawal from that place he had directed an
officer not to "use so much exertion to rally" the regiment, "as he did not
desire to keep them there to be slaughtered." However, Guiney's purpose
while the Ninth served as rear guard for the retreating Federal column was
to buy time and prevent the encirclement and capture of his regiment. For
that purpose he charged the Rebels nine times, and won praise for the
maneuver by onlookers. The third charge was that Guiney pled illness 36
hours before the battle of Malvern Hill.[94]*

*Captain John W. Mahan had a different recollection of events and
swore to them in an affidavit to be used should Guiney be brought before
a court martial.*

I, John W. Mahan Captain of Company D, Ninth Regiment of
Massachusetts Volunteers, of the age of Twenty-one years, being
duly sworn on oath do say—
I am Captain of Company D, Ninth Regiment of Massachusetts
volunteers—at present I am detailed on the recruiting service for
the state of Massachusetts. I have been in the regiment ever since

---

[92] Major General Fitz John Porter to Governor John A. Andrew, HeadQuarters
5th Army Corps, Harrison's Landing Va., Aug. 6 1862; located in Ninth Massachusetts File in the Executive Department Letters, Massachusetts State Archives,
Boston, Massachusetts.

[93] Lieutenant Colonel A. G. Browne, Jr. to Major General Fitz John Porter,
Boston, August 5, 1862; located in Patrick R. Guiney Military Service Record,
National Archives, Washington, D.C.

[94] Charges and Specifications against Colonel Patrick R. Guiney by Captain
Timothy O' Leary, Head Quarters Ninth Massachusetts Volunteers, August 9,
1862; document located in Patrick R. Guiney Military Service Record, National
Archives, Washington, D.C.

its organization and been in every skirmish and battle in which my regiment participated

Was in the Battle fought at Mechanicsville, Gaines' Mills and Malvern, and was present—all the time when the regiment was engaged. At Gaines' Mill, in consequence of Colonel Cass being compelled to give up Command of the regiment, Colonel Guiney who had been on the field and at his post with his regiment assumed command, and led the regiment in nine successive charges up the hill near the hospital where line of battle had been previously formed; and, which had already been referred to in [Major] General Slocum's official report. Col Guiney was in the thickest of the fight and led the regiment—being conspicuously exposed to the enemy's fire, but, at no time was he absent—when the regiment was under the enemy's fire.

June 28th and 29th Colonel Guiney commanded the regiment—Colonel Cass being still unable to ride his horse.

When the evening of the twenty-ninth Colonel Guiney, who had been complaining of severe indisposition during the day, was so exhausted that he could not ride his horse and gave up command to Major Hanley. On the 30th of June Colonel Guiney was much worse and was obliged to ride in the ambulance . . . [letter broken]

. . . retrace their steps and take position upon Malvern Hill, Colonel Cass said to Colonel Guiney, "I know how to feel for a sick man—You had better remain in the ambulance, as I feel a little stronger and feel it is my duty to go with the regiment," or words to that effect. None of us knew whither we were going, but our regiment was posted at the extreme left of a battery of field artillery, in front of a large Mansion on the hill. We altered our position again on the evening of the 30th and laid down in the Wheatfield near the house alluded to, and more to the right. The next day; the first day of July, our regiment shifted positions several times while supporting the battery. Colonel Cass was very sick and several times gave up command to Major Hanley but, as many times returned to take command himself. At one time during the day Colonel Cass said to me that he would send and see how Colonel Guiney felt and see if he was able to relieve him for an hour or two, while he took a nap,—at the same time expressed his opinion that he thought Colonel Guiney was too sick to do so. Colonel Cass afterwards informed me that the messenger could not find Dr. [Stephen A.] Drew or the ambulance in which Colonel Guiney lay,—adding, "It is just as well—he cannot be able for duty," or words to that effect.[95]

Col. Cass was wounded in the early part of the fight at Malvern or rather soon after the musket-firing commenced. I did not see Col. Guiney afterwards until I saw him in Boston, as having been taken to the Hospital myself I did not see him when he called to see the regiment—after its arrival at Harrison Landing.

I remained in the Hospital only a short time and when the enemy opened two pieces of artillery upon our camps at Harrison's Landing, being unable to walk on the wounded leg I rode to the front with the regiment and remained doing duty all the time until ordered on recruiting service.

> John W. Mahan
> Capt. 9th Mass. Vols.
> Aug. 16th 1862

Suffolk August 16, 1862

This day the within named John W. Mahan personally appeared before me at Boston in said County, and he being duly sworn deposed that the within statement by him subscribed is true, and subscribed to the same in my presence.

Taken, to be used at the trial of Col. Patrick R. Guiney of the 9th Regt Mass. Vols. by court martial upon charges preferred against him.

> Hon W. Doherty
> Justice of the Peace

In early September, the regiment's Chaplain Scully wrote Governor Andrew, "The regiment is going on well. Our new Colonel is very much beloved by the men and most of those foolish officers who signed their

---

[95] A resident of Woburn, Surgeon Stephen W. Drew joined the Ninth Massachusetts on August 27, 1861 and was discharged for disability on December 6, 1862. *Massachusetts Soldiers, Sailors*, 1: 617.

names to that infamous libel have apologized and are prepared at any time to do so publicly."[96]

Eventually, Guiney was cleared of any wrongdoing, and all but two officers who signed the original letter to Governor Andrew signed the following recantation printed below. The whole affair caused Guiney a great deal of personal tension and stress, and is a major theme in his letters home for the next several months. The actions of the enlisted men and their apparent enthusiasm for Guiney, such as cheering his return to the regiment and the gift of a sword from Company H, seems to support the view that this was an attempted coup by a clique of officers, and that Guiney retained the confidence of his soldiers.

Camp of the 9th Mass Regt.
Sept 19 /62

We the undersigned officers having been given to understand that a different construction from what we intended has been placed on certain portions of a document in reference to Colonel Guiney forwarded to the Governor of Massachusetts (which we are informed has been published and widely circulated) and that accusation of Cowardice has been laid to his charge. As far as our personal knowledge is concerned we desire to state that no action of his would justify such a charge being made against him.

We do this in simple justice to Colonel Guiney, and regret the unnecessary publicity to which has been given without our consent, to a document of a private nature.

John M. Tobin Comdg Co J
Michael Phalen Adjutant
Archibald Simpson 2nd Lt Co G
Nicholas C Flaherty Lieut Co. D.
Matthew Dacey Lt. Comdg Co. B.

---

[96] Father Thomas Scully to Governor John A. Andrews, near Washington D.C., September 4, 1862. Original is located in the Ninth Massachusetts File in the Executive Department Letters, Massachusetts State Archives, Boston, Massachusetts.

William A Phelan Lt. Comdg Co. A
William B. Maloney Comdg. Co E
Thos Mooney
Thomas K. Roche Lt. Co. H.

[In Guiney's hand is written:]
—the other signer [referring to Lieutenant Edward Timothy] is absent. Keep <u>Safely</u> these originals.

PRG

On August 3 Guiney left Boston to rejoin the regiment as its new colonel. He found it decimated after the carnage of the Seven Days, mustering but 250 men.[97]

Harrison's Landing, Va.
Aug. 6th 1862

My Dear Jennie:
I arrived here yesterday afternoon once I found many of the <u>disappointed</u> officers and malicious traducers dull, savage and morose. The men rushed out to meet me, and gave me the heartiest and loudest welcome. The officers had written a most slanderous communication to Governor Andrew about me. I pronounced them <u>liars</u> to their teeth. The cowards did not show any disposition to fight, but they threaten to have me tried by <u>court martial</u>. I am in good condition now, and feel just like a long and stirring row. They say that they will prefer charges for calling them liars—not for any other cause. There may be nothing of it. I'll handle them easy.
I am expecting my sword. Is Loolie well? Remember me to Lizzie Hale, Miss Crespy, etc. This is a nasty note. I'll write again in a day or two. The weather is very hot. All quiet.

---

[97] *The Pilot*, August 9, 1862. Regan diary, July 7, 1862.

N.B. My speech at Roxbury was sent to McClellan with a view to injure me.[98] Ha! Ha! how foolish malice makes men and women.

P. R. G.

Camp 9th Mass.

Harrisons Landing
Va, Aug.6th 1862[99]

Governor:

I do not write this with any view of eliciting a reply from your Excellency unless your leisure from numerous and public duties, as well as your own inclination, will suggest the propriety of it. But I feel impelled to say a few words on that which is the world to me—my honor. In my absence, I understand a communication was addressed to your Excellency by one of my officers who were not wounded in any battle and some of whom are known to have been guilty of gross misconduct in battle on the matter of which conduct they have every reason to fear and none to love me. But your Excellency does not desire any narration of wrong. I'll trouble you with none. My simple purpose is to pronounce that document utterly false, and in every particular.

I do hope that under these circumstances such communication will not deprive me of that which I highly esteem—the good opinion of your Excellency. Facts and the praise of my Generals I set defiantly against the selfish motives and malicious utterings of those who should be taught to speak otherwise of their superior officer.

P. R. Guiney
Col. 9th Mass.

---

[98] While in Boston, Guiney made a speech stating that the Federals would go to Richmond under Major General John Pope. Patrick R. Guiney to Jennie Guiney, Barnett's Ford, August 29, 1862.

[99] This letter is located in the Ninth Massachusetts File in the Executive Department Letters, Massachusetts State Archives, Boston, Massachusetts.

Head Quarters 9th Regmt.
Mass. Vols
Harrison's Landing, Va.
Aug. 9th 1862

My Dear Jennie:
  You will find enclosed in this package the sum of sixty five dollars which belongs to one of my men. He gives it to me to keep
for him. Bank it in my name. His name and descriptive is William
Sweeney, private, Co. D.[100] If he should call upon you for it—and
I should not be in existence—you will know him by reference to
this letter. But if you banked our own in your own name, do this
in similar manner.

I have the honor to be
your Husband, etc.
Guiney

  I am almost bursting to say lots to you but I am too busy with
duty and a few dirty commissioned devils.

Head Quarters 9th Mass.
Harrison's Landing Va.
Aug. 10th 1862

My Dear Jennie:
  I am moody + sad to-day. The ruffians who have so long and
maliciously pursued me are about to succeed in bringing their
falsehoods to an investigation. It is not the dread of being tried
for these offences (if I am convicted of which I ought to be shot),
but the thought of having my own countrymen seek my life or at
least my disgrace forever, that makes me sad to-day. I shall be busy
with my defence for sometime; and while these accusations are
on trial before a court martial I shall be busy and if you should
miss my letters it is on account of my labors against the most
causeless envy and ignorant malice that ever sought the [meim or

---

[100] William Sweeney survived the war and mustered out with the rest of the
regiment on June 21, 1864. Macnamara, *Ninth Regiment*, p. 475.

reim?] of any man. Oh! Jennie, how deeply it affects me to think that the country I loved from my inmost heart should produce such base vipers as these fellows are! but so it is. I am for the first time in my life disappointed.

Your little watch is safe. I wear it. We are to move away from here I know not where we are going to.

> Ever Yours
> Guiney

> HeadQuarters 9th Mass Vols.
> Harrisons Landing Va.
> Aug. 12 1862[101]

John A. Andrew, Governor of Massachusetts

Your Excellency:

I have not transmitted to you any nominations for commissioned offices in the Ninth because my brigade commander is still, and has been ever since I returned, absent at Washington. Of course, you would expect his approval before considering such nominations as I might make in a favorable light. Indeed, with our present number of men here, I can get along conveniently and well and until we get an increase in numbers, with the present numbers of commissioned officers on duty.

I feel prompted to say to your Excellency a word more on the subject of a libelous document sent to you about myself.

It is due to Generals Porter and Griffin, yourself and me, that an investigation be had. It will soon take place. I will, also, be put on my defense for making a supposed public assault upon the Peninsula Campaign of [Major] Gen. McClellan.

The result of this, Governor, will be a most triumphant vindication of my conduct and only add another official compliment to the list of those with which I have been honored.

> Very Respectfully
> Your   Excellency's   Obt.
> Servt

---

[101] Ninth Massachusetts file, Executive Department Letters, Massachusetts State Archives, Boston, Massachusetts.

P.R. Guiney
Col. Comdg. 9th Mass.

*The regiment remained at Harrison's Landing until daylight of August
15, when it joined its corps in marching over badly cut up roads, with
only short breaks, until 11:00 p.m. That night, the Ninth bivouacked on
the shores of the Chickahominy. After breakfast on the 16th, the regiment
crossed the river on a pontoon bridge. During the march, Guiney kept his
companies in good order. By agreement with Brigadier General Griffin, he
gave his men short intervals of rest to prevent straggling. After passsing
through through Williamsburg, the Irishmen marched in great heat
through Yorktown on the 17th and, by August 18, passed through Big
Bethel to reach Hampton. On August 19 the Irishmen relocated to Newport
News, received a contingent of 65 recruits from Boston (probably induced
to join by a recent bounty of a hundred dollars given by the city of Boston
to every new volunteer for the Ninth, in addition to a thirty-eight-dollar
Federal bounty), boarded the steamer* John Brooks, *and headed for Acquia Creek.*[102]

*Arriving at the wharf at Acquia Creek in the forenoon of August 20,
the Irishmen immediately boarded railroad cars and headed to Falmouth,
near Fredericksburg on the Rappahannock, where they bivouacked until
August 24. The regiment then marched up-river to Ellis' Ford and remained until August 27. There, Guiney placed a guard to protect a nearby
residence housing a number of ladies, and he joined several other officers
in visiting them one evening. One outspoken Southerner defiantly vowed
never to surrender until forced to eat bark off the trees. Upon finishing her
tirade, she cordially invited her visitors to return any time!*[103]

*While sitting on a hill overlooking the Rappahannock River with some
officers from Brigadier General Griffin's staff and other regiments of his
brigade, Guiney was surprised by the approach of the entire H Company.
Lieutenant Thomas K. Roche (who signed the letter to Andrew and later
its retraction) presented Guiney with a sword, calling it a "small token of
their esteem for you personally, as well as their admiration for you as an
officer, a soldier, and a gentleman." Guiney happily addressed the company at some length. A segment of his remarks recorded in* The Pilot:

---

[102] *The Pilot,* July 26, 1862. Regan diary, August 17, 18, 1862. Macnamara, *Ninth
Regiment,* pp. 179–82.

[103] *Annual Report of the Adjutant General . . . 1862,* p. 120. Macnamara, *Ninth
Regiment,* pp. 188–89.

My fellow soldiers—With deep and inexpressible pleasure I accept from you this beautiful and costly sword. What could be more gratifying to me after seventeen months of active service in the quiet camp, on the march and in the red battlefields of the Peninsula, than to be presented with this magnificent sword, so typical in its use and beauty, of our duty and our cause, and this too, by you, my comrades. Nothing on earth.

The memory of this, if I am spared, will outlive the gold mounting, the silver scabbard and the endurable steel. I would that I had words to mirror to you the emotions of my heart—but I have not, nor time. Company H, I have ever looked upon with pride. [Here, Guiney talks about the company's experiences, and loss of its commander, Captain Jeremiah O'Neill at Gaines' Mill]

This is a splendid present you have unexpectedly given me. It is rich, costly, beautiful, and exquisite in finish. I am at a loss which to admire most, the magnificent article itself or the feelings which must have actuated you to surprise me with it. I shall devote it, so far as is possible for me to do so, to the purposes which you indicate. I beg leave again to thank you for this generous compliment to myself, and to say, that while I command the Ninth, I shall endeavor to preserve its honor in the field, its discipline in the camp; to make its future, as well as its past, a testimony of Irish devotion to the vindication and establishment of human liberty.

Afterward, the men gave three cheers for their Colonel. Guiney reports in his letter that this occurred on August 29, but several other accounts place it before then—possibly as early as August 23.[104]

On August 27 the men broke camp early in the morning and marched parallel to the Orange and Alexandria Railroad until they reached Warrenton Junction and pitched their tents in the dark. At 3:00 the next morning, the regiment was on the move, passing through Catlett's Station to arrive at Bristoe's Station, where the Irishmen heard artillery fire from the battle of Brawner's Farm in the distance and saw the debris of recent clashes between Major General John Pope and the Confederate forces under Major General "Stonewall" Jackson.[105] *Frustrated with McClellan's lost*

---

[104] Regan diary, August 23, 1862. Letter signed "Amicus" in *The Pilot*, September 13, 1862. Amicus places the event on August 25, 1862. Furthermore, the regiment's marching order placed it not in the vicinity of the Rappahannock, but near Bristoe Station–Manassas Junction on August 29.

[105] Regan diary, August 27, 28. Macnamara, *Ninth Regiment*, p. 189. Long, *The Civil War Day by Day*, p. 256.

opportunity before Richmond, President Lincoln turned to Pope to lead his Army of Virginia to the Southern capital.[106]

On August 29 the battle of Second Manassas began. Brigadier General Griffin's regiments headed toward Gainesville, where they came under Rebel artillery fire, and one member of the Ninth reported that the Confederates had loaded some of their cannon with railroad spikes and glass insulators from nearby telegraph poles. The next day the brigade marched to Centerville and took position on the road south of the town as the battle of Second Manassas raged. Major General Porter engaged the Rebels around 3:00 in the afternoon, but Griffin's brigade remained idle. Then, Confederate Major General Longstreet pitched in and turned the Federal flank, and the fresh brigade was needed on the field to cover the retreat of troops heading to the rear for more ammunition. The Ninth never directly engaged the Confederates, and soon retired to Centreville.[107]

Bivouac at Barnett's
Ford on the Rappahannock
Aug 29 1862[108]

My Dear Jennie:

We have had no mail for ten days. I received one letter from you at Hampton near Fort Munroe—this is the first moment of which I could answer it. As there is a messenger going down to Fredericksburg tomorrow I will send this by him. I am anxious to hear the fate of the two money packages which I addressed to you from Harrison's Landing. You spoke of receiving <u>one</u>. <u>Which one?</u>

Now my Dear Jennie you seem much troubled about my "adversity." No! I am not in adversity—<u>I</u> <u>never</u> <u>can</u> <u>be</u>. I feel that I am always <u>right</u>. And when a man feels so what can afflict him? This may seem presumptive—but, of course, I mean as to my conduct

---

[106] A West Pointer and Mexican War veteran, John Pope's reputation was based on his opening of the upper Mississippi River to Federal control in spring 1862. After bungling the operation at Second Manassas, Pope went to quash a Sioux revolt in Minnesota and played no further part in the Civil War. Warner, *Generals in Blue*, pp. 376–77.

[107] Regan diary, August 29, 30, 1862. Long, *The Civil War Day by Day*, p. 256.

[108] It seems Guiney was mistaken either in the date or location given here, especially considering the discrepancy of when Company H presented his sword.

as a man and soldier—not as to my God whom I may offend in every act and word.

I wish you to call upon my Dear friends Treanor, Searle, Murphy etc. and as I have not time to write to either of them just now, thank them, in my name and affection, for their worry, <u>true</u> and <u>practiced</u> friendship in my behalf. I have received letters from them and it seems that they think I am under <u>arrest</u> and charges preferred against me. It is not so. I am not under arrest. I never have been. No charges have been yet preferred against me. These wretches have <u>endeavored</u> to prefer charges and Gen. Porter on account of <u>that</u> <u>speech</u> listened to them with much favor as also did Gen. McClellan. The charges no doubt would have preferred and I would have been under arrest—but the order to march came and broke up the arrangement. It was a perfect <u>stunner</u> to them all. They were fast to try me for saying that we were "going to Richmond under Pope" and while they were agitating my punishment, lo! an order from Washington comes and tells them, if we go <u>there</u> at all to <u>go</u> <u>under</u> <u>Pope</u>. We are now under Pope; but I support McClellan and Porter will be along here soon and although they will be under Pope, too, yet they will be over <u>me</u>; so I expect that efforts to punish me will be renewed. They had better put in an additional charge against me—that of being a <u>prophet</u> without inspiration. But time will tell all. The Regiment is well. Some of the officers are under arrest and <u>some</u> will go home <u>in</u> <u>disgrace</u>—a fast vengeance is before them.

[Lieutenant Michael] Flynn came on and met us at Fort Munroe; but himself and Hanley are both gone to Washington <u>sick</u>.[109] This shoves all the work on me and I feel almost used up. Tobin is under arrest and no doubt will be deprived of his commission. He left me at Newport News and did not rejoin me until we arrived at Fredericksburg.

Tonight I have been presented with a most magnificent sword by the men of Co. H (the Milford Co.). The sword cost one hundred dollars. It is the most splendid one I ever saw. I was completely taken by surprise. How gratifying it is to me to be so much thought of by my brave comrades who fought <u>with</u> me and <u>did</u> <u>not</u> <u>skulk</u> <u>away</u> <u>in</u> <u>danger</u> and hide themselves in hospitals and barns! O! what an answer this is to the base traducers.

---

[109] A Boston clerk, Michael Flynn mustered in as a sergeant and eventually became captain to date on February 8, 1863. *Massachusetts Soldiers, Sailors*, 1: 670.

A great number of those who signed that slanderous document are very sorry. They say Tobin and O'Leary misled them. If I should have an investigation they will speak the truth and the archinstigators will get their deserts.

How is my Dear little Loolie?

There has been a fight going on about ten miles from here these last two days but I do not know the result.

You must manage about a residence yourself love—continue in Roxbury though. Give my kindest congratulations to Mrs. McElroy.

Direct as usual to Washington.

Yours Ever
Guiney

On September 2, the Ninth withdrew toward Fairfax Court House and proceeded to Vienna, reaching Minor's Hill and the old campground the next day. They received another group of recruits, but in remembering fallen comrades that had occupied the camp months before, many veterans were saddened in realizing how high casualties had been in recent months.[110]

Sept. 4 /62

My Dear Jennie:

I am at Miners' Hill Va. Am well—we are in the old camp.

Guiney

In September, General Lee decided to invade Maryland with his tattered but combat-hardened army, and Major General McClellan, now back in command of Federal forces, moved to counter this blow. On September 12, the Ninth joined its brigade in crossing the Aqueduct Bridge into George-town and moving through Washington via Pennsylvania Avenue and

---

[110] Regan diary, September 3, 4, 1862. Macnamara, *Ninth Regiment*, pp. 198–99, 201. Macnamara, *Bivouac*, 116. Flynn, *The Fighting Ninth*, p. 26.

*out Seventh Street into open land. Despite tremendous heat, the Irishmen
continued through Silver Springs and bivouacked at Leesboro for the
night. Here, some of the men enjoyed hot meals indoors, provided by local
citizens for a half dollar a plate. On September 13, the Ninth marched
through Rockville, Middlebrook, and Nealsville, camping at Clarksburg
that afternoon and enjoying more good food provided by local civilians.
The next day the Fighting Ninth continued with its brigade through Hyat-
tstown and Urbanna to halt at Monocacy Station; on the 15th, the march
proceeded through Frederick and stopped at Middletown. By September 16
the regiment passed through Turner's Gap and marched over beautiful,
scenic land through Boonsboro and Keedysville. At the end of that day,
the Ninth reached the vicinity of Antietam, where a tremendous battle
would occur the next day.*[111]

*While preparing for battle on September 17, Guiney provided a moment
of grim humor for his comrades. An observer recalled, "No heartier laugh
ever rewarded Irish wit than that which shook our sides when Guiney,
the handsome Colonel of the Massachusetts 9th, bedecking himself in the
gorgeous apparel of a brilliant sash, was reminded that it would make
him a capital mark for the enemy's sharpshooters, and replied, 'and
wouldn't you have me a handsome corpse?' "*[112]

*Had McClellan delivered a coordinated assault with the bulk of his
army that day, he very likely could have overwhelmed General Lee's force.
Instead, his attacks were disjointed, and Major General Fitz John Porter's
powerful V Corps remained in reserve in the center of the Federal line.
Major General Morell's division waited behind a thirty-foot ridge a short
distance in front of McClellan's headquarters at the Pry House. Around
4:00 p.m. the division received orders to support the attacks of Major
General Edwin V. Sumner's II Corps, but after moving a half mile the
regiments received orders to return to their previous positions.*[113]

*The next day, Major General Morell's Division relieved Major General
Ambrose Burnside's IX Corps holding the Federal left. On the 19th, Brigadier General Griffin's brigade double-quicked into Sharpsburg and formed
a battle line near Boteler's Ford. Although nearly every house in the village
had been damaged by artillery shells, bullets, and looters, friendly ladies
gave members of the Ninth some fruit and coffee that the Rebels had not*

---

[111] Macnamara, *Ninth Regiment*, pp. 204–205, 207, 209. Flynn, *The Fighting Ninth*, pp. 26–27.

[112] Francis J. Parker, *The Story of the Thirty-second Regiment Massachusetts Infantry* (Boston: C. W. Calkins & Co., 1880), p. 101.

[113] Macnamara, *Ninth Regiment*, pp. 212, 216.

taken. *McClellan did not pursue Lee's retreating army, and by September
20 the Irishmen settled into picket and guard duty. The Army of the Potomac lay in camp, stretched for miles along the Maryland side of the Potomac River.*[114] *On September 24 the Fighting Ninth crossed the river on a
reconnaissance mission and captured three prisoners, three caissons full
of ammunition, and an artillery forge a little past Sheppardstown.*[115]

*During the lull following Antietam, Guiney sent to the headquarters of
the Thirty-second Massachusetts one of that regiment's men, under arrest
for marauding. The Ninth's provost guard had caught the soldier with a
side of veal and had turned the meat over to Guiney's headquarters.*[116]

*In the following letter, Guiney refers to a new Irish flag made in Boston
to replace the ragged, battleworn colors of the Fighting Ninth. Made of
green silk bordered with gold fringe, in each corner on both sides it bore the
mottoes "Erin go bragh," "Duty to God and Our Country," "Faithful
unto Death," and "United We Stand, Divided We Fall." On the front was
a harp and Irish wolf dog, above which was inscribed "9th Regiment of
Mass. Vols.," and on a scroll below, "Gentle when stroked; but fierce when
provoked." The reverse portrayed an eagle and shield with the motto "E
Pluribus Unum" and an inscription, "Presented to the 9th Regiment Massachusetts Volunteers, by their friends, Sept. 1, 1862." The staff, sur-
mounted by an Irish pike, had a pendant at top with a streamer in
national colors and bearing gilt stars. It arrived October 9, although the
men would miss the old banner that had waved over them and witnessed
action on several fields.*[117]

Headquarters 9th Mass.
Near Thorsburgh, Md.
Oct. 2, 1862

My Dear Jennie:
Your kind notes of the 21st and 26th inst. are in my hands. That
of the 26th alarms me very much. You sick and Loolie too. Do
hurry on to me the intelligence that you are both well again. I

---

[114] Regan diary, September 19, 1862. Macnamara, *Ninth Regiment*, pp. 221–26.

[115] Regan diary, September 24, 1862.

[116] Parker, *The Story of the Thirty-second Regiment Massachusetts Infantry*, pp. 113–
14. Parker further comments that regimental provost guards were uncommon
in the army, and an army directive eventually prohibited them.

[117] *The Pilot*, September 20, 1862. Regan diary, October 9, 1862.

fear that my neglect in not writing to you for so long may have troubled you. I am always sorry too late. I never feel guilty until I reflect afterwards. But never mind now—Do apprise me that you are both recovered. And "tell me all about Loolie."

I am well myself and the regiment is doing splendidly. We are here on the bank of the Potomac idle. Where or when we will go next I know not.

I did not write to Mr. Campbell because in his letters to me in speaking of that trouble (now almost forgotten) he said "if this be true" you are not worthy etc. Now how extremely unkind this was in him. I was very much offended with my friend Campbell. Why should a man of his good sense be mistaken in reference to a document so plainly scandalous? I would not care so much but I had looked to Mr. Campbell as one of my friends.

"The Green Flag" has not arrived yet. The man who was to bring it on is somewhere in Alexandria. No doubt he will be here soon.

My address you know is always Washington D.C.

Yes! Jennie I did and do "know a woman whose name is Jennie Doyle." She is a darling—lives at 21 Vernon St. Roxbury Mass. and had the misfortune to marry a scapegrace who has the impudence to subscribe himself

Your Husband

Head Quarters
9th Mass Vols.
Oct. 5th 1862

My Dear Jennie:

Yours of the 28th ultimo is received. I have written to Campbell. In reference to that communication which I sent to Searle, I say in the most positive manner that I do not wish it to be published in the form of a "circular" or theatrebill. I will not put myself on a level with my debunked vilifiers by pursuing a course similar to theirs. If it has not yet appeared in that forum forbid its publication. I told Searle to publish it in the Post. I wish so much of my communication as is proper for the public eye as well as that paper which the officers signed and which I enclosed, to appear in some respectable paper—<u>nowhere else</u>.[118]

Let my enemies go on—they can do me no harm. I do not wish them spoken of to me—I defy them. Friends are enemies and enemies are friends. This is the definition of the world. They neither can inspire my love or rouse my hate, Jennie. Let them rip! Dishonor can never be fixed upon me. Of course I expect to take my chances as to everything else.

Do send on my things immediately. I wish I could send you on some money, but I have only <u>two</u> <u>cents</u> in my pocket for the past month, and if I could have found anything so cheap that it might be purchased for such a sum I would not have any. I expect our paymaster out every day. I will send some when I get it. Did Mr. Sech [?] ever get up that song? If so, send me out a copy. O' Donnell of Lewiston has been out here to see me. He has gone back. Plunkett is here mute as an old soldier. Father Scully returned to-day after an absence of two weeks in Washington—sick. The regiment is now full and looks splendidly. Scanlan, after loafing a month in Washington came to camp yesterday. I put him under arrest, and he will be tried by <u>court martial</u>. O'Leary has been going it here for some time, but the other night he got so drunk and disorderly that I also put him in arrest.[119] He will

---

[118] Guiney is referring to the retraction signed by nine of his officers on September 19, 1862 and reprinted earlier in the chapter.

[119] Captain Timothy O'Leary proved troublesome in future incidents. He abused and overextended his leave in spring 1863, for which Guiney placed him under arrest. Adjutant M. W. Phalen charged Captain O'Leary with conduct unbecoming an officer and a gentleman for activities conducted at Culpepper, Virginia on October 3, 1863. Captain O'Leary allegedly entered the house of Mrs. Lucy Gibb against her will and falsely portrayed himself as a provost marshal, with authority to search any house he pleased. Inside Gibb's residence and in front of her and her two daughters, Captain O'Leary used profane language and claimed he knew the house was one of ill fame. Captain O'Leary was also brought up on charges in spring 1864 for conduct prejudicial to good order and military discipline. It was alleged that Captain O'Leary admitted enlisted men to his quarters for drinking and carousing on the evening of March 13, 1864. As Officer of the Day, Captain Flynn ordered the men to their respective quarters, whereupon Captain O'Leary replied that he "would send all but one and that one should remain as long as he pleased." Later that night, a drunken Captain O'Leary disturbed the camp by marching up and down the street between officers' quarters, singing in a loud voice. A court martial, convened at Liberty, Virginia and presided over by Lieutenant Colonel Luther Stephenson, found O'Leary guilty of the charge but not the specifications, and held that O'Leary should be reprimanded by Guiney, released from arrest, and restored

be tried soon. You see I have enough on hand for pastime. <u>Do</u> remember me ever so kindly to Lizzie, Miss Crespy, Mrs. Merrill. Mrs. (I can hardly bear to call her "Mrs." it sounds so old woman-ish) McElroy. Kisses to Loolie! lots of em!

Guiney

The new green flag arrived, and the regiment turned out in a square for a presentation ceremony. Guiney made brief remarks and, when the old banner was brought to the center of the square, he announced that he would send it to Boston. A few of the officers—Lieutenant Edward Finnoty, Lieutenant Matthew Dacey, Captain James McGunnigle, Lieutenant Archibald Simpson, Captain Michael Scanlan, and one or two others—opposed this move, and they decided to remove the old colors from Guiney's tent. Later that day, Finnoty took the banner, but Lieutenant Colonel Hanley saw this and told him to return it. Guiney came over and repeated the order, but Finnoty took the flag to the tent where the other conspiring officers were and threw it to Scanlan. The soldiers on guard then came and demanded the flag, which Finnoty relinquished only after tearing a corner of it and placing the fragment in his pocket. The old colors were then returned to Guiney's tent, and Finnoty was placed under arrest.[120]

On October 16 Brigadier General Griffin's brigade went on a reconnaissance with five other regiments, all under command of Brigadier General Andrew A. Humphreys.[121] The Federals crossed at Boteler's Ford and arrived in Sheppardstown, where a brief skirmish sent some Rebels scurrying back. That afternoon a thunderstorm and heavy rains ended the mission. Some of the force bivouacked near Kearneysville, but the Ninth and some

---

to duty. P. R. Guiney to Jennie Guiney, Log House at Camp, April 2, 1863. Charges and Specifications against Captain Timothy O'Leary by Adjutant M. W. Phalen, n.d.; General Orders No. 23, Headquarters First Division, V Corps April 13, 1864; both located in Captain Timothy O'Leary Military Service Record, National Archives, Washington, D.C.

[120] John King to "Friend John," Sharpsburg, October 14, 1862; located in Patrick R. Guiney Military Service Record, National Archives, Washington, D.C.

[121] A West Pointer and engineer, Andrew Humphreys went on to lead a division through the Maryland campaign, Fredericksburg, and Chancellorsville. Transferred to the III Corps, he fought bravely and well against the Confederate attacks at Gettysburg on July 2, 1863. He went on to serve as the Army of the Potomac's Chief of Staff, and in November, 1864, took command of II Corps and led it to Appomattox. Warner, *Generals in Blue*, pp. 240–41.

other regiments opted to return back to their camp, where they dried them-
selves and had hot coffee and hardtack.[122]

                                          Head Quarters
                                          9th Mass Vols.
                                          Oct. 18, 1862

My Dear Jennie:

I received yours of the 12th inst. today on my return from Virginia. We were gone two days and had quite a brisk time with our
old acquaintances the rebels. We drove them into Virginia about
twelve miles in the direction of Martinsburgh and fought them or
rather they fought us every mile of the road. They only had a
small force and our troops had some splendid fun with them. I
do not know the losses on either side. I saw a number of rebels
dead by the road side and I must say that they were the best and
most intelligent looking rebels I ever saw dead or alive. I met with
only the loss of one man, Thomas Mullen Co. H very dangerously
wounded by a shell which burst in our midst and most singularly
hurt no more.[123]

My Dear, you will not think of coming out here. It is no place
for you. We are off every few days somewhere and everything
seems unsettled. The nights are cold—nothing but scanty canvas
to cover us. When we settle, if we do at all, <u>for the winter</u> I will
want you to come out—not otherwise. In the mean time, send my
things to Washington D.C. per Express.

I have not received any envelope enclosing stamps. I have received <u>Journals</u> and Lithographs, music, etc.[124] There is a band
out here belonging to the regular army who are practicing the air
and will play it soon in public. The officers and men like the affair
very well. I do not fancy the <u>words</u>, but the music is fine. But the

---

[122] Macnamara, *Ninth Regiment*, pp. 229–30. Flynn, *The Fighting Ninth*, p. 28.

[123] An Abington laborer, Private Thomas Mullen recuperated and rejoined the
regiment, but deserted on April 1, 1863. He rejoined the regiment on February
8, 1864, was wounded on May 5, 1864 at the Wilderness, and was eventually
discharged for insanity. *Massachusetts Soldiers, Sailors*, 1: 666.

[124] This is possibly a piece of music called the "Irish Volunteer" by S. Leonce.
Published by a Boston firm, an advertisement in *The Pilot* said it was dedicated
to the Ninth Massachusetts, and had a good likeness of Guiney on the cover. *The
Pilot*, October 11, 1862.

words are not so bad when we reflect that the portion of the Irish people who enlist are generally of the "Mickey O'Flaherty" sort of people. The aristocratic snobs are still at home. Mickey's sentiments are fine—correct—pathetic—patriotic!

Do not, I pray you, mention any more about that robust and fame-seeking widow [Mrs. Cass] to me. I have demanded a large regimental fund of her which she has belonging to the Ninth. Her husband had it in his possession. It was some two thousand five hundred dollars. She does not seem inclined to part with it, but she must or take publicly the consequences.

I have been feeding an old horse which was used by Colonel Cass and which, I think, also belonged to the regiment. She wants me to pay for him. I wrote to her to take him off—and that I would not feed him any longer. She is, therefore, I suppose, rampant. Well, it will do her good to shake her up once in a while. I hear [George W.] Dutton is Major.[125] I am glad of it.

Lt. [Edward] Finnotty and Capt. O'Leary have been tried by Court Martial and are now awaiting sentence.[126] I told you I'd handle those fellows at the proper time. I have, and will. O'L. was tried for Drunkenness—Finnotty—for Disobedience. Flynn is slightly ill—all other officers well. Scanlan will go home soon sure.[127] Please find the Post in which Searle published that document and send it to me.[128] I do not get the Post now. I received letters to-day from friend Treanor. Apologize for me to Mulrey. I

---

[125] A Stoughton machinist, George W. Dutton mustered into the Ninth Massachusetts as Captain of Company K. Guiney requested that Governor Andrew promote Captain John W. Mahan to replace Hanley as major (Hanley was the new lieutenant colonel). However, Dutton was the senior captain and, despite other letters to him, Andrew appointed Dutton to the position; it was the general rule for qualified senior officers to receive the promotion. Dutton had been wounded in the thigh at Malvern Hill, but a doctor verified that he was fit for duty and he accepted the commission for major to date from August 26, 1862. He resigned March 28, 1863. *Massachusetts Soldiers, Sailors*, 1: 676. Patrick R. Guiney to Governor Andrew, August 26, 1862; Colonel James McQuade to Brigadier General Charles Griffin, near Stoneman's Switch, April 27, 1863. Both letters are located in the Ninth Massachusetts File in the Executive Department Letters, Massachusetts State Archives, Boston, Massachusetts.

[126] Boston shoemaker Edward Finnoty mustered into service as a sergeant and became a second lieutenant to date September 11, 1861. He resigned and was discharged February 28, 1863. *Massachusetts Soldiers, Sailors*, 1: 658.

[127] Now a captain, Michael Scanlan resigned on October 15, 1862. *Massachusetts Soldiers, Sailors*, 1: 624.

[128] Guiney is referring to the retraction signed by nine of his officers on September 19, 1862 and reprinted earlier in the chapter.

have not time to write much. What is the news? I shall dream of
you and Loolie tonight.

Adieu love
Guiney

*After receiving the new regimental banner, Guiney presented the old one
to Massachusetts along with the following letter to Governor Andrew. Guiney also expressed appreciation for Governor Andrew's efforts to repeal
most of the discriminatory laws aimed at Irish immigrants and passed
with Know-Nothing support in the 1850s. In the instance referred to here,
Andrew succeeded in getting the state legislature to annul the Twenty-
third Article of Amendments of the Massachusetts Constitution. Passed in
the 1858–59 legislative term and ratified on May 9, 1859, this provision
held that "No person of foreign birth shall be entitled to vote, or shall be
eligible to office unless he shall have resided within the jurisdiction of the
United States for two years subsequent to his naturalization. . . ."*[129]

Head Quarters 9th Mass. Vols.

Camp Near Sharpsburgh
Md. Oct 22, 1862[130]

John A. Andrew
    Governor of Massachusetts

Your Excellency:
    On behalf of my command I have the honor to present to the
Commonwealth of Massachusetts the Irish flag which was origi-

---

[129] Governor Andrew held a pro-Catholic stance and took other actions to
show his support for this group and cultivate a following among its voters, such
as requesting that the state legislature grant a charter for the College of the
Holy Cross and attending the school's commencement. Baum, "The 'Irish Vote'
and Party Politics in Massachusetts," 126. *Acts and Resolves Passed by the General
Court of Massachusetts in the Year 1863* (Boston: Wright & Potter, 1863), pp. 42,
44.

[130] This letter is located in the Ninth Massachusetts File in the Executive Department Letters, Massachusetts State Archives, Boston, Massachusetts.

nally given to us in June 1861, by our friends and more especially by the personal friends of my gallant predecessor, Colonel Cass. The regiment has borne this flag in ten engagements. Sometimes when all else looked vague and battle-fortune seemed to be against us, there was a certain magic in the light of this old symbol of our enslaved but hopeful Ireland, that made the Ninth fight superhumanly hard. The memories which cluster around these shreds are indeed very dear to us. We need not ask Your Excellency to hold them sacredly.

Along with the tender of this flag to the state, I beg leave to offer to Your Excellency personally the warmest thanks of myself and command for your generous efforts to expunge from the Constitution of Massachusetts that provision which would make political distinction between us and our brothers in hope, conviction, disaster, and victory.

> I have the honor to be
> Your Excellency's Most
> Obedient Servant
> P. R. Guiney, Col
> Comdg. 9th Mass. Vols

> Head Quarters 9th Mass.
> Near Sharpsburgh, Md.
> Oct. 23, 1862

My Dear Jennie:

Yours of the 19th inst. received. We are preparing this evening to leave this place—to go whither I know not. I hope to victory, decisive, final! I want the rebels whipped quickly and eternally.

About buying house, you may do as you think best—I will approve. Be careful of sharks and mortgages. So you lost your rent! Well, didn't I often tell you how I disliked to have anything to do with others in house matters of this sort. Let her go, poor creature. If she has got a son, I'll make Loolie humbug him sometime for the rent she owes you! Unless this move prevents I can send you from six to eight hundred dollars soon—next payment. I regret Mrs. Merill's trouble very much. She is so kind and full of sympathy herself for others.

But <u>Adieu</u>
Guiney

In the following letters, Guiney expresses disgust at efforts to replenish the Regular Army by recruiting from among the volunteer regiments. By autumn of 1862, the Regular Army division under Brigadier General George Sykes had been reduced to a fraction of its original force, and Sykes felt that over three thousand recruits would be needed to fill his ranks. In October 1862 the War Department issued General Order No. 154, permitting Regular officers to recruit from among the volunteers. The recruits were to serve three years or the balance of their term and were to receive a one-hundred-dollar bounty, with twenty-five dollars payable in advance. Furthermore, noncommissioned officers were assured of quicker promotion through the ranks. November 5 was the deadline for such recruitment to cease.

The states swiftly expressed anger with the War Department's measures, claiming they sabotaged local recruitment efforts. The plan also exacerbated tensions already existing between volunteer soldiers and their Regular counterparts and, in the end, proved a failure.[131]

Head Quarters
9th Mass. Vols.
Oct. 25, 1862

My Dear Jennie:

Yours after 20th inst. received. We are still near Sharpsburgh Md. but expect to move from here every day. If we remain (unexpectedly) I will probably go into Washington for a day or two when I may send for you by Telegraph to meet me there. But this is a <u>mere hope.</u>

As to that house affair, I am willing that you should do whatever you think best. I cannot send you the money, however, for some

---

[131] Timothy J. Reese, *Sykes' Regular Infantry Division, 1861–1864* (Jefferson, N.C.: McFarland & Company, 1990), pp. 158–59.

days after the first of the month. My advice is: 1st do whatever you
find best for yourself and child. 2nd for my interest if I survive I
have a little fear that I may go home sooner than would be advis-
able in view of incurring so large an indebtedness as price of a
house. I feel uneasy here under my Generals (some of them) and
I must say that I am becoming disgusted with the prevailing Military Statesmanship which is every day exhibited here. I may resign
at any time, especially if my men are allowed to famish for want
of blankets and overcoats. I try hard to get them but no. No one
here seems to be in <u>deep</u> <u>earnest</u> in the Quartermasters Dept. I
cannot bear such treatment of my brave men. I complain but it is
no use. If men wish for clothing they can get it by enlisting out of
volunteer regiments <u>into</u> the regulars. The men do sometimes.
Some volunteer regiments have lost dozens of men in this way. I
have lost only <u>two</u> thus far, but it is getting cold. Our Generals are
regulars and favor the regular army—volunteers may go to the
devil as far as <u>they</u> are concerned. I could say a thousand things
that you never dreamed on in the North but enough.

If you buy that house be sure and get safe title <u>in</u> <u>your</u> <u>own</u>
<u>name too</u>—not in my name. In buying you should remember that
taxes will be very high hereafter and that real estate will become
of less value than now but <u>hurrah</u> <u>for</u> <u>a</u> <u>home</u>!

I am well, and hope to hear from you every <u>five</u> <u>minutes</u> and <u>to</u>
<u>see</u> <u>you</u> soon somewhere.

Guiney

Head Quarters
9th Mass. Vols.
Oct. 25 1862[132]

My Dear Treanor:

Yours of the 21st inst whence your strictures as to my recommendations are severe and unreasonable. Cass entailed upon me
the burden which I necessarily labor under. I am here <u>to do the</u>

---

[132] This letter is located in the Ninth Massachusetts File in the Executive Department Letters, Massachusetts State Archives, Boston, Massachusetts. A friend
of Guiney's, Bernard Treanor was a Boston lawyer who helped organize various
Irish regiments, including those in the Irish Brigade. Conyngham, *The Irish Brigade*, p. 51.

best I can for the service with the material in my hands. Could I make 1st Lieutenants of Sergeants? No sir. No general would endorse such nomination, no Governor would commission such [illegible word] even if on recommendation by me, while commissioned officers, 2d Lieutenants, were in the regiment. . . . The recommendations made by me were not (except very few) made as matter of choice, but of necessity. . . . So long as there was a 2d Lieut. in the regiment I could not recommend an enlisted man for 1st Lieut.

As to these men ever being witnesses against me, pray, be easy. I defy the world. They who do right need do nothing for fear. . . .

But, My Dear Treanor, allow me to say that I am not anxious about anything but to do my duty while here. The service is becoming disgusting to me, not on account of our country! No! but for other reasons. There is a want of all serviceable brains—in whom, I will not say lest this letter be read by the censors. My men, in common with many other regiments, are without necessary clothing. I am trying to get supplies, but it seems in vain. Our superiors are encouraging volunteers to abandon volunteer organizations and to become regulars—the willing slaves of some inchoate tyrants. Our volunteers (I fear purposely) are being famished into the regular service. Some of my men have gone. In other regiments around us whole companies have been broken up—disorganized for such purpose. And this order so detrimental to discipline, so insulting to the volunteer—is issued from the Adt. General, Office of Washington. The regulars are after my men. Irishmen are preferred by them. Consider how painful this is to me also that my convictions are in opposition to those of many who are over me, and that a prevailing desire here is that a military dictatorship must be established—the idea of which I abhor, and you will not be surprised if I were soon with you in Boston. I cannot say to you all I would if free to speak. I chafe under the restraint. The patriot-hero Kearney did not say enough of truth, and perhaps, said too much that was personal.

When the Governor's letter comes here I will attend to Plunkett's case.[133] Plunkett left the service with the compliment from

---

[133] Captain Plunkett had resigned August 7, 1861 and he re-enlisted in the regiment on August 14, 1862; he soon received commission as a second lieutenant dated September 26, 1862 and first lieutenant January 8, 1863. He was wounded at North Anna River on May 23, 1864. *Massachusetts Soldiers, Sailors*, 1: 630, 637.

Col. Cass endorsed on his resignation that "he did not wish to lose him as he was a most reliable officer." But Plunkett, disliking Cass, personally persevered (which was his one offence) and against the will and protest of Col. Cass, had his resignation accepted. I want Plunkett commissioned. I do not hesitate to say that he is better fitted for commission than any line officer in the Regiment. He can control men and he is <u>manly</u> in everything. I hope the Governor will not hesitate. Now, my ever Dear friend, do not, I beseech you, think of me in any changed light, but look upon me now as heretofore, as being <u>true</u> in all things, and judge of me only by a glance of the inexorable circumstances under which I am placed.

Ever Yours Guiney

In fact, it was not only the matter of clothing and supplies which caused some distress within the regiment. Other frustrations abounded, as Timothy Regan wrote:

Considerable dissatisfaction prevails in this regiment on account of the promotion of some of the recruits to be noncommissioned officer, to the prejudice of some of the old members of the regiment, who consider themselves entitled to promotion on account of their long service, and experience. Some of the old members talk of going into the regular army (which they can do on application) if the practice is not discontinued. Colonel Guiney has heard of this, and today [October 26], while on battalion drill, he formed the regiment in a hollow square and talked to the men on the subject. He said that he hoped none of his men would go into the regular army, as by doing so they would forfeit the honour of being volunteers, which, he said, was the only honour he could see in being a soldier at all. That they would then be soldiers by profession and not entitled to the same honour as the man who enlists in their country's time of needs, and when the emergency is passed returns quietly to private life. He said also, that if any man had cause of complain, to come to him and that justice should be done him.

The diarist continues:

I am satisfied that the Colonel is not to blame, but that it is the doings of some of the captains who send for their friends to join their companies with a view of promoting them to be noncommissioned officer, and then to engineer them into lieutenancies.[134]

On October 27 Major General Morell was assigned to command troops remaining in the upper Potomac area, and leadership of the division devolved on Brigadier General Daniel Butterfield.[135] Marching orders finally came at 3:00 p.m. on October 30, rousing the army from its encampments along the Potomac. The Ninth moved at 7:00 p.m. and halted at midnight around three miles from Harper's Ferry. Under a bright moon, the men could see Harper's Ferry and the picturesque scene of the Potomac River coursing through the mountain gap. The next day, the Irishmen crossed pontoon bridges over the Potomac and Shenandoah rivers and bivouacked at Pleasant Valley, a few miles from Harper's Ferry.[136]

Meanwhile, still in Boston on recruiting duty, Captain John Willey tried to cause trouble for Guiney. He penned another letter to Major General McClellan, in which he recalled Guiney's speech which claimed that the Federal army would go to Richmond under Major General Pope. Although in Massachusetts and far away from the Ninth, Willey further implied that the regiment was in poor condition. Guiney's brigadier, Charles Griffin, immediately intervened and wrote a brief note that "The Regiment has improved very much under Col. Guiney within the last two mos. In regard to the letter from Capt. Willey—Comment is unnecessary," and the matter ended.[137]

On November 2 the Fighting Ninth moved forward to Snicker's Gap, where it spent an extremely cold night. They remained there until November 6, when they marched from Snickersville to Middlebury and camped three miles outside the town. Meanwhile, on November 7, President Lincoln relieved Major General McClellan and put the Army of the Potomac under command of Major General Ambrose Burnside. Major General Jo-

---

[134] Regan diary, October 26, 1862.

[135] Flynn, *The Fighting Ninth*, p. 28. Macnamara, *Ninth Regiment*, p. 230. A New York lawyer and businessman, Daniel Butterfield was wounded at Gaines' Mill and, thirty years later, received a Congressional Medal of Honor for his service there. When Major General Joseph Hooker took command of the army, Butterfield served as his chief of staff, continuing in this role at Gettysburg. He later served in Sherman's Atlanta campaign until sickness caused him to leave the field. Warner, *Generals in Blue*, pp. 62–63.

[136] Regan diary, October 30, 31. Macnamara, *Ninth Regiment*, pp. 231–32.

[137] Captain John C. Willey to Major General George B. McClellan, Boston, October 27, 1862; Brigadier Charles Griffin [no address], HeadQuarters Second Brigade Butterfield's Division, November [?] 1862; both located in the Patrick R. Guiney Military Service Record, National Archives, Washington, D.C.

seph Hooker replaced Major General Porter in charge of the V Corps. That same day, the Irishmen tramped to White Plains, where it snowed in the afternoon, and proceeded to New Baltimore the next morning. On November 9, the Ninth Massachusetts reached Warrenton and remained here until November 17.[138] Earlier, on November 14, Burnside reorganized his army into three grand divisions, with the III and V Corps in the Center Grand Division under Major General Hooker; Brigadier General Butterfield now assumed temporary command of the V Corps. Hooker reviewed the V Corps the next day, but many of the men were sullen at the loss of Major Generals McClellan and Porter, and not so much as a cheer welled in anyone's throat.[139]

The Ninth marched on to Warrenton Junction and remained there until November 20, and continued on to Hartwood Church on the 21st. The next day they proceeded to Stoneman's Switch near Falmouth, around three miles from Fredericksburg.[140]

> Head Quarters
> 9th Mass Vols.
> Camp Near Falmouth, Va.
> Nov. 25, 1862

My Dear Jennie:

I received three letters from you within two days. I receive no papers whatever from any source.

You think I do not write so as that I may have the sport of curing and heart-break when I <u>do</u> write. Well, Jennie, what an idea! It may be so. You know I had not much time to plague you while we were courting so a little alternate <u>breeze</u> and <u>sunshine</u> now will not be amiss occasionally. For some reason or other I do sometimes like to vex those I love—it is a shame, but I <u>am possessed</u>—of an Irishman, not a d-l.

As you are so kind Jennie, I will ask you to send me some flannel drawers and shirts—not many you know. Have the material <u>thick</u> at all hazards. I am not particular about style—but have them fit my neck which is certainly a half inch thicker than it was when I

---

[138] Macnamara, *Ninth Regiment,* pp. 232, 234. Flynn, *The Fighting Ninth,* p. 28.
[139] Regan diary, November 15, 1862.
[140] Macnamara, *Ninth Regiment,* p. 237.

was at home last. Arrange them so that I can button on white collars. The shirts which I brought out with me are so small for me that I cannot wear them. I have grown much stouter. Send me a few pairs of stockings and some <u>pomade</u>. Ain't I fancy for a soldier? If Major Dutton has a spare corner left, put in a few <u>drops</u> of brandy. Since we left Sharpsburgh, I have had nothing either necessary or luxurious but a pipe, hard bread, and coffee. I have lived splendidly on them though.

Plunkett has his commission in his pocket. Let the North End howl! I do believe that my enemies (deluded creatures) will never cease until they help me to a generalship. Opposition is sure to elicit the truth. I will be the gainer. Never mind them—they are really my most valuable friends.

I expect to receive my boxes from Washington in a few days. Are you in that house yet? I am very thankful to Mulrey, will write him soon. No prospect of a fight <u>here</u>, no pay yet. I would speak to you about Father Scully but I had rather not. He left us at Sharpsburgh. I am <u>satisfied</u> with the removal of McClellan and Porter. <u>More</u> of their sort ought to go. It is dangerous to leave any of that <u>clique</u> here. They may serve Burnside as they served Pope. O! God, when will men sink their petty prifemeneus[?] and think only of success to our Arms?

The Regiment is in splendid condition and discipline. I have a thousand most flattering compliments from equals and superiors. I provided clothing for the men at last. <u>I</u> <u>do</u> <u>not</u> <u>think</u> <u>I'll</u> <u>resign</u> <u>at present</u>.

I shouldn't wonder if some morning I found myself a "General." God, I think, was always with me, and I believe my course to be ever onward! But I am content as I am for the present.

How is <u>dear,</u> <u>sweet,</u> <u>little</u> Loolie?

Guiney

Head Quarters 9th Mass.
Nov. 30 1862

My Dear Jennie:

Yours of the twenty third inst. is received. We are encamped close to the dingy village of Falmouth situated on the immediate

bank of the Rappahannock. We were here last summer when we
were on our way to join Gen. Pope, after evacuation of the Peninsula. Fredericksburgh is on the opposite bank and looks splendidly. We desire possession of this latter place for hospital
accommodations for our sick, but the rebels have it yet—we envy
them, but it's no use—they have it yet. I seldom have seen a place
in Virginia worth speaking of and I should not have said so much
of this locality were it not that in my opinion, it is probably to be
the resting place of both armies for months to come. America is
here in her two forms of power and civilization. Which shall conquer? or shall this stream divide them forever? This is an awful
pause. The air is permeated with rumors of peace, armistice etc.
My way would be now, at this moment, to bring out, conscribe,
force, and push to the front, flanks, and rear of the enemy, the
(as yet) unused might, and inevitably overwhelming physical
power of the loyal states. Now is the time. The rebel Gladiator has
been fighting all along, and, strong as he was, he may be now
overwhelmed in his fatigue if met swiftly by our fresh levies. Vigor
now is victory forever! Where is the genius to inspire and direct
it? I know not. We have had all through some good generals but
no great ones. We are, I fear, still so, but I hope my fear is groundless. Perhaps my opinions are too hastily formed and it may be
that I do not appreciate fully our own weaknesses. Certainly, my
opportunities to form correct judgments have been very limited,
comparatively. My inclination is not to find a fault, but my passion
is to beat that rebel army (Richmond is no military consequence)
and I am impatient for an American Wellington!

My Dear Jennie, you must not notice, in any manner, these
poor creatures who talk disparagingly of this regiment and of myself. Now be sure and observe this. Neither should you encourage
any of my friends to notice them. Such men as that Scanlan could
do one no service by speaking well of me, and their ignorant and
malicious denunciation is a great personal compliment to me in
the judgment of all decent people. What do I care for a drunken
rabble? Thank God, my circumstances no longer force me into
any acquaintance or association with them. I was very poor once.
That tells a long story, It is, I hope, at an end. Therefore you will
tell my Dear friend Fallon, of whom I am delighted to hear, that
it is my wish no notice be taken of these contemptible fellows. An

approving conscience, the respect and confidence of my superior officers and the esteem of my brave comrades is enough for me. It will seem so to all when they reflect that I go on in the severe path of duty not caring whether I am loved or hated, so long as I am right.

No paymaster yet—expect him every day. All the recruiting party from this regi . . . [letter ripped here]

Camp near Falmouth, Va.
Dec. 4, 1862

My Dear Jennie:

Your letter of the thirtieth Nov. Shawmut Avenue house (our house) received this evening. How sorry I am, my Dear, to hear that you are unwell, and also little Loolie? This must not be. You have no right to be sick. I won't stand it. Come, Jennie, get up! Stir yourself! Shake up Loolie. Both must be well by next letter. Disobey a Colonel if you dare. You know the consequences if you do. I will have you court martialed and sentenced "to once more have rosy cheeks, waving black curls, splendid form and"—O! Jennie, do not tempt me to go into particulars of what I will do if you do get better at once! If Loolie is not better immediately, do her up in a bundle and send her out to me for a dose of kisses I'll repeat so often that the poor cherub will be tortured into health!

I suppose you have received a letter from me since you wrote. But no matter, it's no harm to stir me up once in a while. I fancy I see you when you attempt to scold me. O! If I had hold of you when you were at it, wouldn't I make you take it back and laugh! Wait a while. I'll—I will, Jennie, sure.

No paymaster here yet. I tried to go to Washington to get my pay and send it on to you, but my friend Hooker would not let me go. Well, we must wait and be patient.

No fighting here yet. The rebel camps are in sight just beyond the river. Father Scully says he intends to resign. He is in Georgetown, D.C. His health is very poor, he says. The fact is he is not hardy enough to live out here. All well. Good bye, Love.

Guiney

It turned extremely cold on the night of December 6-7, as four inches of snow fell on the troops and water froze in their canteens. Before dawn on December 11, the Ninth marched toward Fredericksburg with three days cooked rations. Engineers were attempting to build pontoon bridges over the Rappahannock, a procedure greatly slowed by the sharpshooting of Brigadier General William Barksdale's Mississippians on the opposite bank. Two Federal regiments and a massive artillery barrage eventually cleared the Southerners out and the engineers completed the bridges, while the Ninth remained north of the river.[141]

On December 13, Major General Burnside assaulted the Confederates atop Marye's Heights, a strong natural position crowned with much artillery. With Major General Sumner's Right Grand Division attacking the Heights and the Left Grand Division under Major General Franklin assaulting below the city of Fredericksburg, Major General Hooker's Central Grand Division was held in support until it, too, was needed in the forlorn charges.

The Ninth and its division, now under Brigadier General Griffin, crossed the pontoons between 2:00 and 3:00 p.m., meeting along the way many of the wounded of the Irish Brigade after their brave, ill-fated charge up the Heights. At one point, Brigadier General Andrew Humphreys rode by and the Massachusetts men cheered him, and he responded in cavalier fashion by doffing his cap and bowing. The Fighting Ninth moved parallel to Marye's Heights and endured heavy Rebel artillery and rifle fire, losing sixteen casualties at this time. A shell fragment struck Guiney's sword scabbard, breaking it cleanly in half; it proved a narrow escape from serious injury to his leg.[142]

With regimental flags driven into the ground, Guiney's men lay down in a depression in the ground as a murderous hail of shells and bullets poured upon them. Upon the sun's setting on the bloody day, a staff officer rode to Guiney and conveyed that his general wanted the regiment to charge Marye's Heights. Guiney, realizing that such an assault would only mean the useless shedding of his troops' blood, replied, "You go and tell your general that I take orders from my immediate superiors." The aide left without speaking a word, and that was the last Guiney or the regiment heard on the matter. Eventually, the carnage ended with nightfall and the regiment remained in their position. The Ninth lost a total of 27 men—

---

[141] Regan diary, December 6, 11, 1862. Macnamara, *Ninth Regiment*, pp. 241–42.

[142] Regan diary, December 13, 1862. Macnamara, *Ninth Regiment*, pp. 255–57.

comparatively light considering the thousands of Federal casualties that day.[143]

Fredericksburgh, Va.
Dec. 15, 1862

My Dear Jennie:

I send you a word this morning not because I have leisure I assure you, but to quiet any apprehension which you might entertain for my safety in the battle of the few past days. A report was current the 1st that I was <u>killed</u> 2nd that I was <u>wounded</u>. I fear one or both of these have gone home. It is certain, Jennie, that I was not "<u>killed</u>," neither was I wounded. I am well. These reports arose, I presume, from the circumstance that a shell burst very close to me and smashed my sword-scabbard into fragments leaving only a piece hanging on the belt. This was the one presented to me by one of the companies and of which you may have seen an account in the <u>Pilot</u>. The battle was severe, and I am sorry to say not successful for us. But we'll try them again. I enclose you a list of casualties occurring in my command Dec. 13th. Have it published.[144] Plunkett fought finely, and is well.

Yours,
P. R. G.

On December 15 Brigadier General Meagher invited Guiney and his officers to attend a presentation of three Irish silk flags to the New York regiments of his brigade. Despite the heavy casualties the Irish Brigade had experienced but a few days earlier, the affair was happy and cheerful. The next day, Major General Burnside's army began its retreat across the river and by December 17 the Ninth was back in its camp before the battle. Meanwhile, a sword belonging to Captain William Madigan, killed at Gaines' Mill, was found on a Rebel officer captured at Fredericksburg by

---

[143] Regan diary, December 13, 1862. OR, vol. 21: 135. Macnamara, *Ninth Regiment*, p. 258. Macnamara, *Bivouac*, p. 160.

[144] Part of the letter itself was printed on the front page of *The Pilot*, describing Guiney's narrow escape as his sword deflected the shell fragments. *The Pilot*, December 27, 1862.

the Sixty-second Pennsylvania. Guiney received it from that regiment's adjutant, to be sent to Madigan's family.[145]

Camp Near Falmouth, Va.
Dec. 18, 1862

My Dear Jennie:

I wrote you a brief note from Fredericksburgh just after the battle. I enclosed list of casualties which in two or three particulars was erroneous. It turned out in a more careful survey of the facts that two men reported killed were still living although badly wounded. I have sent on to Adjutant Gen. Schouler a correct list, and when persons make enquiries of you, refer them to him.[146]

I am quite well and have pitched my tent on the same spot where it was before the fight. I will endeavor to get in to Washington soon so as to send on money to you.

At the last battle the troops generally fought bravely. Some few regiments broke. The "Ninth" was splendid in action. We were fortunate too. We went up in line over an open plain and driving the enemy back to his entrenchments where in a sudden we struck against the enemy's strongest works lined with heavy artillery. We were sent in as reserve to another Brigade which was ordered to storm these works. The Brigade could not carry the works and it was found to be impossible for us to do more than to hold our position which we did from afternoon 13th to morning 16th.

I felt as every soldier in the army who looks back at the events of that day with an impartial eye—indignant. I feel now too deeply that our troops—our brave troops—are not—and seemingly not to be, skillfully led. I despair of Generalship for us!

---

[145] Regan diary, December 16, 17, 1862. Macnamara, *Ninth Regiment*, p. 267.

[146] William Schouler was born in 1814 in County Renfrew, Scotland, and arrived in America with his father the next year. He edited several papers in both Massachusetts and Ohio, where he served as adjutant general. In 1858 he resigned to return to Massachusetts and in 1860 was appointed adjutant general of Massachusetts by Governor Banks. During the war he proved an efficient administrator and hard worker who greatly aided the Massachusetts war effort. P. C. Headley, *Massachusetts in the Rebellion* (Boston: Walker, Fuller, and Company, 1866), pp. 106–107.

I have received letters and papers from you. I will send home my broken scabbard soon. My <u>boxes</u> have not yet come.

I would like to spend Christmas with you but it is no use to hope for that. You and Loolie must drink some <u>wine</u> that day for me.

Adieu
Guiney

On December 20 Guiney replied to a letter of Assistant Military Secretary Major Henry Ware. Ware wrote on behalf of the mother of James and Edward Petty, inquiring about her sons, and Guiney informed and assured him:

The boys have been sick with typhoid fever, but are now nearly recovered. I hope to see them entirely well in a few days. They are in a regimental hospital. Every kindness and attention within our power to bestow upon them has been and still continues to be given. Assure Mrs. Petty that her boys are not friendless here. . . .[147]

Washington, D.C.
Dec. 24 1862

My Dear Jennie:

At last I succeeded in getting a Leave of Absence for 48 hours. I managed to get some money (which by the way is very scarce here) and I send you on six hundred dollars. If you want anything else, <u>buy</u> it and let the house go to the devil. I am afraid that yourself and Loolie are in want of many things for your comfort. Mind you, Jennie—your personal comfort is of more value and importance to me than all the world. And with this money which I send you I wish you <u>first</u> to see to yourself. You must dress better. Be happy for the world with its teeming promise is before me.

---

[147] Patrick R. Guiney to Major Henry Ware, Head Quarters 9th Massachusetts volunteers, December 20, 1862. This letter is located in the Ninth Massachusetts File in the Executive Department Letters, Massachusetts State Archives, Boston, Massachusetts. Although James survived the war, his older brother Edward Petty was killed in action on May 5, 1864 at the Wilderness. *Massachusetts Soldiers, Sailors,* 1: 636.

How much I would like to be with you tomorrow but cannot—I wish you my dear bosom-angel "A Merry Christmas."

Adieu
Guiney

Christmas passed quietly in the Ninth, with longing for peace and family. The next day, the V Corps received as its new commander Major General George Gordon Meade, formerly of the Pennsylvania Reserves. On December 30 the regiment broke camp and joined the rest of the division on a reconnaissance toward Kelly's Ford. The Ninth bivouacked that night in a plowed field, where a heavy mist fell and saturated their blankets by morning. The Ninth continued on to Kelly's Ford on New Year's Eve, driving away Rebel pickets across the river and capturing nine prisoners. The Irishmen then returned to camp in the evening, having marched 54 miles in 31 hours, and celebrated the passing of the year with some whiskey and much-needed rest.[148]

---

[148] *Annual Report of the Adjutant-General of the Commonwealth of Massachusetts . . . For the Year Ending December 31, 1863* (Boston: Wright & Potter, 1864), p. 576. Regan diary, December 30, 31, 1862. Macnamara, *Ninth Regiment*, p. 271. Macnamara, *Bivouac*, p. 176.

1863: ". . . the pain of separation from you draws heavily upon the heart-strings."

Camp 9th Mass.
Jan. 6, 1863

My Dear Jennie:

I am in possession of several letters from you as well as papers received since I wrote last. You will overlook the delay in my writing when I tell you that I have been awaiting the arrival of Major Dutton with your presents and those went to me while I was in Maryland so that as I hoped, I might be able to gratify you by an acknowledgement on their receipt. But alas! Major Dutton has arrived, but not a box![1] What misfortune we have in these matters. Still, I hope to obtain them soon.

My Dear, I can scarcely give an opinion as to the future [of] this war. I hope for success. I fear defeat. Of this, however, feel assured: our army will fight bravely and deserve success. If the nation dies the monument expected to commemorate its fall should be inscribed—"The Republic which had the world at its service, expired for the want of a General to lead its armies." How the thought of our defeat pains me! Yet, I cannot shake off the impression of events. If we could only be successful how proudly I could live afterwards in the knowledge of my humble participation. If we fail I never can be half the man. The charm of life will be gone. Even now the "Star Spangled Banner" sounds like a wail to me. God is above us, though, and no Christian should despair.

If the army should have a rest I will see you during the winter or spring. I may have an opportunity soon. I am anxious to get that picture of Loolie. Send it by mail. I will send you money as rapidly as possible. The government has cut down our pay very much. By the way: I wish you to go privately to Mr. [Joseph W.] Dudley, City Treasurer, and inquire the amount of money which was paid by the city to you while I was commissioned.[2] Send me the item, I will pay it back at once. Do this promptly. [In margin, the following is written] I meant to have done so long ago but forgot up to this writing.

Guiney

---

[1] Major Dutton returned on January 3. Regan diary, January 3, 1862.

[2] Joseph W. Dudley served as treasurer and collector of the City of Roxbury at this time. *A Catalogue of the City Councils*, pp. 204–14.

The men passed their time in quarters, although Major General Burnside's review of V Corps provided some excitement on January 8. However, Guiney grew very sick with a bad cold and throat problems. The night after Fredericksburg, he reported having a severe cold, and his condition was worsened during the recent reconnaissance to Kelly's Ford. By January 6 Guiney had a sore throat which prevented his active command of the Ninth and he requested a twenty-day leave to return home, stating that he would remain in camp if the service required but that he felt he would recuperate and return to effectiveness sooner if he rested at home. A few days later, the Ninth's doctor, J. F. Sullivan, examined Guiney and found that he suffered from severe bronchitis, "much aggravated by the exposures of camp life."[3]

Guiney received his leave of absence to return home and he departed on January 12, returning on February 4, in time for a snow and rain storm that lasted several days. In Guiney's absence, the regiment participated in the famous, ill-fated Mud March which began on January 20. For several days they sloshed through muck and mud, until the movement ended a few days later with the troops back in their winter camps.[4] On January 25 the Army of the Potomac experienced yet another command change, as Major General Joseph Hooker assumed charge at President Lincoln's orders. Meanwhile, with Colonels McQuade and Sweitzer on leave, Guiney acted as brigade commander from February 5 to the end of the month.[5]

The Ninth's camp had neatly laid out company streets with gutters on each side to draw off rain and snow water, and the men's quarters had fireplaces for heat and cooking purposes. Meanwhile, Major General Hooker abolished the impractical grand division organization and took special pains to improve the rations and supply of his troops, so that they eventually enjoyed "salt pork, fresh beef, soft and hard bread, beans, rice,

---

[3] Regan diary, January 8, 1863. Patrick R. Guiney to Lieutenant Colonel Dickinson, Head Quarters Ninth Massachusetts, January 6, 1863; Written statement of Surgeon J. F. Sullivan, Camp Ninth Regiment Massachusetts Volunteers, January 9, 1863; both letters are located in the Patrick R. Guiney Military Service Record, National Archives, Washington, D.C.

[4] Regan diary, January 12, 21, February 4, 5, 6. Macnamara, *Ninth Regiment*, pp. 272–73.

[5] Ninth Massachusetts Infantry Regiment Letter and Order Book, Record Group 94, National Archives, Washington, D.C., 17, 32. Colonel Jacob Sweitzer commanded the Sixty-second Pennsylvania Infantry. When that unit's first commander, Colonel Samuel L. Black, was killed while leading his troops at Gaines' Mill, Sweitzer took over until he was wounded and captured. Upon his release from Libby Prison, Sweitzer was promoted from lieutenant colonel to full colonel. Powell, *The Fifth Army Corps*, p. 115.

coffee, sugar, tea, salt, soap, candles, potatoes, onion, and lots of other things."[6]

Head Quarters 2nd Brigade
Feb. 11, 1863

My Dear Jennie:

At last I have news to tell you about those boxes. The smallest one of the two boxes which you addressed to me at Sharpsburgh, has arrived here. The bottles were all smashed and my dressing gown and pantaloons were preserved in jelly! I expect the other Sharpsburgh box along with boots in a few days. Do you hear anything of Dutton's boxes?

I am getting along well and my health is good—although I am more susceptible of cold than I formerly was.

There is no news afloat here just now. The army seems dreary and partially dead. We want a good shaking up of some kind. I like Hooker, but he inspires no enthusiasm. The Army of the Potomac was spoiled in its youth—its education was idolism—not worship of the true God—McClellanism, not devotion to the nation in its unfractured greatness. I find but very few whose views are congenial to me. I am weary of expressing my opinions. I would like to serve on to the end—to the triumphant end—but how painful in the midst of men who are constantly talking down the Government! Griffin still holds his command—annoys me when he can—especially when my back is turned. I think a good deal and sleep little—sometimes I conclude to resign—then again I conclude to stay. At any rate, I am not so happy as I was. I think I see the South independent—They are becoming more United—the North more divided every day. If the process goes on what must the result be in a year?

If the country is to be broken—then we will have no country to love or serve. Every man must find food for his affections in his own house. Will we be safe from want if tribulation should soon come? It often has seemed to me that events in the future impress me in advance of their coming. I hope my fear is groundless, but the northern people are a failure and the Southern a success. My

---

[6] Regan diary, March 14, 1863.

head gives me this idea—my heart would reverse it. It isn't much use to quarrel with the inevitable whatever it may be. God rules in Peace and War—in the circumstances and the catastrophe.

When you get little Loolie asleep kiss her for me.

Believe me, My Dear Jennie, ever thoughtfully and fondly yours,

Husband

In the following letter, Guiney refers to a number of officers who overstayed their allotted furlough by obtaining "sick leave" certificates while home. Army policy allowed for only a few officers of each regiment to go at a time, and the next group scheduled to visit Massachusetts could not depart until the absent members returned. This fostered no small measure of discontent among the regiment's officers, and Guiney forwarded a signed petition of protest to his superiors.[7]

Head Quarters 2nd Brigade
1st Div. 5th Corps
Feb. 16 1863

My Dear Jennie:

I am in receipt of your letter written in answer to my first after returning. The Major [Dutton] does not know the name of the man to whom he entrusted the boxes in New-York. They may turn up sometime but it is no use to worry about them now. The other Sharpsburgh box has not yet come but I expect it along every day. In reference to that deed I think you had better get Mr. Gaston to make it out.

How are those knaves and arrant humbugs enjoying themselves? Hanley is a handsome baby! Does he find any one to admire him? The other three claim to have been suddenly seized with a multitude of diseases and do not intend to come back for some time yet. They received leave from Griffin while I was gone. They never could have received it if I were here. Not content with that however, they got some quick surgeon to certify that they were sick and received extensions I suppose. Well, you see the

---

[7] Macnamara, *Ninth Regiment*, p. 277.

honorable class of men with whom I am associated. I have ceased
to trouble myself much about whatever they may do. Nothing re-
strains me from leaving the whole tribe and Griffin, its chief, but
the fear that friends might misconstrue my motives. How long I
can endure this thing I cannot tell. I feel like giving out sometimes. However, there is some sport in the affair of these officers.
The officers here cannot get away until those absent come back.
Hence they are indignant and signed a protest which I sent up
this morning. I had nothing to do with it but to send it forward.
In fact I regard them all as Kilkenny Cats, no great consequence
which conquers. I am an amused spectator and could, with perfect composure, take a carpenter's rule and measure the animal's
receding tails!

We are having beautiful weather here just now, but there is no
stir in the army. "All quiet" etc. I had some visitors from Roxbury—Mr. [John W.] Marston and Mr. [L. Fostner] Morse.[8] They
took one of my luxurious dinners with me.

How is my little pet? Let me know all about her. Is Flynn married yet? You remember that Capt. Willey of this Regiment—he
has been dismissed the service at last.[9] Remember me to Lizzie,
Kate, Mrs. Fitzpatrick and the Old Lady. I am sorry for poor Katey
Reed. I never thought she would come to that! But I won't go on
with this subject lest I—something I don't know what.

I wish I could make that visit of mine over again—I was excessively unhappy—but I think I would be wiser now. Cannot go,
though—Good bye Jennie.

                                                    Guiney

                                        Hd Quarters 2nd Brigade
                                        Feb. 23, 1863

My Dear Jennie:
    I received two letters from you two days ago—one in reference
to your Dear Brother's death—and the other speaks of those
boxes.

---

[8] Both served with Guiney on the 1860 Roxbury Common Council. *Catalogue
of City Councils*, p. 211.

[9] On February 7, 1863, the War Department issued Special Orders No. 63; one
of its provisions dismissed Captain Willey, with loss of pay and allowances due
him, for absence without leave. Ninth Massachusetts Infantry Regimental Letter
and Order Book, Record Group 94, National Archives, Washington, D.C., 26.

My Dear Jennie: words which I could offer you in sympathy for your affection would be cold ere they were read by you for they should be warm when uttered. Tears I cannot shed for any one (so it seems to me). But of this be assured Jennie, that affliction endears you to me, as it would me to you. The world has been unkind to me in youth—very unkind, hence I cannot always weep when you do—what my heart has wished is to love and be loved—and if the loss of your loved brother has made you more dependant upon me, your affliction will develop in me a stronger affection for you and a deeper interest in the fulfillment of your wishes. I almost envied the brother that shared your affection with me. If this seems selfish I cannot help it. But God be with him and he with God! He was one of the few who redeem the character of man. I wish I was like him but I never can be—I fear. Write me whatever else you hear in reference to his death—and his marriage.

About that box—there was no coat nor boots in it—nothing but what I told you before. Perhaps coats and boots may be in next one. If coat or boots were in the same box with dressing gown and pantaloons they are certainly lost—stolen in fact.

Pardon this hastily written note if it seems to you an inadequate reply to your two welcome long letters.

Ever yours
Guiney

Head Quarters 2nd Brigade
Feb. 26, 1863

My Dear Jennie:

Your note of the sixteenth inst. I received last evening. I am rather sorry that those people who call upon you to describe the ovations to O'Leary and others should not find it convenient to converse upon different subjects.[10] If there is any one thing I am

---

[10] His North End friends presented Captain Timothy O'Leary, a ringleader in the attempted coup against Guiney, with a sword and belt on February 21, 1863. Eneas Smyth, who enjoyed less than cordial relations with Guiney, delivered the address. He insulted Guiney by claiming of O'Leary, "your independence of character . . . [has] brought down on you from officers, your superior only in

sick of it is this eternal prattle about myself and my enemies. Let them be left to me. In the end they will get their deserts. As a matter of fact these fellows are not my enemies at all for they well know my motives have been good and that I never injure anyone on personal grounds alone. But the unarmed traitors of the North End encourage them in seeing hostility to me, because I am for the government in all its measures—and they know that I am. Then another cause of Irish opposition to me is sending that green Flag to the State House.[11] Well, let them rail on! When I see fit to make myself heard, thank God, I am able to make myself understood by the public. In the mean time, Jennie, I must admit that these little things are annoying—but I have endured them so long (as you say) they fall lightly upon me now. There is one incident which I confess did hurt my feelings very much—that was to see in the Boston Pilot that I was denounced for many crimes of the commission of which I never dreamed. If, after reading the article, Donahoe had come in my way, upon my soul Jennie, I would have killed him—or beaten him so badly that his best friends would not have known him for six months. John C. Tucker told the truth of Donahoe when he said he had a soul so small that the Almighty could not find it on the Day of Judgement.[12] I suppose he was well paid for his word. As to the presentations to O'Leary etc. they are the standing jokes in the regiment among officers and men. There is a report here that O'Leary has been presented with a gold shears by his admirers in token of his skill—as a tailor. But of course this is a joke. Poor Hanley! Were it not for certain things, I would cause him to be dismissed as a worthless humbug. But when I think of this, I ask myself, with

title (otherwise your inferior) a mean, unmanly persecution, which must have been, to say the least, oppressive and unjust. . . ." This is ironic considering the amount of hostility Guiney endured as a result of his political sentiments and his split from the typical Irish-American position. *The Pilot*, February 21, 1863.

[11] Guiney sent a letter dated October 22, 1862 to Governor Andrew, tendering the Ninth's tattered, battleworn Irish flag to the state of Massachusetts since the regiment had received a new one. Governor Andrew responded with a letter complimenting the brave service of the Ninth and assuring that its flag would be preserved. Guiney to Governor Andrew, Camp near Sharpsburg, October 22, 1862 in Ninth Massachusetts File in the Executive Department Letters, Massachusetts State Archives, Boston, Massachusetts. *The Pilot*, November 22, 1862.

[12] John C. Tucker was a leader in organizing Boston's Montgomery Guards, an Irish-American volunteer militia company disbanded in 1838 because of anti-Irish sentiment. Lord, *History of the Archdiocese of Boston*, II: 251–53.

whom shall I fill his place? Alas! I have none better who could be appointed. He is well understood here. The men have a perfect contempt for him, Scanlan, O'Leary etc.

Now, my Dear, let us talk about other matters. You ask me why I was unhappy when at home. Well, dear, I scarcely can tell, I had been thinking for a long time of seeing you—you only. In all the wretched moments during which I was obliged to associate with those who were not congenial to me, I thought of the time when I should see you and have many trials with patience in that thought. I thought of the perfect happiness—which I would enjoy with you when at home. But when I got home—first the news of that movement disconcerted me for I correctly realized that Hanley and Dutton would both fail in the hour of necessity and that Griffin would release O'Leary and put him in command.[13] Then again instead of meeting you only, at home I met three others whom I had not pictured to myself as a part of home. I also met Father Scully and my Mother both of whom I would avoid. Then that miserable little Mahan bringing a woman of bad character into my home, and his likeness on the mantle-piece in our parlor. You, Jennie, were all I could ask or my heart ever craved, but do pardon my weakness (silly as it may seem) when I tell you that my picture of home, in other aspects, was a picture merely. I hope I shall grow wiser and less sensitive; but while the process is going on, do, my Dear cherished darling, pardon a nature for which I can scarcely be held responsible.

This letter has already exceeded the usual length and I will only stop to enclose you forty dollars which was deposited with me by one of the men. You can use it as I will settle with him some pay day when he wishes his money. I expect to get a box tonight from Adam's Express. I am still in command of the Brigade, but I also have to give my attention to regimental affairs as Dutton is sick again. I am kept pretty busy I assure you. I had a sharp talk with my friend Griffin the other day—I was assured that he had something against me and that I knew what it was. Well, I do. He did not make much in the conversation. I answered him curtly and disconnected him with my apparent coolness and assumed dignity. But I must close Dear wife with kisses for you and Loolie.

Guiney

---

[13] Guiney refers to the so-called Mud March, begun by Major General Burnside on January 19 and abandoned a few days later. Long, *The Civil War Day by Day*, pp. 313–14.

Head Quarters 2nd Brigade
Feb. 28, 1863

My Dear Jennie:

I received your note last night informing me that you had been
ill. Why didn't you tell of this before? I am quite vexed with you.

You say something about coming to see me. Well, <u>now</u> is your
time if ever. We will probably stop here some few weeks and I fear
that warm weather will find us in another active campaign.

I do not <u>insist</u> upon your coming because I fear you will not
enjoy your visit but My Dear, you will be welcome here if you think
well of it. There is in fact no use of me dodging the question, <u>will
be glad to see you here</u>, so come!

If convenient bring a riding dress although on account of the
mud it may be of no use. At any rate bring <u>warm</u> clothing—you
must calculate upon a tedious journey. Come now or never! In
Washington you call upon Capt. Parker of [Brigadier] Gen. Martindale's staff and give him my compliments—he will furnish you
with ticket on steamboat and rail to Stoneman's Station.[14] If you
write me as to your starting, I will have some one to meet you at
Acquia Creek. If you're coming Jennie, <u>come at once</u>—quick.

Etc., Etc.
Guiney

*Jennie did come, arriving on a rainy March 10, and by March 13 the
men had constructed for her a log house covered with canvas and a floor
boarded by wood panels from hardtack boxes, near a row of hemlock trees.
A sentinel kept guard outside the door to ward off intruders, although
Timothy Regan wrote humorously in his diary, "It is probable that the
Colonel is to have a free pass at all times."*[15]

*Then, the men of the Irish Ninth turned to preparing for the upcoming
St. Patrick's Day festivities. The entrance of each company street became
decorated by an arch of holly and evergreen. Furthermore, Guiney set aside
the present officers of the regiment, and allowed the enlisted personnel to
elect their own officers for the day. St. Patrick's Day dawned bright and*

---

[14] A West Pointer and former district attorney, Brigadier General John Martindale served as military governor of the District of Columbia at the time. Warner,
Generals in Blue, pp. 312–13.

[15] Regan diary, April 10, 13.

sunny, and after breakfast, Guiney gave an oration on Saint Patrick's life, the celebration of his feast day, and the duties of men to their native and adopted countries. Then, the Ninth turned out for a dress parade and, drawing into a hollow square, listened to speeches and remarks by both old and "new" officers, and gave cheers for Major General McClellan, Major General Hooker, President Lincoln, Guiney, Ireland, America, and Massachusetts. Afterward, the men were dismissed to receive the first of three whiskey rations, and Guiney invited the new officers to his quarters, complimenting them on the dress parade and chatting before each left after shaking hands with both the colonel and his wife.[16]

Then, the men engaged in several games: trying to climb a greased pole which had fifteen dollars and a ten-day furlough at the top (no one succeeded), attempting to catch a greased pig, and foot and sack races. A number of horse races took place after the midday meal, but an accident put an end to this activity. Quartermaster Thomas Mooney's horse collided with that of a participating surgeon of the Thirty-second Massachusetts. The doctor got up with a dislocated or broken arm, but both horses were killed, and Mooney was rendered unconscious by the blow; sadly, he died on March 27, 1863. Late in the afternoon, the regiment enjoyed a mock parade, and a member of Company F parodied Guiney's manner and voice while acting as regimental commander. A large crowd of spectators watched the spectacle, and the men ended the day in high spirit.[17]

Guiney was understandably lonely when his beloved Jennie departed camp a few days later, although he accompanied her as far as Baltimore.[18]

Head Quarters
9th Mass. Vols.
April 1st 1863

My Dear Jennie:
I wrote you yesterday but I miss you so much that I must commune with you tonight again. You cannot imagine the dreariness of my house—it looks so deserted, I cannot bear to stay in it.

---

[16] Regan diary, March 16, 17, 1863.

[17] Regan diary, March 17, 1863. *The Pilot*, March 28, 1863. Macnamara, *Ninth Regiment*, pp. 278–79, 430. Macnamara, *Bivouac*, p. 179.

[18] Patrick R. Guiney to Lieutenant Colonel F. T. Locke, Camp Ninth Massachusetts Volunteers, March 27, 1863; located in Patrick R. Guiney Military Service Record, National Archives, Washington, D.C.

Nothing can ever supply your place there—it was made for you and now that you are gone, it ought to fall. I am so lonesome at night and at table—if I had a dog to bark once in a while—something to break the silence—something to annoy me and to give my thoughts back to me, I should feel better. Jennie, did you pay my fare—did you purchase a through ticket for me on that train? If you did not, I went free—I went with you and my heart still hovers around you—My Darling, I never can love you half so much when you are with me. Then there is nothing to be desired but when I lose sight of you then the pain of separation from you draws heavily upon the heart-strings.

There is no particular sign of a movement yet. Indeed the indications are that we will be here for some time to come.

Quite a rivalry is going on as to the Majority of the Regmt.[19] Tobin has written to Mrs. Cass to secure her influence, but the best man will probably get it. Perhaps I will be allowed a word in that matter, but, Jennie, how goes matters at home? How are yourself and Loolie and how is James' wife? Send a long letter to

Your Husband

Log House at Camp
April 2, 1863

My Dear Jennie:

I have a few moments of leisure and I gladly devote them to you. I am waiting for your first letter with the most stormy impatience. When will it come?

Captains O'Leary and [James F.] McGunnigle arrived in camp this afternoon—both placed under arrest.[20] Will I ever get

---

[19] Major Dutton resigned due to wounds sustained at Malvern Hill and was discharged on March 28, 1863. *Massachusetts Soldiers, Sailors*, 1: 676.

[20] Presumably, they had been the officers who abused their leave of absence by obtaining extensions. Both proved problematic to Guiney; Captain O'Leary had been a ringleader of the attempted coup against him in the summer of 1862. Boston bootmaker James F. McGunnigle entered the service as first lieutenant, received his commission for captain dated June 28, 1862, and was wounded at Spotsylvania on May 12, 1864. Guiney consistently misspelled his name as "McGuinegle" in his letters. *Massachusetts Soldiers, Sailors*, 1: 678. For more on O'Leary see footnote 119 of the previous chapter; for more on McGunnigle, see footnote 48 of this chapter.

through with these men? It is unpleasant to me to be the instrument of injury to any one—but I must be, against my natural inclination.

My Dear—Do not make much exertion in that matter of <u>Provost Marshal</u>. If it comes easily, let it come—God is good to me and I feel that the best will happen.

I am very anxious to hear of your seeing Mrs. [Sarah] Doyle and whether she feels happier.[21] I know you will be kind to that poor afflicted soul. Those who are sorrowful and heart-broken are sometimes thrown in our way to test the Question whether we are good or base.

Since you left me, my Dear, I have been very lonesome, and, more than on any other occasion, I miss you. The good Father [Peter] Tissot was here to see me to-day.[22] I was over to see my friend [Brigadier] General Meagher yesterday but he had gone to New York.

Make the sign of the Cross on Loolie <u>with</u> <u>kisses</u> (not Oriental), for me. Remember me to Lizzie and Kate.

And believe me fondly

Yours
Guiney

Head Quarters
Log House
April 4, 1863

My Dear Jennie:

I received yours of the 1st inst. this evening. How glad your dear letter made me! Was it not fortunate, my dear, that you went

---

[21] Sarah Doyle was Guiney's sister-in-law.

[22] Father Peter Tissot, S.J. was born in Savoy, entered the Society of Jesus at Avignon, and volunteered for foreign mission with hopes of being sent to the United States. He arrived in 1846 and taught science at Fordham University in New York. He joined the Thirty-seventh New York "Irish Rifles" when the Civil War erupted. When Scully resigned, Tissot volunteered his services to minister to the men until a replacement came. Major General Philip Kearny deemed him "the model chaplain of the Army of the Potomac." He eventually returned to Fordham, where he served a brief term as vice rector from January to June 1865. Robert I. Gannon, *Up to the Present: The Story of Fordham* (Garden City, N.Y.: Doubleday & Company, 1967), pp. 17–18, 66.

home just when you did to alleviate poor Loolie's sufferings and to make her happy? Our dear child is so precious to me that I would rather see the red-flash of the Judgment-day upon us all than to lose her. You and Loolie happy and well and that is a satisfaction which leaves me without a wish. I know the difference between your care and kindness and those of others, and Loolie knows them too.

I hope most fervently that Mrs. Doyle is with you ere this and that she is more happier than she was. I am really interested in her and feel that she will be much better in heart and spirits when she meets you. Tell me all about her in your next.

I am reading the Miserables by Victor Hugo. The interest increases with every line. It is a splendid assault upon society as it is, and a powerful invitation to be good. There are some expressions in it which are objectionable, but I like it for its grand purpose— Philanthropy.

Captain Mahan has arrived in camp with two recruits. What a product for 8 months labor.

Although your letter is hopeful on the point, since you left I have given way to the belief that I am not to be appointed Provost Marshal. Well, let fate operate.

Give my love to Mrs. Doyle (if she is with you) and kiss our little cherub for me.

Guiney

Head Qrs 9th Mass Vols.

Camp near Falmouth Va.
April 5th 1863[23]

Col. James McQuade
Comdg 2nd Brigade

Colonel,

In compliance with your request that I furnish a detailed statement of the circumstance attending the punishment of private

---

[23] This letter is located in the Boston Public Library Rare Book and Manuscript Collection, Boston, Massachusetts.

Denis McCarthy, late Quarter Master Sergeant and private John B. O'Hara, late Sergeant, both of this command, I beg leave to submit the following.[24]

O' Hara left this camp Jan. 27th 1863, on ten days furlough, returned March 22nd 1863, so that from the fifth day of February to the 22nd of March, forty-five (45) days, he was absent with out authority. No intimation was ever made to me in writing or otherwise, that his furlough was extended, or that he was sick, or in any other way disqualified for duty during the whole or any part of these forty five days. Indeed this I know to be the fact, from information which I could not doubt, that he was during this time walking in the streets, attending exhibitions, visiting friends outside of Boston etc. Having no official information that he had received any authority for his absence, other than that which he received though these Head-Quarters, and being to the effect that he was able to travel, I regarded him as absent without leave during the aforesaid forty five days; indeed he was officially reported to me by his Company Commander as "dropped from the rolls as a deserter Feb. 20th 1863, and by me was officially reported as a deserter to the Provost Marshal General of this Army. In passing, Colonel, allow me also to certify a fact which is known to the whole regiment that this same O'Hara, being their Orderly Sergeant of Co. A left his place in line when the regiment first went under fire at Fredericksburg and did not rejoin the command until we were withdrawn to the City. It will be asked why did you approve a furlough for such a man in violation of Gen. Order No. 3 A. P.? My answer is that when his furlough was approved I was not in command, and if I had been disapproved if presented.

McCarthy left this camp Feby 2nd 1863, on ten days furlough, returned March 22nd 1863, having been thirty eight days absent without authority. During his absence he forwarded through the mail the enclosed paper which I believe to be a forgery; but even this (if genuine) would not cover his absence.

---

[24] *Massachusetts Soldiers, Sailors, and Marines of the Civil War* does not provide much information on these men. In Company A there was a Sergeant John B. O'Hara who was an expressman from Boston, wounded at Malvern Hill on July 1, 1862. Company B had a Private Dennis McCarthy, a Boston stereotyper. Both are listed as having mustered out with the rest of the regiment on June 21, 1864. No mention is made of the incident recorded in this letter. *Massachusetts Soldiers, Sailors,* 1: 623, 629.

The President's Proclamation was not officially promulgated to me until March 26th 1863, four days after punishment had been inflicted.[25] The soldiers themselves did not comply with its provisions and were not sent to me as therein provided, for which reasons it was my duty to treat them without reference to the proclamation of March 16th 1863. By every rule known to me by the terms of their own furloughs, by innumerable precedents in this Army, and by one hundred and fifty five (155) precedents in this Regiment, I was bound to treat them, punish them for <u>desertion</u> under the milder name of absence without leave. Their punishment was this: reduction to the ranks, one night in the guard house, one day from Reveille to Retreat tied by the hands (with intervals of rest) each labelled skulker. One month's pay was to be deducted from each of them, but this portion of the punishment assigned has not been carried into effect, and is reserved; whether they lose pay or not will be determined by their behavior in future. I am quite sure that this punishment was neither cruel or unusual.

By the Provisions of Gen. Order No. 3 A. P. the absence of these men deprived their comrades of the privilege which [they] themselves were abusing. In this way they were not only guilty of desertion, but also of an offence against the Regiment. It may not be an inapt comment upon my course towards these men to state that since this punishment was inflicted, men who left this camp on furlough come back promptly on <u>the</u> <u>tenth</u> <u>day</u>.

You will allow me, Colonel, if you please, to add to the foregoing a few words of a personal character. I made up my mind long ago that Irish soldiers cannot be governed by a military dove with the rank of colonel. They need to be handled as severely as justice will permit, when they do wrong. I have punished these men and others with the sole motive and purpose of improving the efficiency of the Regiment. [Brigadier] General Griffin under whom I have served so long and yourself know as to the failure or accomplishment of my design. The gentleman [Eneas Smyth] at whose instigation this investigation is had is unknown to me personally. He assailed me once before in my official capacity, and seems to be one of that class of men who delight in slandering officers who do or honestly endeavor to do their duty. He is the chief of a small

---

[25] This refers to President Lincoln's amnesty to all absent soldiers who returned to their unit by April 1. Boston *Post*, April 14, 1863; April 17, 1863.

but vicious faction who vegetate and develop in the purliews of a place in Boston called "North-end," and every one of whom comes within the scope of the first part of the third paragraph of the proclamation to which I have referred. I have not the least doubt that when he wrote to his Excellency the governor of Massachusetts he found his inspiration in his politics and dipped his pen in a Confederate inkstand.

I have the honor to request as a personal favor that this statement may be made a part of any report which may be sent to his Excellency the Governor of Massachusetts, and to subscribe myself

> Very respectfully
> Your Obt. Servt.
> PR Guiney
> Col. Comdg 9th Mass. Vols.

> Log-House at Camp
> April 6, 1863

My Dear Jennie:

I received the enclosed letter from Mr. [Senator Henry] Wilson.[26] An answer has been sent. You will please preserve the Senator's letter.

I expected to hear from you tonight—but did not. Ah! Jennie, Don't commence that imitation of your neglectful husband. Write often.

The President was here today receiving this Corps. I wish you were here darling. I am down upon Hooker for sending the Ladies off. The wretched <u>Old</u> <u>Bach</u>.

There is no immediate prospect of a move.

By the way, that "Eneas Smyth" has complained to the Governor about my punishment of those two deserters, and the Governor has referred the matter to my <u>friend</u> Griffin. I am sorry that the Gov. noticed that clique at all—but no matter, the deserters <u>have</u> been punished, and the statement which I made to Griffin will be sent to

---

[26] Henry Wilson represented Massachusetts in the United States Senate from 1855 to 1873. He joined the Know-Nothing party in 1854, hoping that it could be liberalized so as to promote the cause of abolitionism. Wilson later helped found the Republican Party and was elected Ulysses S. Grant's vice president in 1872. His letter to Guiney has not been located. Johnson and Malone, eds., *Dictionary of American Biography*, 20: 322–25.

Gov. Andrew who will read no doubt my opinion of the North End faction to Mr. Smyth, who will be delighted thereat!

Give my warmest regards to Mrs. Doyle and warmest kisses to sweet little Loolie.

Ever yours
Guiney

On April 8, President Lincoln reviewed the Army of the Potomac, and the soldiers turned out with glistening sabers and polished cannon. As the Ninth passed the reviewing stand holding the President, several governors, and some members of Congress, the band played "Saint Patrick's Day In The Morning," and the troops marched by in high spirits, hopeful of up-coming victory.[27]

Log-House at Camp
April 9, 1863

My Dear Jennie:

Your very kind and long letter of the 4th inst. received this evening. Since it seems out of the question that I am to go home soon, with you, I will make the best of our separation.

Perhaps when I see Mr. Wilson I can come to an understanding with him as to what is best. I wrote him a letter the other day. Give my regards to Mrs. Doyle and the other Ladies, Flynn and Plunkett well—send regards.

I will write to Searle tomorrow. Have you seen the letter I sent to Mrs. Mooney? I am to be repaid in slander, I suppose. Adieu to you, love from

Yours

Log-House Where
You Were Once
April 11, 1863

My Dear Jennie:

I am very well and write this to tell you that I procured a little Cat the other day to cheat me into the belief that I was in a

---

[27] Regan diary, April 8, 1863. Macnamara, *Ninth Regiment*, p. 284.

house—in a home. She was a playful creature, but for some reason or other she left me this morning—"Twas ever thus" etc.

I expected a letter from you this evening, but none! Oh! Jennie, Jennie!

Love to Loolie and warmest regards to <u>our</u> sister Sarah.

Ever Yours
Guiney

The regiment continued in camp, and some of the officers passed time by holding horse races. In the afternoon of April 12, horses owned by Major General Sykes, Brigadier General Griffin, Colonel Sweitzer, Lieutenant Colonel Hanley, Adjutant Michael Phalen, and Guiney were run.[28]

Log-House at Camp
April 12, 1863

My Dear Jennie:

I am in possession of four letters from you the last one dated April 8th. I entirely agree with you love that we are just learning to love and appreciate each other now—We are passing from impassioned affection to that more enduring and intelligent appreciation of each other which is what I understand by true love. The one is individual, worldly, animal—the other is better, more happy, purer, Heavenly! Well, my dear, it is no wonder. The fact is we had no time to understand each other before marriage. I have often thought that delay would have been better in our case. But <u>it's</u> <u>done</u>, Jennie, and what a fool I am to be, like Maud Muler, speculating upon what "might have been."

I regret very much that my N. E. friends have seen fit to introduce your name in connection with my horrible cruelties.[29] But there is a good deal of wisdom in your saying that the burden is light upon each and would be heavy upon one. As to that McCar-

---

[28] Regan diary, April 12, 1863.
[29] "N.E." refers to the North End.

thy being a brother to Mrs. Lappen, I say I would have treated my brother as I did him under the same circumstances.[30]

So the N. Enders are aroused! Yes, I know they went to the governor, but the Gov. referred the matter to Griffin, and the Gov. and Gen. Griffin and the N. Enders have all received my reply ere this. Didn't I put on to Mr. E. Smyth? If they really wish to find out who I am, <u>they</u> <u>had</u> <u>better</u> <u>continue</u> <u>stirring</u> <u>me</u> <u>up</u>.

I clip the enclosed from <u>Salem</u> Gazette.

The Regiment is in fine condition and all is quiet and as I wish it. The War for Major though is hard. I think all will be right. Kindest remembrance to folks at home.

P. R. G.

Log-House at Camp
April 13, 1863

My Dear Jennie:

Ere this reaches you the probability is that the little house so long (<u>short</u>, I should say) blessed with your presence, will be deserted. Everything goes to confirm the idea that we are off in a few days. Pray, my Darling, that success will be our fortune this time. No one here seems to know where we are going to—but it is certain there is something important in the wind. I do believe that I shall drop tears when I am leaving this little canvas-covered cot when I leave it forever. O! my dear, you never know what a charmed remembrance I shall have of your presence in it. I never do feel when you are gone. I cannot explain the feeling which crowds upon me tonight, Love. I think I see you here all the time and yet I cannot feel you—you walk across the room and yet you neither speak to me nor touch me. I wish I had your hands to clasp on your waist, or your cheek to kiss. But separated we must live, for a while at least. Be assured of one thing my Dear, that if a battle should occur before you hear from me again, that I will come out of it with glory or wounds—or perhaps, both. Still, we may not fight at all.

The regiment is in splendid condition, and whatever the "Cop-

---

[30] See Guiney's letter to Colonel James McQuade dated April 5, 1863.

perheads" of North End say, is for <u>me</u> heart and soul—except a few soulless officers for whose appointment I am not responsible, and would not be for the world.[31] Mahan is back, and quite mad because I do not recommend him for Major.

Do, my Dear Jennie, in the warmest manner possible, give my regards to our dear sister Sarah, if she is with you. Flynn is writing epistle to "his Mary" at the other end of the table. He annoys me, so I bid you—<u>Adieu love.</u>

Guiney

Log-House at Camp
April 14, 1863

My Dear Jennie:

Your note of the 10th inst. and also one by Capt. Phalen received this evening.

I am so glad that you have met our sister Sarah. Your description of her is in exact conformity with the idea I had formed of her appearance and character. I shall remain anxious until I receive her picture.

Capt. Phalen has said something about all at home, but I have not had much time to speak with him since his return. He told about Loolie and her kisses for me. God bless the little cherub! I will kiss her yet.

O'Leary has been tried also McGunnigle but I have no doubt

---

[31] During March–May, 1863, Captain Michael F. O'Hara and Lieutenants William B. Maloney, Edward Finnoty, and Nicholas C. Flaherty tendered their resignations. Guiney fully endorsed their wishes and, believing their commissions could be filled by more effective and deserving men, recorded this opinion as he forwarded each resignation up to corps headquarters. Only Finnoty's resignation was accepted, however, and this probably because he had been under arrest since autumn 1862. Copperheads were Northern Democrats who opposed Lincoln and continuation of the war, supporting instead a compromised peace with the Confederacy. *The Pilot* asserted that such Peace Democrats were "the only true representatives of Republican freedom today in this country" and predicted that "time will vindicate the justice of their conduct." Ninth Massachusetts Infantry Regiment Letter and Order Book, Record Group 94, National Archives, Washington, D.C., 32–35, 39–42, 44, 53–54. *The Pilot*, April 4, 1863. For more information on the Copperheads, see McPherson, *Battle Cry of Freedom*, pp. 494, 591–98, 761–73.

that if punished at all the sentence will be very light if not a total acquittal. Thus it is in this Army—the greater scamp the more favor and friends.

As you already understand, we have not moved. The tremendous rain storm still raging prevents such a thing—

My Dear—My Darling Wife, I hope you are enjoying yourself at home and with our little child. There seems to be a long, severe, and decisive campaign ahead of us, and I will feel much better if, whether I write to you often or not, you give me frequent assurance that you are well. When I turn my face away from these noisy scenes, I only see you and <u>our</u> child in the world.

My love, I wish I could press you to my bosom tonight. If Sister Sarah is still there bid her <u>adieu</u> for me—Remembrance to Lizzie.

> Ever fondly yours
> Guiney

> Log-House at Camp
> April 16, 1863

My Dear Jennie:

Your note of the 11th inst. and also copy of <u>Journal</u> received this evening.

Hon. Henry Wilson was here to-day, he made but a short call upon me as he was in a hurry to get back to [Major] Gen. Hooker's quarters. He expressed a desire to assist me in any way in his power, but as Col. [William S.] Tilton of the 22nd Mass. was with him, I could not say anything to him of a personal nature.[32]

As an active campaign is now daily expected to open, I will not take—in fact I cannot take time to look after my personal interests. Probably next fall will occur the first rest which we will have after starting. <u>Then</u> I will stir myself, although I have no hope of

---

[32] A Boston merchant, William S. Tilton began the war as a first lieutenant and adjutant of the Twenty-second Massachusetts Volunteer Infantry, and by October 4, 1861, was its major. He was wounded and captured by the Confederates at Gaines' Mill on June 27, 1862; upon his release he was promoted to lieutenant colonel. On October 17, 1862 Tilton was commissioned colonel of his regiment and commanded the Twenty-second Massachusetts until mustered out on October 17, 1864. He received a brevet promotion to brigadier general of volunteers to date on September 9, 1864. *Massachusetts Soldiers, Sailors*, 2: 651.

being treated with even common fairness in the mean time, yet all may be well.

Send my fatigue suit on as soon as possible to Mr. F. [?] in Washington. [Brigadier] Gen. Griffin and Col. McQuade think I served the deserters right. All well here.

If here, I will write again tomorrow. Regards to folks and kisses to pet, and O! Jennie, what a caress for yourself—

Adieu Love—
Guiney

Log-House at Camp
April 18, 1863

My Dear Jennie:

Yours of the 15th inst. enclosing photograph of sister Sarah, received this evening. I like her picture very much—she looks spotless, possessed of womanly pride, and like one who spurns, with her whole nature, everything that is not good and noble. By the way, she seems to me a little puritanical, gentle yet austere— like one having fixed principles in life—yet full of heart, impulses and soul. She would find great happiness in the Catholic Church. I wish she were not a cold Protestant.

I really am once more anxious about our little pet—poor little cherub! Tell me Jennie, that she is well and as she says herself, "Gay and happy" again.

Ever yours
P. R. Guiney

In April the Boston Post *printed a letter signed "Vidette" which recounted and justified Guiney's arrest and punishment of Sergeants McCarthy and O'Hara on charges of desertion, argued that Guiney's brigadier, Griffin, approved of the measure, and mentioned that Copperheads in Boston were attempting to use the issue to attack Guiney. "Vidette" also praised Guiney as maintaining the regiment in the fine state of discipline inaugurated by Colonel Cass. Eneas Smyth, from the North End, countered with a letter that criticized Guiney's disciplinary measures as despotic and doubted that the Colonel had not yet heard of Lincoln's*

*amnesty to all who would rejoin their commands. Smyth also argued that,
"If a Washington paper, or a Boston one, had a small little notice of
certain reasons why Col. Guiney should be made a Brigadier (God save
us) the very efficient Colonel would have heard it in ten hours," and called
Guiney a "political and skedaddling Colonel. . . ."*[33] *As indicated by the
following letters, the issue of McCarthy's and O'Hara's punishment would
persist for some time, as Guiney's political opponents used the matter to
attack the colonel in the public forum. (Guiney consistently misspelled
Smyth's name as "Smith," but the correct spelling has been rendered in
this transcription.)*

Head Quarters
9th Mass. Vols.
Camp Near Falmouth
April 22, 1863

My Dear Wife:

Your letter of the 18th inst. received this evening—containing
slip from the <u>Post</u>. It really does not amount to much as against
me, and so Mr. Smyth's friends think—even say out here that he
damaged himself by the letter. However I have sent the original
of the enclosed copy to Col. Green of the <u>Post</u>—also one to Searle
with a letter. When I get home I shall have a year's business on
hand sure. Poor Smyth will pay for his ignorant and malicious
ravings some day in the future. But Love, I must cut this interview
with you short since I am quite busy, and have only time to ask
you for a <u>modern</u> <u>kiss</u>.

Guiney

Log-House at Camp
April 24, 1863

My Dear Wife:

Your dear good letter speaking of the ceremony at the Church
of the Immaculate Conception [has been received]. How I would
love to be there with you darling in that Heavenly blaze of light. I
am sure you must have been very happy—and I am happy in the

---

[33] Boston *Post*, April 14, 1863; April 17, 1863. See also Patrick R. Guiney to
Col. James McQuade, Falmouth, Va., April 5, 1863.

thought of your peace and blessedness. Father [Joseph B.] O'Hagan who is out here as Chaplain in a New York regiment a Jesuit Father and an old friend and companion of my two friends at the College [of the Holy Cross], told me about the grandeur of the scene in the church, and asked me yesterday if you had not spoken of the magnificent spectacle![34] I told him, no, but I expected you would in your next letter—and sure enough to-day I received your description. I wish the light in my soul was as bright as it is in yours tonight! But we may share it yet together.

Plunkett and a lot of officers are around the table joking—and poking fun at Eneas Smyth and the Boston sore-heads so I cannot write you much tonight. I see that they have tried their hands at slander in the Pilot again.[35] The whole thing is harmless to me. What military philosophers they are! A Colonel and a sergeant in a "difficulty." Well, such nonsense. We have no difficulties here—we settle things without difficulty in the Army.

The move has not taken place yet as you see by the heading of this. I expect to be on picket tomorrow or next day.

Send my regards to sister Sarah, when you write, also, to sister Mary—give respects to Lizzie and Kate—Kisses to Loolie—little diamond of my heart where she is firmly set in golden Love and where her lustre will be ever bright as the stars!

"Ever of Thee," Love
Guiney

---

[34] Father Joseph B. O'Hagan, S.J. was born August 15, 1826 in Clogher, County Tyrone, Ireland, and joined the Jesuits while in America. After studying at Louvain University, he returned to America after the Civil War's outbreak and received appointment as chaplain of Brigadier General Daniel Sickles's Excelsior Brigade. A friend of O'Hagan's, Guiney sought his services in the absence of a chaplain for the Ninth. After the war, O'Hagan took office as president of the College of the Holy Cross in 1872. His diary, which runs from February 1 to February 19, 1863, can be found in the Dinand Library Archives, College of the Holy Cross, and its contents were published in Rev. William L. Lucey, ed., "The Diary of Joseph B. O'Hagan, S.J., Chaplain of the Excelsior Brigade," in Civil War History Vol. 6, no. 6 (December 1960), 402–09.

[35] This refers to an article published in The Pilot entitled "Difficulty in the Ninth Regiment" and signed "Videbimus." The article criticized Guiney's punishment of Sergeants O'Hara and McCarthy for being absent without leave. An earlier article published in the Boston Journal supported Guiney's action as justified, meritorious, and fostering a sense of discipline in his regiment. This Journal piece, also published in the Boston Post and signed "Vidette," inflamed those who opposed Guiney in the regiment. The Pilot's article criticized Guiney's pun-

P.S. I enclose a letter to me from the sisters of <u>Notre Dame</u>.

P. R. G.

April 24, 1863

My Dear Jennie:

The officers have held a meeting to-night and denounced the cowardly <u>clique</u> who dared to assail me. I will send the proceedings when completed. They have voted me complimentary resolutions and also purpose to make me a valuable present. <u>Good</u> has come out of <u>evil</u>, and I feel fully avenged. What a raking Mr. Smyth got. But more bye and by.

Yours Love
Guiney

Log-House at Camp
April 25, 1863

My Dear Jennie:

Your note of the twenty first inst. received this evening. Why, my dear, I thought I told you that I received your pictures—I have received <u>two</u> of yours and one of Sarah's. So Darling, if you [illegible words] too. Oh! Don't love. It's too bad—come here and <u>kiss</u> me Dear.

I think I receive your letters regularly—one almost every night.

The officers are to complete their arrangements tonight for a grand presentation to me. The address I have seen and it is more severe upon the North End than I would wish. Hanley, Tobin and of course O'Leary stand <u>neutral</u>. But the vast majority—in fact 25 of them sign it. The men are indignant also and are contributing for my present.

Tomorrow morning I go on picket as <u>General Officer of the</u>

---

ishment as "extreme" and questioned his motives and conduct. See also Guiney's letter to Colonel James McQuade dated April 5, 1863. *The Pilot*, April 25, 1863.

<u>outpost</u>—acting Brigadier again as Col. McQuade is again unwell. I will be absent <u>four</u> days, but letters coming to me by mail will be sent out to me. My post will be a little beyond that place that you and I rode to the day it rained upon us. By the way Darling I have often thought since how cruel I was to urge you to ride <u>faster</u> that day when all the time you were <u>suffering</u> <u>pain</u>. But I did not know it Love, and was afraid you'd get wet on the way home. Never mind we'll have a morning ride in the future when I will try and be reasonable, if not <u>polite</u>.

There is no move yet and I still inhabit the house—the <u>deserted</u> house. My <u>little</u> <u>cat</u> even left me. The flag still waves over the bed—but there is no such charm in it as there was. Griffin appears more friendly—he is now in Washington.

Ever fondly
Your Husband

On April 27 Major General Hooker began to move his infantry, planning to give battle to General Lee's army; the Ninth joined its brigade on route to Chancellorsville and bivouacked near Hartwood Church that night. On the 28th, the troops reached Kelly's Ford and crossed the Rappahannock on pontoon bridges the next morning. The Ninth then proceeded to march until reaching Ely's Ford on the Rapidan, and crossed the swift stream. One member of Company E lost his footing here and was carried downriver, and would have drowned had not Brigadier General Griffin himself plunged in to save the man. The next day the division marched to Chancellorsville and took position in Major General Hooker's battle line, stationed with the rest of the corps on the Federal left near the Rappahannock. The V Corps remained unengaged during Confederate Lieutenant General "Stonewall" Jackson's crushing flank attack of May 2, and the next day, Major General Meade's corps moved closer to the Chandler House to cover a withdrawal of the Federal troops. Companies E, G, and H advanced at the double-quick under Lieutenant Colonel Hanley to drive a battalion of Southerners from a nearby embankment, and received three cheers from its brigade. The sector remained quiet on May 4, although the Ninth joined its brigade in conducting a reconnaissance, and helped push back the Rebel skirmishers to uncover their main line of battle. On May 6 the V Corps acted as rear guard for the retreating Army of the Potomac, and the Ninth reached its old camps later that day; the regiment had only

sixteen wounded from the campaign, while the entire corps suffered but
669 casualties.[36] *In his letter, Guiney blames the campaign's failure on*
the rout of the XI Corps in the face of Lieutenant General Jackson's on-
slaught on May 2, and the defeat of a wing of the army under Major
General John Sedgwick on May 4. Guiney expressed tremendous satisfac-
tion and personal admiration for Major General Hooker, however.

At Camp
Near Falmouth, Va.
May 7, 1863

My Dear Jennie:

After an absence of ten days on the other side of the Rappahannock, we are once more in our old camp. How many hours or
days we will remain here I am not able to say nor surmise. I found
my log house a <u>wreck</u>. I am now in an old tent pitched where I
was when you arrived here the first day.

I suppose the news papers have given all particulars of the recent battles. At any rate, my Dear, I am not in a mood to speak of
them. <u>We</u> <u>are</u> <u>whipped</u> <u>again</u>—not in battle exactly, but for want
of numbers. Sedgwick lost all we had gained. He had not men
enough to hold the heights of Fredericksburgh—so when he was
driven nothing remained for us but to abandon Chaunceyville
[Chancellorsville] as the possession of Fredericksburgh was the
purpose of our flank movement. On that point, it is true that if
we had defeated the enemy at Chaunceyville in any one of the
battles fought there, Sedgwick's disaster would have been of less
consequence. We certainly would have gained a great victory were
it not for the cowardice of the 11th Corps—a German corps
which was formerly commanded by [Major General Franz] Sigel
but now by [Major] Gen. [Oliver O.] Howard of Maine.[37] The

---

[36] Regan diary, May 3, 11, 1863. OR, vol. 25, pt. 1: 505–509, 516–17. Macnamara, *Ninth Regiment*, pp. 296–301.

[37] The XI Corps had a large number of Germans in its ranks and among its
officers, and many considered it a "foreign" corps. The German-born Franz
Sigel fled to America after participating in the Revolutions of 1848. By spring
1862 he was commissioned a major general in the Federal army. Although not
very valuable on the battlefield, he was a source of pride to the North's German
population, and many enlisted to "fights mit Sigel." A West Point graduate from
Maine, Oliver O. Howard lost his right arm at Seven Pines. He led the XI Corps

Dutch Corps ran. The rest of the Army fought well. Hooker made the best movement (and did it in the best manner) that has been made during this war. He deserved success and was beaten by two things—want of numbers, and the disgraceful flight of the flying Dutchmen. I saw Hooker himself working like an enlisted man at the guns. I almost wept for him when I heard the retreat was ordered. I shall admire him forever.

As to our own loss in the regiment it was not serious. I lost fourteen or fifteen only—none of them died on the field—and perhaps all will ultimately recover. The "Ninth," on account of its being reliable was kept in support of the Artillery most of the time—hence it is that we did not suffer more. I had all sorts of commands during the battles—sometimes I had the whole Brigade under me—sometimes three regiments—sometimes two regiments—sometimes my own regiment. Griffin placed me in command of the Brigade once when he could not find McQuade nor Sweitzer. McQuade's horse ran off with him and all his staff followed—it was fun to see them dashing to the rear. Sweitzer went astray and several other mysterious things occurred of that nature all of which made more work for me. I have not slept two successive hours for the past ten days.

My health is good love, but of course I am very tired and weary—in fact, heart sick over our defeat. O! God, when shall our defeats cease?

Flynn and Plunkett are well—Plunkett goes for peace—he says "it's no use."

We are expecting to move every hour. I will write again as soon as possible. My love to Loolie—

Guiney

Following the battle, a meeting of officers from the Ninth Massachusetts convened on May 7 to condemn the recent attacks on Colonel Guiney

---

through the Chancellorsville and Gettysburg campaigns and later reinforced the Federal army at Chattanooga, Tennessee with his corps. While participating in the Atlanta campaign, Major General William T. Sherman put him in command of the Army of Tennessee following the death of its commander, Major General James B. McPherson. After the war, Howard served as first commissioner of the Freedman's Bureau and later helped found Howard University. He became superintendent of West Point. Warner, *Generals in Blue*, pp. 237–38, 447–48. McPherson, *Battle Cry of Freedom*, pp. 641, 654.

in the Boston newspapers. In an address to their colonel, they expressed "unbounded confidence in your high military qualifications displayed in many a dangerous emergency," and credited his efforts for maintaining a high sense of morale and discipline in the regiment. The next day, Guiney replied with gratitude toward these officers and scorn toward his oppponents, and claimed that his "sense of duty, a love for the reputation of my countrymen—an abiding ambition to serve this Republic, alone prompt me in the enforcement of discipline."[38]

Head Quarters
9th Mass. Vols.
May 8, 1863

My Dear Jennie:

Last evening after mailing my letter to you I received a whole armful of letters. They made me very happy indeed—it was so refreshing after my fatigue to converse with you so long.

I received the clothing the day before we left camp. I wore the suit through the march. It was cool and nice. All fit well but the vest is a little tight.

The Regiment raised [$]500.00 to purchase presents of horse equipments etc. for me. They also presented me with enclosed address.

I received a whole flood of letters from friends—Mulrey, Searle and others. I cannot answer them now—No time. Please tell friend Mulrey to excuse me. Every thing goes well here. Griffin has said to Gov. Andrew that O'Leary is not fit for Major—and said the same of Mahan. But he recommended Tobin. What a change! I stick to the Adjutant [Michael Phalen]—he is the best man.[39]

We are under orders to move where I know not.

I wish I was with you and little pet in that garden but the wish seems vain now.

McQuade was badly hurt by a fall from his horse while the horse was running away. I saw him this morning—he will recover.

---

[38] Boston *Post*, May 16, 1863.

[39] Adjutant Phalen was also a signer of the letter to Governor Andrew, and later put his signature on its retraction.

My Dear, You will please go to Whipples and get a dozen of my cards de visite send me six. Many ask me for them.

Send my regards to sister Sarah when you write.

Ever fondly
Your Husband

P.S. Splendid horse that cost [$]300.00 has been purchased for me today. I will send home the little "Whitie" if you like.

P. R. G.

At Camp
May 9, 1863

My Dear Jennie:

Yours of the 5th inst. received this evening. I suppose you have heard from me ere this. It does not take me long to write you when I know you are anxious about my safety. I never was better in my life—This afternoon I had a ride on my new horse. I like him very much—The little "Whity" is very jealous of him. It would amuse you to see the doleful look he casts at me on the back of the other. After all I hate to part with my little Whity and I now think I will keep him here unless you wish him at home.

Capt. [Patrick W.] Black—the Lord Chesterfield of the Ninth has gone home for a few days and will, no doubt, call upon you.[40]

How does Loolie progress in her hoeing and digging? I hope she will grow and bloom like the flowers—but never fade.

Guiney

---

[40] Patrick W. Black studied law before the Civil War. He mustered in as the Ninth Massachusetts' commissary sergeant, and received commissions for second lieutenant dated to August 26, 1861 and first lieutenant dated to March 1, 1862. He was promoted to captain on October 20, 1862 and discharged July 28, 1863. He mustered into the Twenty-eighth Regiment Massachusetts Volunteer Infantry on March 29, 1864 and became a captain in July of that year. He mustered out of the military in July 1865 and received brevet promotion to major to date from April 9, 1865. *Massachusetts Soldiers, Sailors*, 1: 617; 3: 252. Philip Dormer Stanhope, 4th Earl of Chesterfield (1694–1773), was an English writer and statesman who helped define the aristocracy of his age by his actions as a man of letters and a citizen of the world.

On May 10, perceiving the low morale of some of the troops following the Chancellorsville debacle, Guiney had a special order read to the men at dress parade. In it he expressed his gratification and satisfaction at the manner in which the men did their duty, and thanked a number of officers and especially Companies E, G, and H for their repulse of a Confederate force on May 3.[41] On May 12 Guiney counted 519 men present for duty in the regiment.[42]

Head Quarters 9th Mass.
May 13, 1863

My Dear Jennie:

Your note of the ninth inst., and two previous letters have come to hand since I wrote to you last. I expected that you would have received my first letter before the ninth and I am real sorry that you are so worried by delay in our mails.

When the last movement took place we were <u>immediately</u> <u>withdrawn</u> from picket and sent on with the army.

I was near Gen. Whipple when he was shot by a sharpshooter.[43] He was a great loss. He was a very pious Catholic—a convert to the Church. It seems that [Thomas J. "Stonewall"] Jackson the rebel General is dead. I hope it is true—yet I feel no personal enmity—to so gallant a soldier—the <u>general</u> we may abhor—but the <u>individual</u> is another thing. I only wish the "Confederacy" had died with him.

[Brigadier] General Meagher and staff were over here in all their splendor last evening, and presented us with a most magnificently embroidered Green flag. We now have <u>three</u> Green flags.[44] So you see he was not shot—neither did his Brigade fire a

---

[41] Macnamara, *Ninth Regiment,* p. 304.

[42] Ninth Massachusetts Infantry Regimental Letter and Order Book, Record Group 94, National Archives, Washington, D.C., 54.

[43] Major General Amiel Whipple, a West Point graduate of the class of 1841, directed the Third Division of the III Corps at the time of his mortal wounding. Near Chandler House on May 4, he sat on his horse writing an order for Colonel Berdan's sharpshooters to clear out an annoying Rebel sniper when the Confederate fired and hit him in the abdomen. The bullet exited near his spine and he died in Washington on May 7. Ernest B. Furgurson, *Chancellorsville 1863* (New York: Alfred A. Knopf, 1992), p. 295. Warner, *Generals in Blue,* p. 554.

[44] The other Irish flags were the original one received in Boston in 1861 and one sent to the regiment in the autumn of 1862. The flag referred to in Guiney's

single shot in the battle. However, the enemy's artillery, as in our own case, did the Brigade some damage.

So Father Whelan is about again.[45] Well, I can fancy your feelings. I suppose he is still the same.

Guiney

Camp
May 16, 1863

My Dear Jennie:

Your welcome favor of the 13th inst. and also your favor of the 11th came to hand today. I send you the original of the address of the officers with signatures attached. You may allow friend Searle to publish it with the names if he pleases in the Post.[46] Those that were sent to papers were mere copies.

Yesterday one of my commissioned baboons presented me with a set of frivolous charges against myself.[47] The charges were very silly but insulting. I immediately locked him in arrest, and will

---

letter was intended for the Twenty-ninth Massachusetts of Meagher's brigade, but Lieutenant Colonel J. H. Barnes protested that his unit was not of Irish descent and refused to bear it on the field. Brigadier General Meagher had the "2" removed, transforming the banner into a flag for the Ninth Massachusetts, and presented it to Guiney. Macnamara, *Ninth Regiment*, p. 285.

[45] In 1857 Father Daniel Whelan relocated from the Brooklyn Diocese and was assigned to Lewiston in the Portland Diocese until his dismissal in July 1862. Notes of Rev. William Lucey, S.J., Dinand Library Rare Book Room, College of the Holy Cross.

[46] The address, dated May 7, expressed "unbounded confidence in your [Guiney's] high military qualification displayed in many a dangerous emergency," claimed that the regiment's high state of morale and discipline was due to Guiney's leadership and attention, and condemned negative remarks published about him in the Boston *Post*. The address and Guiney's reply were published in both the *Post* and *The Pilot*. Boston *Post*, May 16, 1863. *The Pilot*, May 23, 1863.

[47] On May 15, Adjutant Michael W. Phalen, Captain Michael Flynn, Captain Thomas K. Roche, Lieutenant Michael A. Finnerty, and First Sergeant John P. Murphy signed a letter stating that they were "not acquainted with any information tending to prove Colonel Patrick R. Guiney guilty of the charges preferred against him by Captain James F. McGunnigle . . . [and] we believe them to be utterly false." Michael W. Phalen et al., Camp of the Ninth Massachusetts Volunteers near Falmouth Virginia, May 15, 1863; located in Patrick R. Guiney Military Service Record, National Archives, Washington, D.C.

have him tried [f]or his impertinence.[48] His name is Capt. Mc-
Gunnigle. The North End crowd are hard pressed for something
about me and doubtless this will give them a new sensation. The
charges are about the "White horse," "Cruel punishment of
O'Hara" and "having soldiers for servants" all of which I have a
right to have and do except the Cruelty.[49] He must be a good
officer the meanest personal enemies can find nothing against
but such things—poor fellows! They are met and foiled at every
point. The Adjutant's wife is dead—he is gone home. He felt
dreadfully at the sad news. I send you copy of an order I issued
yesterday which meets the case of the heroes.

[no signature]

[In the margin Guiney has written:] Love to Loolie

Camp
May 18, 1863

My Dear Jennie:
Your kind note of the 14th inst. received this evening. Under
present circumstances I am not able to comply with my former
promise to send home the "White horse."

---

[48] Guiney specified that Captain McGunnigle preferred false charges against
his commanding officer, "animated by a malicious and personal spirit," and for
"writing deliberate falsehoods in relation to his commanding officer." A few
days later, Guiney added to these charges when Captain McGunnigle left his
quarters, breaking his arrest and confinement to his tent. Guiney also charged
the captain for straggling in the marches and battle of Chancellorsville, and
added that Captain McGunnigle was not "able to discharge his duty as commander of his company for the want of intelligence, education, and executive
ability." Guiney was unable to have Captain McGunnigle dismissed from the
regiment, even after the Ninth's Surgeon Sullivan found the captain medically
unfit for full military duty due to several painful ulcers on both his legs. Charges
and specifications preferred against Captain James F. McGunnigle, Camp of the
Ninth Regiment Massachusetts Volunteers, May 15, 1863; Charges and specifications against Captain James F. McGunnigle, Head Quarters Ninth Massachusetts
Volunteers, May 18, 1863; Written statement of Surgeon J. F. Sullivan, Camp
Ninth Regiment Massachusetts Volunteers, June 11, 1863; Patrick R. Guiney to
Brigadier General James Barnes, Head Quarters Ninth Massachusetts Volun-
teers, June 11, 1863; all are located in James F. McGunnigle Military Service
Record, National Archives, Washington, D.C.
[49] See Guiney's letter to Colonel James McQuade dated April 5, 1863.

I have not seen the address in print yet but expect it every day.

I am not in a mood to converse with you tonight Love. I am vexed about several things here—but all may come out right in a few days.

P. R. Guiney

[underneath, he wrote and crossed out:] Col. Cmd.]

Camp

May 19, 1863

My Dear Jennie:

I wrote you some sort of a note last evening. I was quite vexed at the time. Col. Sweitzer who happens to command the Brigade now, undertook to release Capt. McGunnigle from close confinement without consulting me. To this I objected and told him if he persisted "I would resign my commission immediately." He then revoked his order and concluded to let me have my own way. All right again.

I am just going over to bid Gen. Meagher farewell—he has resigned and is going home.[50] Give Loolie a shower of kisses for me. No sign of a move yet.

Guiney

The Ninth went out on picket duty on May 20, with its reserve encamped in a pleasant grove of cedar trees and a good water supply nearby; the men returned to camp by May 23. On May 27 the Governor of Michigan, Austin Blair, came to visit the Fourth Michigan, and the entire brigade turned out for his review.[51]

At Camp

May 27, 1863

My Dear Jennie:

I received your note of the—inst. this evening.

If you have not already started—I wish you to come on at once.

---

[50] Brigadier General Meagher tendered the resignation on May 14, and on May 25, the Ninth marched to the railroad station to bid him farewell as he headed home. Regan diary, May 25, 1863. Warner, *Generals in Blue*, p. 318.

[51] Regan diary, May 20, 23, 27, 1863.

I will try and meet you at Washington but if I do not, go and see either Mr. Wilson or Mr. [Senator Charles] Sumner about pass.[52] I am afraid of Loolie's coming, but if you think best bring her on—Lizzie I do not see how I can provide quarters for, but if she will 'soldier it out'—let her come. Great many Ladies are coming every day—

Guiney

By May 28 the regiment had finished their new camp, with gutters dug and trees planted on each side of the company streets. However, after all this work, the Ninth received marching orders and moved a few miles upriver at 5:00 p.m. At sunrise on May 29, the regiment relocated to Ellis Ford with orders to guard it along with the Thirty-second Massachusetts, while the Sixty-second Pennsylvania and Fourth Michigan secured Kelly's Ford. The Confederates occupied similar positions on the opposite side. With Colonel Sweitzer on leave, Guiney commanded the brigade until June 5.[53]

Head Quarters at Ellis
Ford On the Rappahannock
June 1st 1863

My Dear Jennie:

Not having heard from you for some time, I am afraid that you started for Washington before receiving my dispatch—Oh! how sorry I will be if such be the case. Just as I was fixing up a splendid residence for you and Loolie the order to march came—and here

---

[52] An influential Massachusetts abolitionist, Charles Sumner was elected to the United States Senate in 1851 and represented his state there until his death in 1874. Two days after delivering a passionate speech to the Senate on May 19-20, 1856, concerning violence between pro- and anti-slavery forces wrestling for control of Kansas, Congressmen Preston Brooks of South Carolina—the nephew of Senator Andrew Butler, who was severely criticized by Sumner—walked into a nearly empty Senate Chamber and beat Sumner over the head thirty times with a gold-headed cane as the surprised Senator could not escape from his desk. Johnson and Malone, eds., *Dictionary of American Biography*, 18: 208–214.

[53] Regan diary, May 28, 29, June 1, June 5, 1863. Macnamara, *Ninth Regiment*, p. 307.

I am looking across the river at the rebels and in such an unsafe and exposed position that I could not wish you here.

Our Brigade is scattered up along the river—I am stationed 18 miles from Falmouth—Sweitzer is going to Washington tomorrow—I will command the brigade (empty honor).

Everything goes on well here and I am living high on milk and nice fresh butter. I shall get fat right off as soon as I hear from you.

Guiney

Head Quarters 2nd Brigade
at Ellis Ford
June 5, 1863

My Dear Jennie:

I received your note acknowledging receipt of my letter and dispatch from—Old Camp. Our circumstances are so changed—we are so far off and so near the enemy—and it would be so difficult for you to get up here—and our stay here may be so short that I feel compelled to forego the joy of seeing you and our dear little pet. I feel dreadfully disappointed—but Hooker will have his way. I am well—and as you see—in command of the Brigade again.

Guiney

The morning of June 5, the Ninth rejoined the rest of its brigade at Kelly's Ford, crossed it on June 8 and remained there until June 13. One night a Rebel band played "Dixie," "Bonnie Blue Flag," and other Southern airs, so a Federal band broke out their instruments and replied with "Yankee Doodle," and the "Star Spangled Banner." The Confederates concluded by playing the sentimental camp favorite, "Home Sweet Home," and the Union band joined in. Upon conclusion of the concert, men on both sides sent up three cheers.[54]

General Lee led his Army of Northern Virginia north to invade Pennsyl-

---

[54] Regan diary, June 5, 11, 1863.

vania, and Major General Hooker's Federals followed with a pursuit marked by excruciatingly hot weather, dust-choked roads, and great fatigue. On June 14, the Ninth marched to Beaversville and reached Manassas Junction the next day. June 17 dawned extremely hot as the men undertook an uncomfortable march to Gum Springs, and four men of the division died of sunstroke. The Ninth proceeded to the pleasant town of Aldie and bivouacked there for the night of June 19. On June 21 Brigadier General Griffin's division supported Major General Alfred Pleasanton's cavalry and, after passing through Middleburgh, the Irishmen deployed as skirmishers in beautiful open country. The next day the Federals fell back toward Dover and remained here for the night. On June 23 Griffin's division returned to V corps at Aldie.[55]

Camp at Aldie, Va.
June 23, 1863

My Dear Jennie:

We left Kelly's Ford June 13th and a few days before leaving that place, I wrote you a short note which in common with the whole contents of that particular mail bag was captured by the rebels.[56] Since that time we have been so very busy flying about in so many directions that I have had no opportunity of writing you. Indeed there has been no mail communication whatever with Washington of late and it is doubtful when I will be able to get this on the road home. I can fancy your feeling at this long intermission and you can fancy mine when I tell you that we all have been deprived of the "News from home" for the past two weeks. We are, as you see, located at a place called Aldie—on the Bull Run range of Mountains. We have just returned from Middleburgh where we have been up supporting the Cavalry who, by the way, have been doing all the fighting of late. Our turn will, no doubt, soon arrive. Lee is <u>somewhere</u> that's all I know of him. We occasionally meet small parties of rebels, but the main rebel Army has kept out of sight thus far. Hooker is after Lee with a sharp

[55] Regan diary, June 14, 15, 16, 17, 1863. Macnamara, *Ninth Regiment*, pp. 307, 309–11. Parker, *The Story of the Thirty-Second Regiment Massachusetts Infantry*, p. 162.

[56] The Regan diary reports the mail carrier missing and feared captured since June 9, 1863. Regan diary, June 13, 1863.

stick and will keep prodding him until he fights a general engagement. My own opinion is that Lee wants Harper's Ferry as depot of supplies for his Army which he intends to throw into Maryland + Pennsylvania. He can't have it. If the truth were known, Hooker, I think, would prefer that Lee should go in to the Loyal States. Our men would fight better there and final victory would certainly come to us. What's the devastation of a state to the conquest of Lee's army?

At Middleburgh yesterday I saw a little child who was in look—in words and action—in all her little pouting, rollicking ways, the picture of Loolie. How I did hug the little rebel!

Affairs in the regiment stand the same as ever—I have my own way in everything here. But I have all the work to do. Hanley is dull and indolent as usual. Mahan is gone off somewhere on "sick-leave."[57] Heaven knows when I'll see him again. Didn't the Governor give me a valuable Major? Doctor [James F.] Sullivan is also off—on "sick leave." He is about as sick as I am—and I never was in better health. Flynn, Plunkett, Phalen and all others are well.

As soon as we get settled down again (Heaven knows when) I will write to my darling often.

When the mail does come I expect a shower of letters from you.

> Farewell love
> Guiney

> Camp at Aldie, Va.
> June 25, 1863

My Dear Jennie:

I wrote to you yesterday but as I sent the letter by a chance messenger Heaven knows if it will ever reach you. This evening I am informed that mail communication is again opened with Washington so I will send this through the ordinary channel and hope it will reach its destination. I have not heard from you for three weeks—in fact no mail has come here during that time.

---

[57] John W. Mahan filled the vacancy of major, his commission dated March 30, 1863. *Massachusetts Soldiers, Sailors,* 1: 635.

We expect to move tomorrow or next day—probably into Maryland or on the line of the Potomac. It is said here that Lee is at "Antietam."

There is nothing new going on here—everything going on well in the regiment. Hanley is sick (?) and also Dr. [John] Ryan so that myself and the Adjutant are, as usual, doing the business.[58] Dr. Sullivan + the Major are still absent in Washington. Flynn and Plunkett are well. Lieut. [Frank] Lawler is sick in camp.[59] The recent marches went hard with us all, the weather was so hot. It is cooler now.

While on picket on the river the other day I learned that two rebels who were opposite on similar duty were cousins of mine— their name is O'Brien from Mississippi. They had a long talk with one of my men and said they knew all about me etc. I remember the family very well.

O! Jennie, how anxious I am to hear from you—every one here is in a fever to hear from home—Plunkett says he will resign if Hooker don't get him a letter within two days.

Yours,
Guiney

P.S. I have some money to send you but there are no means of sending it.

P. R. G.

Pursuit of General Lee and his army continued on June 26, as the V Corps left Aldie, passed through Leesburg, and crossed the Potomac River at Edwards Ferry into Maryland. The next morning the Ninth advanced through Poolsville, Beallsville, and Barnesville, crossed the Monocacy River, and went through Buckeystown to bivouac at Ballinger's Creek. Here the men saw fields of grain and rolling hills, with mountains in the

[58] Assistant Surgeon John Ryan mustered into the Ninth Massachusetts on December 13, 1862 and served until the regiment mustered out on June 21, 1864. *Massachusetts Soldiers, Sailors,* 1: 617.

[59] Frank Lawler enlisted in the Ninth Massachusetts as a private on August 12, 1862. Appointed sergeant, he received promotion to second lieutenant to date February 13, 1863. He was dismissed August 3 of that year. *Massachusetts Soldiers, Sailors,* 1: 634.

background, forming a beautiful sight. Guiney awoke the next morning to find that many of his men had gone into nearby Frederick during the night. With Adjutant Phalen, some drummers, fifers, and the remaining members of the regiment, Guiney went into the city to retrieve them.[60] *On the morning of June 28, V Corps commander Major General Meade received orders from President Lincoln to relieve Major General Hooker and assume command of the army; Major General George Sykes took over the corps.*

On June 29 Brigadier General Griffin's division marched through Frederick and other towns with flying colors and drums beating. Many of the houses flew the Federal flag, and friendly civilians gave fruit and refreshment to the troops. One elderly gentleman came five miles to pump and distribute water to the soldiers, wishing to do something for those who would drive the Rebels out of the Keystone State. The Fighting Ninth went into camp near Johnsville that evening. The next morning, the Irishmen passed through Union, Union Mills, Frizzleburg, and Devilbliss to bivouac near Milesville. On July 1, the Ninth passed over the Mason-Dixon line. Guiney addressed the regiment, telling them that they were about to enter Pennsylvania and that every man would have to do his duty, and with banners unfurled and music playing, they crossed. At Hanover, the sounds of battle could be heard in the distance. By 8:00 p.m. the Irishmen were advancing toward Gettysburg via Hanover Road, stopping for the night at Bonaughtown.[61]

The next morning, they reached the battlefield to find elements of the XII Corps skirmishing with Confederates of Lieutenant General Richard Ewell's corps. The V Corps left Captain Frank C. Gibbs' Battery L of the First Ohio Volunteer Light Artillery and the Eighteenth Massachusetts in their support. Then, Brigadier General James Barnes, commanding the division in Griffin's absence, ordered Colonel Sweitzer to dispatch another regiment for the picket line. Originally, the Thirty-second Massachusetts was to be detailed for this duty, but its colonel requested that his regiment be excused since it had little experience or instruction in skirmishing, and the Ninth was chosen instead.

Guiney led his 470 men to the open fields near the Deardorff buildings on Brinkerhoff Ridge, where he deployed into skirmish line facing northwest and waited for Union cavalry to relieve him. After the war, Guiney wrote to Joshua Chamberlain, then colonel of the Twentieth Maine, and recalled:

---

[60] Macnamara, *Ninth Regiment*, pp. 312–13. An article written by Guiney for the *Saturday Evening Gazette*, in Guiney scrapbook, page 1.

[61] Regan diary, June 29, July 1 1863. OR, vol. 27, pt. 1: 599-600. Macnamara, *Ninth Regiment*, pp. 314–15.

Both flanks [of the Ninth] were thus unconnected and exposed. Just then Gregg's Cavalry bivouacked in my immediate rear, and I found myself protecting an inactive cavalry force large enough, and assuredly brave enough to take care of its own front. In the mean time the battle raged on our left—and it was plain that our beloved corps was doing what it had never done—fighting without us. Towards evening, however, Lieutenant [T. Corwin] Case of [Brigadier] General Griffin's staff arrived with instructions that I should move to join my Brigade, and to conduct me thither. The enemy's Artillery gave us some attention as we passed along the immediate rear line towards the left.[62]

The fighting they had heard was Lieutenant General Longstreet's attack on the Federal flank, and the other three regiments of Colonel Sweitzer's brigade—the Thirty-second Massachusetts, Fourth Michigan, and Sixty-second Pennsylvania—got caught in the maelstrom of the Wheatfield, entering that vortex of hell to reinforce the Federals here. The Ninth rejoined its brigade after it had withdrawn from the Rebel onslaught; the three other regiments entered the battle with about a thousand men and lost 466 of them.[63] Guiney recalled:

When we arrived at Colonel Sweitzer's Head Quarters, we could scarcely be said to join the Brigade; it seemed to me that it would be more appropriate to say that we constituted the Brigade. There were flags of the regiments, a remnant of a splendid regiment around each; there were a few officers near their respective colors; there was a broad visit of death and havoc in front.

The Ninth proceeded under orders to join Colonel William S. Tilton's brigade and deployed on the northeast side of Big Round Top, where the men took cover behind a breastwork of rocks. The colors were planted on a large granite boulder in the middle of the line, and here, the Irishmen engaged in skirmish duty. The brigade remained on Big Round Top on July 3, and on July 4, the Ninth went forward in skirmish line to ascertain the position of the Confederates. They soon found the Rebels arrayed in

---

[62] Patrick R. Guiney to Joshua Chamberlain, October 26, 1865; this letter is located in the Joshua Chamberlain papers, Library of Congress, Washington, D.C. OR, vol. 27, pt. 1: 600, 610. Parker, *The Story of the Thirty-Second Regiment Massachusetts Infantry*, pp. 165–66. Macnamara, *Bivouac*, p. 195. Harry W. Pfanz, *Gettysburg Culp's Hill & Cemetery Hill* (Chapel Hill: The University of North Carolina Press, 1993), pp. 116–17, 154. Today, Route 15 passes through Brinkerhoff Ridge, and development has greatly changed this area.

[63] OR, vol. 27, pt. 1: 602, 613. Harry W. Pfanz, *Gettysburg: The Second Day* (Chapel Hill: The University of North Carolina Press, 1987), p. 294.

battle formation, and retreated after losing three casualties. Heavy rains added to the misery of Gettysburg's carnage, but also meant a cessation of the hostilities. The Ninth Massachusetts came through Gettysburg with only fifteen casualties, thanks to the early morning assignment on July 2.[64]

Brigadier General Griffin returned and relieved Brigadier General Barnes on July 4, and the next day, the division commenced a muddy march toward the Potomac and camped near Emmitsburg at Rock or Marsh Creek. By July 7 they reached Middletown and proceeded by Fox's Gap to Jones' Cross Roads. After engaging in outpost duty here, the division advanced on July 14 to Williamsport and then to Berlin.[65]

In the following letter, Guiney expressed his frustration at what he felt to be a lost opportunity to destroy General Lee's army at Gettysburg.

Camp at Berlin, Md.
July 16, 1863

My Dear Jennie:

Your letter of July 9th reached me today. I am surprised that you did not receive a scrawl which I sent to you from the battle-field of Gettysburgh July 5th. I entrusted it to a civilian who happened to be passing and he promised to post it.

It is no wonder darling that you should complain of my tardiness in writing to you. But really while we were engaged in those recent rapid and all important marches, I could not set myself down to anything of a personal nature even if I had time. But it was, more than all, impossible to mail any letter unless through

---

[64] Guiney to Joshua Chamberlain, October 26, 1865, located in the Joshua Chamberlain Papers, Library of Congress, Washington, D.C.. Macnamara, *Ninth Regiment*, pp. 319–20, 331, 336. Macnamara's account of Gettysburg has to be considered carefully, as he embellished the role of the Ninth in the Round Top region, perhaps to justify the location of the regimental monument on the battlefield. In June 1885 the regiment dedicated its granite monument off Sykes Avenue on the northern slope of Big Round Top, a prime location of the battlefield compared to the isolated position on Brinkerhoff Ridge. The monument can be easily found as one drives along the Gettysburg Battlefield. It is in a small clearing on the northern face of Big Round Top, behind a monument to the Tenth Pennsylvania Reserves, just before the marker for Sykes Avenue and the intersection with Wright Avenue. The Ninth Massachusetts held position on the hill in the woods just in front of the monument.

[65] OR, vol. 27, pt. 1: 605. Macnamara, *Ninth Regiment*, pp. 332, 338.

the agency of the residents. At last the hurry seems to be over, at least for a few days and I hope to be able to write to you and hear from you often. However I regard our stay here as one of a very temporary character. It is said that we are simply awaiting pontoons etc. to cross the Potomac again; but the fact is, if it were an object to cross immediately we could do so at several points without pontoons at all, as we have done on several former occasions. I think the delay here is—1st to arrange the details and elements of a new campaign and 2nd to give rest to this wearied army.

Today I have been very unwell and if we had to march one mile farther I should have been obliged to give up. The heat exposure so long continued, and want of proper food nearly brought on a fever—at any rate I never felt so before in my life. I am better this evening and feel scarcely any trace of that sensation which oppressed me earlier in the day. Lee, you are aware "has escaped" etc. It is no silly job to catch him, I assure you. When once he left Gettysburgh it was impossible to give him any fatal blow. Gettysburgh, the evening of July 3rd were the time and place to ruin his Army. We saw his Army flying from the field, broken, beaten, terrified! O! how I felt the significance of that moment. But Meade allowed it to pass—stood still, and gave us—another years work. In common with thousands I was disgusted to see such an opportunity lost.

Well, the soulless ruffians of New York and Boston I see are making trouble in the very hour of victory. I hope the artillery will exempt them from the Draft forever![66]

---

[66] Guiney refers here to the Draft Riots in New York City, which began on July 13 as mobs stormed the draft headquarters and then commenced looting. The unrest subsided only when Federal troops who had fought recently at Gettysburg arrived in the city; damage from the riot has been estimated at a million and a half dollars. Meanwhile, the trouble in New York triggered rumblings among some of Boston's poor and Irish communities, and on July 14 several angry women in the North End attacked two provost marshals serving official papers. Nearby men joined in and nearly beat to death some policemen going to the provosts' aid. As the mob grew riotous, the police retreated to a station house, now barricaded by the mass of people. Mayor Frederick W. Lincoln, using a police telegraph, deployed three militia companies from the Cooper Street Armory and reinforced them with regular troops from outside the city. When the mob attempted to storm the armory, the soldiers fired with rifles and cannon, killing six and driving off the crowd. The rioters went to procure weapons from several gun shops at Dock Square, but an advance guard of police arrived first and blocked their passage until militia dispersed the crowd. Night came and with it, rumors that violence would be renewed the next day, but there was no

Edward McLaughlin is here and well.[67] Sullivan, Hanley and Mahan are still off—Triumvirate of humbugs! Kiss my little pet for me.

                                                                    Guiney

On July 17 the men of the Ninth crossed the Potomac River on pontoons and camped once again on the soil of Virginia, at Lovettsville. July 18 was spent enjoying the delicious blackberries in abundance here. The next day the regiment moved to Oakland. The Irishmen proceeded to Goose Creek on July 20, pitching their tents in a shady grove of cedar trees on the edge of the clear stream and remaining here to savor more blackberries. On the 22nd the regiment marched and bivouacked at Rectortown and reached Manassas Gap by late afternoon on July 23. Here the III Corps struck the rear guard of a Rebel force holding the gap to cover the retreat of a Confederate wagon train, and the V Corps moved closer to support the Federals in this skirmish of Wapping Heights. On July 24 the Fighting Ninth marched to Orleans, and by the 26th reached the vicinity of Warrenton, passing through the town the next day to camp three miles past it. The marches during these days were conducted in extremely hot weather, and many men dropped out of the ranks suffering from heat exhaustion. On the 28th, with Brigadier General Griffin gone to Washington, Colonel Sweitzer commanded the division and Guiney had charge of the brigade; this lasted until Griffin returned on July 31.[68]

                                                Camp at Warrenton, Va.
                                                July 31, 1863

My Dear Jennie:
    The last letter I wrote to you, I did give you Jessie.[69] I have been regretting it ever since, because I ought to know by this time that

---

further trouble. Mayor Lincoln's swift response, and the action of some Catholic authorities and local pastors, helped alleviate the tension and prevent further violence. O'Connor, *Fitzpatrick's Boston*, pp. 209–12.

    [67] According to *Massachusetts Soldiers, Sailors, and Marines in the Civil War*, there were two Edward McClaughlins who served with the Ninth Massachusetts. One was a twenty-year-old bootmaker who served through the entire three year term of enlistment, but the other was a painter who was taken prisoner at Spotsylvania on May 9, 1864 and died at the prison camp at Andersonville, Georgia. *Massachusetts Soldiers, Sailors*, 1: 635, 666.

    [68] Regan diary, July 20, 26, 28, 31, 1863. Macnamara, *Ninth Regiment*, p. 338.

    [69] The letter is missing from the Guiney Collection at the College of the Holy Cross.

you are far more likely to be right in everything than I can ever hope to be. But it is a fact that I was displeased with the proceeding and should feel so yet if I had not abused you so much about it. Forgive me love. My temper is a nuisance to us both.

General Griffin resigned the other day and went off home, but he is now back again, as the War Department would not accept the proposition. I think he will persist, however, as he is tired of the service.[70]

I hear from Plunkett almost every day. He says he went to see you and found yourself and my "beautiful little daughter in good health."

My "box" has not yet arrived nor have I even received the one sent by Mrs. Holly. They both were to be sent tomorrow to Warrenton but the order has just come to be ready to move tomorrow morning so that I am unlucky as usual in such matters. I have no idea whither we are going.

I wish Darling you would send me an exact statement of our affairs—how much money <u>invested</u> and how much in <u>bank</u> or on hand. I am beginning to be interested in the question of our future comfort.

May God be with you Jennie and with my little pet, through all the perils and turns of life. Pray Love, constantly that He may also watch over me.

Guiney

The Ninth remained near Warrenton until the evening of August 3, when it received orders to march through a dark woods (even though there was a road nearby) to a position on the Rappahannock River. On August 8 the men awoke early in the morning to proceed to Beverly Ford, where they stayed until September 16. The Ninth laid out its camp on the east side of a sloping hill a mile away from the Rappahannock River, planted evergreen trees for shade from the hot summer sun, and enjoyed the nearby water.[71]

Guiney once again held temporary command of the brigade while Major

---

[70] In fact, Brigadier General Griffin would stay until the end of the war, receive promotion to major general and serve as one of the Federal commissioners at the surrender at Appomattox. Warner, *Generals in Blue*, p. 191.

[71] Regan diary, August 3, 1863. Macnamara, *Ninth Regiment*, p. 339.

General Sykes was in Washington, leaving Brigadier General Griffin to command the corps and Colonel Sweitzer, the division.

Camp at Beverly Ford
on the Rappahannock
Aug. 8, 1863

My Dear Jennie:

Last evening I wrote you a note and although I am willing to admit it was a fair portrait of my feelings at the time, yet I have been troubled about it all day, and could not go to sleep to-night until I wrote you a few lines of a different nature.[72]

My Darling, if you knew how my heart is bound up in you, how tenderly I cherish you in my inmost soul—how much—nay, how wholly I rely upon you for my happiness, you, I know, would not say a word to touch with anger or sorrow my sensitive, impulsive nature. I beg of you Darling to say nothing that will displease me, as upon this depends my happiness in this world. Whatever may be your feelings, Darling, retain them rather than make me think I had not the love and respect of her for whom I have both, now as fresh and pure as on that morning at the altar!

Jennie Dear I feel almost heart-broken about the little remark you made in your letter of Aug. 2nd. If I thought you intended to hurt me the whole tenor of my life would be changed. But I cannot yield to such a belief. You are too good and true and sensible to purpose such a cruelty. While I feel subjected to many evil influences, it would be too keen for my endurance to know that you yielded to any spirit of retaliation upon me. No more of this, Love!

My Dear little sufferer after whom I name every bird that sings near me and every brook that ripples and flows by my tent, how is she? How is my sweet Loolie?

Give my warmest regards to Father Whelan and Lizzie and tender my heart felt sympathy to Mrs. Duffy.

Guiney

---

[72] This letter is missing from the Guiney Collection at the College of the Holy Cross.

Beverly Ford on
Rappahannock
Aug. 15, 1863

Dear Jennie:
Your note + Father Whelan's of the 9th inst. came to hand last evening. My position as Brigadier was temporary. Griffin is back again. Hanley, Black, Roche, [Lieutenant Robert A.] Miller and Lawler are all <u>dismissed</u> for absence—Some of them may be restored again but they will have hard work.[73] Mahan is still absent and will also be dismissed unless he returns very soon and makes a good defence. I offered to do something for Miller on your account but he wishes to be dismissed in order to get home—he counts the disgrace nothing at all. Of course I would not do him a kindness against his will. Indeed he is not a proper person for favors. I applied for leave of absence to go home but I was denied it on account of the absence of my gallant colleagues Hanley + Mahan. I have to suffer for their Miss-deeds you see. I was mad enough to resign but did not—We will probably move—Heaven knows whither—from this place within twenty four hours.

I hope you have entirely recovered Love. I hoped to be with you in your affliction + my hope was broken—Did you receive package by Express? My regards to Father Whelan.

Ever Truly Yours
P. R. Guiney

---

[73] Captain Black and Lieutenant Lawler received their dismissals on August 3, Lieutenant Miller on September 14, and Lieutenant Roach on September 30, 1863. A Boston shoemaker, Robert A. Miller mustered into the Ninth Massachusetts as a sergeant, and received his commissions for second lieutenant dated to August 27, 1862 and first lieutenant dated to March 21, 1863. Captain Black was arrested on the charge of drunkenness, but the dismissal was set aside and he was restored to command. However, all vacancies in the regiment had been filled, and even though Black was willing to serve as a second lieutenant, no place could be found for him. Guiney wrote that if anything opened up, he would recommend Black for the commission, since he had been "unjustly dealt with, and he has served long enough and well enough to be entitled to whatever favor is possible under the circumstances." Guiney to Major William Rogers, A.A.G., February 18, 1864; letter is located in Ninth Massachusetts File in the Executive Department Letters, Massachusetts State Archives, Boston, Massachusetts. Macnamara, *Ninth Regiment*, pp. 444, 460, 506. *Massachusetts Soldiers, Sailors*, 1: 629.

Beverly Ford Rappahannock
August 15, 1863

My Dear Jennie:

I dropped you a note this morning, but since, I have received yours of the 12th inst. informing me of the cause of your recent illness. It was too bad Darling but it was one of those misfortunes that should not rest heavily upon our hearts. I am very glad you told me about the matter because however painful it is a satisfaction to <u>know</u>.

It is a great pleasure to me also to observe, Dear, that we are both of a mind about <u>words</u> and their value when weighted in the scales of the heart. We are both forgiven by each other you said nothing Dear but that you "had a mind not to answer my letter" about the presentation. This expression cut me but it really was not so bad as it seemed to me at the time.

Your stamps were also received in good order, but Flynn and the Adjutant [Phalen] stole them from me right off. So I shall have to borrow <u>one</u> of <u>my</u> <u>own</u> to put on this letter.

I am really anxious to know how much we can call ourselves worth. Please send me an exact statement of how much was <u>paid</u> for our home and how much money we have besides that sum. Do not count Flynn's $500.00. Let me know as soon as possible whether you received a package of $500.00 per Express. My regards to the folks and Believe me Truly Yours

Guiney

Camp at Beverly Ford
On the Rappahannock River
Near Sulpher Springs
Aug. 16, 1863

My Dear Jennie:

This evening I received two letters from you and one of them contained flowers <u>pressed</u>—as I would like to <u>press</u> <u>you</u> <u>both</u>—not quite so fatally but persistently and until you both should cry "enough" if you could cry at all—and also containing a little charming epistle from our sweet little pet.

It is impossible, absolutely that you could come to see me. The presence of ladies was to-day strictly forbidden and those that came down here some days ago are ordered to go home immediately. I am sorry, Love, especially as your health might be improved by the visit to this neighborhood. But it is useless to think of it. Gen. Meade is more cruel than my old friend Hooker in that respect. But you must do something to preserve your health—Let me know what you intend. My Love, you talk about "Keeping accounts of expenses" etc. By George! I'll go into hysterics if you do. Pray do not Jennie. I only wanted to know how much we had saved, which, of course, is an item of interest to both of us.

We are still under orders to march but the bugle has not sounded "forward" yet.

We are again as of old and as we ever ought to be, Love, one in all things—even trifles.

Yours and Loolie's always
P. R. Guiney

P.S. Tell Loolie to write again.

If Julia will sign her name and give me her address—I will answer her next billet deaux

—Papa.

Beverly Ford, Va.
Aug. 18, 1863

My Dear Jennie:

I anxiously looked for a letter from you in to-day's mail, but none came, so that I am left in doubt and painful suspense about your health. From what you said in your last note I should think that you had some apprehensions as to your health in future. I hope, Dear, that such apprehensions will prove totally unfounded. But let me say this much that if you are seriously threatened with an illness likely to prove dangerous or permanent, I must be with you. Do tell me love what your fears may be in that respect. I would go home—resign in a moment if my presence with you can contribute to your happiness or alleviate your sufferings. Of course, my staying here, if your health was good, would be mutually advantageous to us. But this advantage cannot be put against the heart—health—and happiness of both or either of us. We have a little of the world's goods now and <u>neither</u> <u>of</u> <u>us</u> <u>need</u> <u>to</u> <u>kick</u> <u>up</u> <u>antics</u> <u>against</u> <u>nature</u>—<u>as</u> <u>I</u> <u>did</u> <u>when</u> <u>I</u> <u>first</u> <u>enlisted.</u> So <u>command</u> me Love in this respect. I tried to get home to see you but, as I told you at the time, I failed on account of others. I am not sure that I could get my resignation accepted, but if there is any occasion for my presence at home with you, I will <u>try</u> hard.

Let me know your views candidly and fully and believe me ever at the service of my beloved wife.

We are still at Beverly you see but we are on tip-toe for a "Move."

Guiney

Camp at Beverly Ford, Va.
August 26, 1863

My Dear Jennie:

Since I wrote to you last I have received three letters from you the last one enclosing stamps.

I am quite well and so are all our friends here. I expect to see Plunkett tonight—he is out here in the neighborhood some-where and will call no doubt ere he returns. MacNamara was here this morning looking well. I reported Mahan's case to-day to War Dept.

Six "Substitutes" are to be shot in this Brigade day after tomor-row for desertion. This shooting men for desertion is something new in this Brigade—but it is better late than never. It should have been done long ago. I hope they will commence to shoot officers for the same offence. This Army, if such a course had been adopted in the first place, would be now from fifty to seventy five thousand men stronger than it is—and would be unconquer-able.

I asked you love for Julia's address and you did not send it to me because you said Loolie <u>was</u> <u>out.</u> Does she live at home at all now? I hope she is not already displaying her feathers with a view to matrimony.

The times are dull here—no fighting—no news—no excitement, so I while away the hot hours of the day with "David Copperfield" and his friends, Uriah Heap and Wilkings McCawber. Love to Lizzie.

Yours
Guiney

Camp at Beverly Ford, Va.
August 26, 1863

My Dear Jennie:

This evening I was made glad by the receipt of two good dear letters from you. I must not forget to mention that I also received a note from <u>Miss</u> Guiney.

You see by the heading of this that Mr. Meriells programme for the army is not carried out. We are still here and the indications are that we will remain here for some time. We are having a gay time horse-racing etc. almost every day. Next Friday I am invited to be present at a grand sword presentation to General Meade. It is too bad that Ladies are not allowed here they would have such a splendid time. It is said that Gen. Birney who is quite a Ladies man and who has his quarters about six miles from here at Sulpher Springs spoiled the arrangement by inviting about half the ladies in Philadelphia down to see him.[74] Meade heard of it and stopped <u>them</u> <u>and</u> everybody <u>else.</u>

McGunnigle withdrew those charges long ago—I haven't thought of the matter these 4 months. Harry is still here and looks primely.

Hanley and Mahan arrived back today—they look hale and hearty.

The conscripts were not shot today—they are to be shot next Saturday—followed by a grand horse race and other sports. The

---

[74] Born in Alabama, David B. Birney was a Philadelphia lawyer and businessmen when the Civil War erupted. He rose in the Army of the Potomac and took command of III Corps at Gettysburg after the wounding of Major General Daniel Sickles. Major General Birney continued on until he contracted malaria, causing his death before war's end. Warner, *Generals in Blue*, pp. 34–35.

six graves will make six nice hurdles for the horses to jump—Ain't I cruel to talk so? But Adieu

Guiney

P.S. You might send me a box by Adam's Express—send nothing in clothing line but shirts flannel + white. Pack jug so it won't break—send whatever you can—Lemons etc. but be sure of the <u>packing</u>. Address to me as follows—

Col. P. R. Guiney
9th Mass. Vols. 5th Corps
Washington, D.C.

It will come right through—

P. R. G.

The deserters Guiney writes of were shot before the entire corps on August 29, 1863, and the incident led to a new chaplain for the Ninth Massachusetts. Major General Meade had sent to the War Department asking for a Catholic priest to minister to two of the deserters. Father Constantine L. Egan, O.P. met with Assistant Secretary of War James A. Hardee and agreed to go, starting on a train from Alexandria the next day. Egan attended to the two Catholics and conducted their funeral, and afterward Guiney invited him to the Ninth Massachusetts. Next day being Sunday, Egan celebrated Mass and announced he would stay the week to hear confessions and celebrate Mass at 7:00 a.m. in a chapel tent erected for him. Brigadier General Griffin suspended drill for Catholic soldiers to attend to their spiritual well being at this time. Egan remained available to the entire corps for ten days, after which time Guiney asked him to stay in the army. The priest received permission from his order's provincial, M. A. O'Brien, to leave his Washington, D.C. parish and serve with the regiment, and he wrote Guiney to procure his commission as chaplain of the Irish Ninth. Egan joined the regiment near Warrenton and Guiney appointed him to the chaplaincy on September 18 and requested Governor Andrew to issue the commission as such and of that date.[75]

---

[75] Patrick R. Guiney to Governor John A. Andrew, Army of the Potomac, October 31, 1863; letter is located in the Ninth Massachusetts File in the Executive Department Letters, Massachusetts State Archives, Boston, Massachusetts. C. L. Egan's narrative of events, as reprinted in William S. Corby, C.S.C., *Memoirs of Chaplain Life* ed. Lawrence Frederick Kohl (New York: Fordham University Press, 1992), pp. 312–18. Macnamara, *Ninth Regiment*, p. 429.

Camp at Beverly Ford, Va.
Sept. 2, 1863

My Dear Jennie:

This evening I received your note of the 30th of August. I am
also in your debt for two received before. The box which you sent
on has not yet arrived but I hope to get it with the <u>usual</u> speed or
a little faster.

Now I will tell you just what things I want in the clothing line. I
want a nice uniform pantaloons (You made me say it) three pair
of drawers (Unmentionables) and three red flannel shirts (outside) and three flannel inside shirts. Now <u>do</u> <u>not</u> send me the
uniform pantaloons as I can get them cheap and made to order
in Washington. There is no tape in the Regiment so you will have
to guess the size of my neck—You measured it with your arms
often enough—Make them about as before.

The final <u>result</u> in Hanley's and Mahan's cases is not yet known.
The only case <u>decided</u> up to this time is poor Black's who was
dismissed the service and has gone off. You say Mahan spoke ill
of me—Well Darling if he did I had rather not hear of it. Those
fellows are <u>entailed</u> upon me—I see no way of replacing them
with better men. You may see—but—I confess I cannot discover
desirable successors for them in the regiment to which my choice
should necessarily be confined. It is true there are good officers
here—but what is the use—Gov. Andrew would as heretofore
probably disregard my recommendation as to person and give
me another Mahan instead of John—Another Hanley instead of
Patrick. I cannot help these matters—so I am satisfied with them
so long as the authorities see fit to leave them here—my duty is
simply to report their mis-deeds. Let them talk and bobble away!
I am no craven that I should fear them—I am not a fool—that I
must rely upon food or ill-will of others for my destiny. If men—
such men—try to make life a hell for me—I feel that there is
enough underdeveloped in me to change the character of the
Creation <u>in</u> <u>toto</u>! Pray do not listen to such rehashes of old yarns
from <u>story</u> <u>carriers</u> whose lips are singed with the malice or mean-
ness of their favorite pursuit.

My conscripts have arrived—a fine set of fellows—I like them
very much and have no trouble with them.[76] Col. Morse gave me

---

[76] The Regan diary recorded that several of the conscripts deserted shortly
afterward. Regan diary, September 8, 12, 1863.

your magazines and a letter from Capt. Phelan.[77] I am sorry Father Whelan cannot get a mission in Mass. but I expected as much for certain reasons.

> Ever Yours, My Love
> Guiney

> Camp at Beverly Ford, Va.
> Sept. 9, 1863

My Dear Jennie:

I did hope that to-day I would receive a letter from you but the mail deceived me. Last night I had a dream of you + Loolie and I supposed it meant a letter today.

Your well-stored box came here this afternoon and all in it was safe except one bottle.

I am fixing up nice quarters in the hope that we will remain here for the winter when I hope that Ladies will be allowed to come, and I can see yourself + Loolie. But as to Loolie I should be afraid to have her come—the Little Silly—lest the cold air of the canvas-tent would be too severe for her. It would be so refreshing to me to breathe the same air with my little pet and to be in the chastening presence of our dear child that I fear I will be tempted to send for both of you when the proper time comes. But no more on this subject until <u>that</u> time does come—O! Jennie, how I long to be with you again.

I am much obliged to Father Whelan for cigars—they are excellent—

I have read a great deal lately—your magazines—"Aurora Floyd," "No Name," "Lady Audley's Secret"—and several other <u>first class novels</u>.[78] So I am particularly sentimental just now and if I should say any more I should probably quote from "Romeo

---

[77] Either Lieutenant Colonel Charles F. Morse of the Second Massachusetts, a young architect from Jamaica Plain, or Colonel Augustus Morse of the Twenty-first Massachusetts, who had resigned his commission on May 15, 1862, and might have been visiting the army. *Massachusetts Soldiers, Sailors,* 1: 84; 2: 596.

[78] *Aurora Floyd* and *Lady Audley's Secret* were written by Mary Elizabeth Bradden and published in 1863; *No Name* was penned by Wilkie Collins. Both were London authors. *Lady Audley's Secret* met with great success, with nearly a million copies sold.

and Juliet" so I'll spare you the pain of standing out on the bal-cony so long.

Guiney

Camp at Beverly Ford, Va.
Sept. 11, 1863

My Dear Jennie:

Your dear letter enclosing violet came to me last evening. I am sorry that you do not know exactly the size of my waist—but it is pleasant to hear you say that you will hazard a guess at it, anyhow. This proves a confidence which could not be given except by practical experience in its measurement. I'll wager my life the things will fit. I'll make you a suit some time, dear, when you are off at a war and I am at home—warranted to fit.

I await anxiously the coming of the snow-flakes so that either here or at home I may be able to see you. Little Loolie, too, how I'd like to hear her prattle near me! The little pet, put her in mind that she owes me a letter. Harry is nice and white and gentle and spirited and Loolie shall ride him when the war is over.

Horse-racing is all the talk and trouble and excitement now. The rebels just across the river are no account compared to— horses. I ran my black against the hitherto victorious horse "Dick" of Lt. Col. Hanley. Mine won, in fact, shot right by his opponent. Tomorrow my horse runs again and I am going to keep him on the track until he beats everything in the Army or is clearly beaten himself.

This morning I received the order from Washington dismissing Capt. Roach & Lieutenants Lawler + Miller.[79] Poor fellows, I dis-like to lose them—bad as they are, but duty must be done. Hanley was not dismissed because I did not recommend such a course. I simply requested that he be recalled to the field. Everything goes well in the Regmt.

I have had letters recently from the perfumed Captain and the honest but uncouth Plunkett.[80]

---

[79] See August 15, 1863 letter.
[80] The "perfumed Captain" is probably Captain Patrick W. Black, whom Guiney called "Lord Chesterfield" in his May 9, 1863 letter.

Flynn + Dr. Sullivan, Phalen and myself are all well.

The news from Charleston looks cheering, but "peace" will not come of it, in my opinion—so it's no account to you and I, it brings us no nearer together.[81] Ever in thought + dreams.

Yours

G

Beverly Ford, Va.

Sept. 15, 1863

My Dear Jennie:

Just as we are nicely fixed up and anticipating very good times—our tents arranged like grottos—mine especially in expectation of your visit this winter—that old pest a "Marching order" comes, and, by tomorrow night, we will probably be many miles from here. The rebels have cleared out, it is said, and gone towards Richmond. Their intention no doubt is to either encircle Richmond and go into the Cotton States, or to induce us further into the interior where our supplies will not be so convenient and where our chances of retreat in case of disaster will be diminished. The latter is probably the motive of Lee.

I did hope to receive those shirts which you are so kindly making for me before leaving, but I fear the hope is vain.

We are expecting Plunkett out every day—indeed, I wish that whole conscript detail would be permitted to return for good.

Everything in the Regiment goes on well—all friends are well—and I have a <u>full</u> if not a very efficient staff.

If we are here tomorrow at ten o'clock a.m. we are to have a grand Division horse-race—mine I expect will come off victor. But why should I bother you, Love, with nonsense like this? In fact, if I had anything else to do—and hadn't a fast horse—I would not engage in it myself, I assure you.

---

[81] On September 6, Union forces had forced the withdrawal of Confederates from two positions in the Charleston defense system, Battery Wagner and Morris Island. Fort Sumter and the city remained in Confederate hands, however, and would continue to do so until 1865. Long, *The Civil War Day by Day*, pp. 405, 638–40.

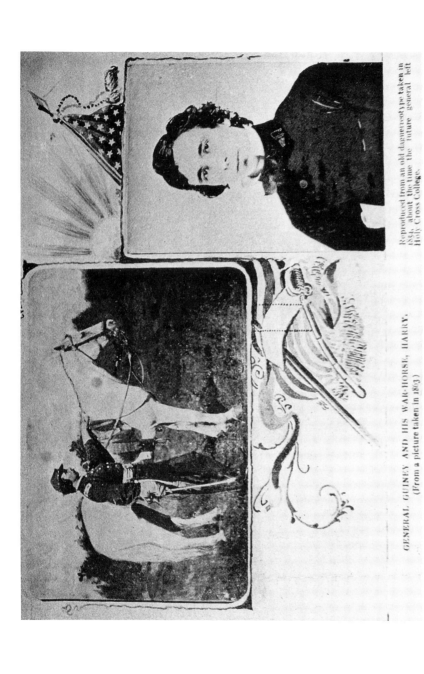

GENERAL GUINEY AND HIS WAR-HORSE, HARRY.
(*From a picture taken in 1863.*)

Reproduced from an old daguerreotype taken in 1859, about the time the future general left Holy Cross College.

From a page of a 1904 Holy Cross alumni magazine. Photo courtesy of College of the Holy Cross Rare Books—Special Collections and Archives. See letter of September 20, 1863.

HIS EXCELLENCY

JOHN A. ANDREW,

GOVERNOR AND COMMANDER-IN-CHIEF

OF THE

Commonwealth of Massachusetts,

To *Patrick R Guiney of Boston in the County of Suffolk, and Commonwealth of Massachusetts*

Greeting:

Whereas, It is provided by a Law of the United States of America, enacted on the twenty-second day of July, A.D. 1861, entitled "An Act to authorize the employment of Volunteers to aid in enforcing the laws and protecting public property," that the Governors of States furnishing Volunteers under said Act, shall commission the Field and Staff and Company Officers requisite for the said Volunteers.

2nd Whereas, The President has authorized and required the Commonwealth of Massachusetts to furnish certain Regiments organized as aforesaid, under and according to the provisions of said Act, to serve in the Volunteer Military Force of the United States, subject to the laws and regulations governing the army thereof, for the term of three years, unless sooner discharged.

Now, Therefore, I, JOHN A. ANDREW, Governor of the Commonwealth of Massachusetts, pursuant to the Authority and Duty aforesaid in me vested, do hereby appoint you *Colonel in the Ninth Regiment*

of the MASSACHUSETTS VOLUNTEERS, called for and organized as aforesaid. You will therefore, with honor and fidelity discharge the duties of said office. And all inferior officers and soldiers are hereby commanded to obey you in your said capacity: and you will yourself observe and follow such orders and instructions as you shall, from time to time, receive from the President of the United States, or others, your superior officers.

Given under my hand, and the seal of the Commonwealth, this *Twenty sixth* day of *July* in the year of our Lord one thousand eight hundred and sixty *two*, and in the eighty-seventh year of the Independence of the United States of America.

By His Excellency the Governor.

Secretary of the Commonwealth.

Guiney's commission as colonel. Photo courtesy of College of the Holy Cross Rare Books—Special Collections and Archives.

Guiney as colonel of the Ninth Massachusetts. Photo courtesy of College of the Holy Cross Rare Books—Special Collections and Archives.

Guiney with 12 of his officers, dated 1863, Culpepper, Va. The officers are identified, from left to right, as Capt. Timothy R. Bourke, Capt. Martin O'Brien, Capt. Michael Flynn, 2nd Lt. William A. Plunkett, 1st Lt. Patrick E. Murphy, 1st Lt. D. G. Macnamara, 1st Lt. Bernard F. Finan, Surgeon James F. Sullivan, 1st Lt. William R. Bourke, Col. Patrick R. Guiney, unidentified, Adjt. Michael W. Phalen, 1st Lt. Timothy Dacey. Photo courtesy of U.S.A.M.H.I., Carlisle Barracks, Pa.

Letter of July 16, 1861. Photo courtesy of College of the Holy Cross Rare Books—Special Collections and Archives.

Louise I. Guiney in autumn 1892, at age 31. Photo courtesy of College of the Holy Cross Rare Books—Special Collections and Archives.

Louise I. Guiney as a young child. Photo courtesy of College of the Holy Cross Rare Books—Special Collections and Archives.

Guiney in 1874 at age 39. He shows the effects of his wound, and on the back, Louise I. Guiney wrote, "dear, dear boy!" Photo courtesy of College of the Holy Cross Rare Books—Special Collections and Archives.

Jeanette Guiney, aged 62. Photo courtesy of College of the Holy Cross Rare Books—Special Collections and Archives.

Dr. Sullivan is in good spirits but he has appeared a little dreamy lately as if he intended the felony (fellowny) of marriage.

Give my love and kisses to Loolie—and regards to Lizzie. By the way do you hear at all now days from James' Widow? I will drop you another line when we halt again.

Guiney

Major General Meade began to move the army on September 16. The Ninth broke camp, crossed the Rappahannock, and marched a dozen miles before resting for the night. The next day the Irishmen passed through Culpepper, now under martial law, and went into camp nearby, engaging in picketing, guard duty, and drill until October 10.[82]

Camp at Culpepper, Va.
Sept. 19, 1863

My Dear Jennie:

Your favors of the 13th + 14th instant were duly received. Also, news-papers—and I must not forget to acknowledge Loolie's note. God bless her Little Heart! May she ever be as proud of being "a good girl" as she is now. I have seen Capt. Phelan's letter in the Post and am much obliged to the captain for his truthful and intelligent rendering of the facts. Mahan—Hanley's counsel—wrote the original slur in the Post.[83] He knew he was lying

---

[82] Macnamara, *Ninth Regiment*, pp. 344–46.

[83] The Boston *Post* printed several surgeons' letters claiming that Hanley was ill with remittent fever. Included was a letter of Brigadier General E. B. Tyler, who indicated that he ordered Hanley to serve for a while as commander of Camp Tyler, a straggler's camp, and that this also detained the lieutenant colonel's return to the Ninth Massachusetts. At the end of the article, the *Post* printed, "Comment upon this case is unnecessary, for the intent of Col. Guiney is too apparent to need explanation. Colonel Guiney is either guilty of the grave military charge of 'making a false muster,' or he has libelled and sought to cast odium upon the honor of a deserving and faithful officer." Guiney states in the above letter that Captain Mahan wrote this. The next day, the *Post* admitted that these remarks were inserted without their knowledge and escaped the editors and that Guiney was "incapable of any conduct unbecoming an officer and a gentleman, or of performing any act inconsistent with propriety and the highest sense of honor." The article concluded, "he [Guiney] has won the reputation of a gallant and faithful officer, and has received repeated and expressive tokens

when he wrote it but I must be abused, of course, so that a dust, a smoke must be raised and incense thrown around the persons of the corrupt and fearless firm of Messrs. Hanley and Mahan.

Mahan has since been discharged the service on my recommendation. He has gone and I trust the atmosphere of the camp will never again be polluted with his presence. Some of the old grumblers are now getting up a subscription for Hanley in token of their sympathy. Plunkett's company (B)—led by McGunnigle etc. are doing the honors. You will soon see another splurge in the Press.

Lee is beyond the Rapidan and we are near Culpepper Village within five miles of the river. The Cavalry had a fight here—but we abide in peace so far. I cannot offer even a surmise as to our future.

If you see Capt. Phelan I wish you would suggest to him that I would like a return of the whole conscript detail as soon as it can be properly effected.—Father Egan—a priest from Washington, D.C. is to become chaplain of the Regmt. I intend to leave the Major position vacant for some time.

Tomorrow or next day, I intend to send you on some money. Flynn has applied for leave of absence and he will probably get it—on the ground of sickness.

When he goes home I do not wish him to stop at our house—as I may find in the course of events—that it would be necessary to treat him as I have others. Indeed more than half the trouble which I have met—I fear has arisen from my supposed intimacy with and friendship for some few officers—so that I—in part—became responsible for their faults. I have made up my mind not to invite any more of this petty and troublesome opposition. When trouble comes in a natural way—Let it come right along.

---

of respect, love and confidence from his regiment." Captain Phelan penned a lengthy letter arguing that under military regulations, Guiney had to report Hanley as absent without leave, since the required permission placing him on medical leave had never issued from Corps headquarters, as needed. Phelan asked, "If the orders under which he [Guiney] was acting were severe was he to be held responsible?" Tensions with Mahan may have stemmed back to April, when Guiney recalled him as "quite mad because I do not recommend him for Major." Meanwhile, Guiney requested Hanley's return to the regiment, indicating that he did not wish to have his lieutenant colonel dismissed. Boston *Post*, September 8, 1863; September 9, 1863; September 15, 1863. Patrick R. Guiney to Jennie Guiney, Log House at Camp, April 13, 1863; Camp at Beverly Ford, Va., September 11, 1863.

I am expecting Plunkett up every day but he has not arrived yet.

Guiney

Culpepper, Va.
Sept 20, 1863

My Dear Jennie:

Yesterday I sent to your address the sum of three hundred dollars by Adam's Express. Today enclosed herewith I send you by mail some pictures for Loolie to look at. The one in which I am taken by Harry's side is faulty in the heavy shade thrown over the forehead and eyes by the visor of the cap. But they cannot avoid that out here. The one in which I am taken with the Doctor is not very good of me but we had several taken, none of which would suit the Doctor so in order to please him I threw myself into an awkward position, thereby, made him as handsome as nature. He looks as if he meant to have a good picture taken—don't he? The one in which Flynn—I send because it is decidedly the best picture of Harry.

There is no sign of a fight here—probably will be none unless Lee attacks us.

Plunkett has not arrived yet. The weather is quite cold especially at night. Flynn will—no doubt—be going off in a day or two. I do not know whether he intends to go home or to stay in Washington. I think he is in consumption and advised him to go into the "Invalid Corps" but he thinks he can get well and will not go into that corps.[84] Do not forget what I told you in relation to him—I have the best of reasons for the view I take of that matter.

Rev. Mr. Egan of Washington is now our chaplain. He is a very good man—a Dominican Friar and a Tipperary Man.

There is a great contest among the numb-sculls for Major. But

---

[84] The Invalid Corps consisted of wounded soldiers unfit for field duty but capable of performing limited tasks behind the lines, such as hospital and provost duties. For more information, see Gary L. Todd's "An Invalid Corps" in *Civil War Times Illustrated* Vol. 24, No. 6 (December 1985), 10–19.

I'll have none at present—when I do recommend I hope the governor will not again disregard my opinion.

My love to all at home
Guiney

Not all of Guiney's letters home were to Jennie—he wrote a letter to Loolie at this time, while she was nearly three years old.

Culpepper, Va.
Sept. 24, 1863

My Dear Pet:
Your nice little letter telling me all about your doll came here to day. Poor little doll couldn't grow some + I don't wonder she fainted + got all dirty in the effort. I am glad you didn't whip her, Loolie, because she couldn't help it. How do you like the pictures of your dada's? Tell your mother to get you a charm for your little pencil and hang it around your neck. You must tell me how you like the white horse "Harry." The little rogue is asleep in one but his eyes are wide open in the other picture.

The next time you go up to see the good nuns my little pet will say to them—"Pray for my dada—he is fighting bad men." Then you must pray "Hail Mary" yourself for me. You know God will give a good girl anything she asks of Him.

When I go home, Dear, you + I and mother will have such a good nice walk together—that is, if the rebels don't cut my legs off—and if they do—we can ride little "Harry."

Your mother gave me all the kisses that you sent + they were all very sweet + like Angels' kisses. Send me more, Dear.

Father

Culpepper, Va.
Sept. 28, 1863

My Dear Jennie:
Your favor of the 25th inst. enclosing stamps came to hand this evening. I am very glad to hear that yourself and Loolie are in such good health and spirits.

You will see from heading that we are still at Culpepper on the north bank of the Rapidan—our old antagonist in diminished numbers occupying the south bank. Our Army is also somewhat diminished in numbers. Reinforcements from us have been sent all round—I understand—to help our friends Rosencranz [Rosecrans] and Gillmore.[85] There are many here who are secretly glad that Rosey got a Whipping, as these western fellows were in the habit of taunting the Army of the Potomac with want of success if not cowardice—while they were brave and successful. The truth is we have always been fighting the best and bravest troops in the South—our Western friends have been dealing with poor ignorant undisciplined troops under Bragg and Pemberton.[86] Now when Lee's troops unexpectedly met the Western Hoosiers, they suddenly found out the reason why the A. P.[87] were not always successful in battle. However, I am sincerely sorry for Rosencranz and his gallant Army—and I am no great lover of the A. P.—but it fights well—no mistake.

It is impossible to tell what the upshot of our stay here will be—things look peaceable here as I write—to-day we had a review by Gen. Cortez of Mexico, This is significant. I think if this war were settled tomorrow, we would declare war against France in Mexico.[88] Will these horrid wars ever end? We had once what was

---

[85] Guiney refers to the reinforcements sent by both General Lee and Major General Meade to the Western theater, where the Confederate army under General Braxton Bragg defeated Major General William S. Rosecrans's troops at Chickamauga, September 19–20, 1863. Rosecrans had served under Major General McClellan in West Virginia in the early days of the war, and was later transferred west. He aspired to command the Army of the Cumberland, and engaged General Bragg at the drawn battle at Murfreesboro at the end of 1862. When his army retreated to Chattanooga following the defeat at Chickamauga, Major General Ulysses S. Grant took over, and Rosecrans did not receive another major military command. He represented California in Congress after the war. Quincy Gillmore was first in his West Point class, and he reduced Fort Pulaski near Savannah, Georgia early in the Civil War. Gillmore then commanded the Department of the South and had charge of operations against Charleston until being transferred with his corps to the Army of the James in the spring of 1864. He ended the war back in the Department of the South. Warner, *Generals in Blue*, pp. 176–77, 410–11.

[86] Braxton Bragg led the Confederate Army of Tennessee at such battles as Murfreesboro, Chickamauga, and Chattanooga, and John Pemberton commanded the Rebel forces captured during the siege of Vicksburg in mid-1863. Warner, *Generals in Gray*, pp. 30–31, 232–33.

[87] Army of the Potomac.

[88] In June 1863 French troops of Napoleon III entered Mexico City and estab-

called an "Age of Reason" but this seems to be an "Age of Blood." My regards to Miss Crespy, Father Whelan—Lizzie, Misses McWilliams (when they come) and kiss to Loolie.

Guiney

Camp at Culpepper, Va.
Sept. 29, 1863

My Dear Jennie:

Your favor of the 22nd inst. just received. I told you, I think in a previous letter, that my flannels had come safely. Didn't you receive it?

I do not propose to make a liar of Dr. [John] Ryan in <u>public</u> but he is one and most base one too, and he, as well as everybody else here, knows it. I cannot be engaged in anything like a quarrel with my subordinates.[89] I do not see him except on parades once in a week—Hanley about as often. I have no personal social intercourse with them. Ryan will suffer <u>sometime</u>. They must look sharp or they will go from here some fine morning in a quiet way.

The cigars sent by Father Whelan were splendid and I wish I could compliment your box in a similar manner but—do excuse me Love—for saying that they had rather a <u>domestic flavor</u>.

You may pay as much as you can afford and will be accepted by the Mortgagor, on the house. The money I suppose might be invested more advantageously if I were at home—but I do not wish you to go upon "Change" nor to the stock-brokers looking for chances so my advice is, Dear, to pay the one thousand dollars next January as you suggest. Be careful and do not leave your self without money, however, for we cannot tell what will turn up in my prospects. For instance, when my term is out, if I should live so long, it will take every cent of the last four months pay to clear up my liabilities so that all we can count upon is the pay for next

---

lished a puppet government, and the crown of a Mexican Empire was offered and accepted by Archduke Maximillian of Austria. The United States strongly protested this and eventually pressured the French into evacuating without the involvement of United States troops. McPherson, *Battle Cry of Freedom*, pp. 683–84.

[89] This refers to Ryan's role in the Hanley incident, discussed earlier. His statement was printed in the September 8, 1863 Boston Post.

four months. Let me know, Dear, the amount of <u>money on hand</u> after paying this one thousand. All well and merry and fat here.

Your Husband

My respects to Father Whelan. What's his address?

P R G

Camp at Culpepper, Va.
Sept. 30, 1863

My Dear Jennie:

Your favor of the 29th inst. received this moment. As you express apprehensions of a battle, I hasten to inform you that circumstances now indicate that a battle is remote if not indefinitely postponed. Matters did look threatening a few days ago but now we are falling back upon the routine of ordinary camp life.

The conscripts which I received are, on the whole, very good material for soldiers. I like them much, and have no fears as to their performance of duty in the field. In fact, discipline is so well enforced that it is safer for them to <u>fight well</u> than to <u>run fast</u>.

Mahan has been restored to his position again. I will tell you sometime or other why I am <u>not</u> sorry. All well here. My love to Loolie.

Guiney

Camp at Culpepper, Va.
Oct. 4, 1863

My Dear Jennie:

I received two letters from you and a news-paper containing proofs of pictures. I have but a few moments to speak with you tonight. The pictures suit pretty well—but I do not wish you to incur any extraordinary expense on them. I wish you would have one copy of the one you like best made, finished, and framed for ourselves. Let others more if they see fit. Tell Capt. Phelan I received his letter and will write him again in a few days. Plunkett and M'c have not answered yet. Mahan came back today restored to his rank. All well here. Father Egan celebrated Mass here today. I like him very much—sure—why wouldn't I? He is a Tipperary man. All friends are well here. No sign of either a move or a fight. We are living on the best of terms with all the world "the rest of mankind" and ourselves.

Yours
Guiney

On October 4, Guiney complained to Major William Rodgers, A. A. G. State of Massachusetts, about his efforts to find suitable people within the regiment to fill commissions:

It has been my endeavor from the start to confine my nominations for promotions to the names of those who were in the ranks of the Regiment—but I must confess that to find the proper material was an effort on my part in many instances. Yet, on the whole, I think it best to adhere to that rule. The regiment, at least comparatively has not suffered in discipline from its workings.

The rule of promotion by seniority presupposes rare intelligence in all, and a wide field for original selection. In these particulars I need not inform his Excellency how deficient my command has been and is. Whence, I must ask that those whom I have recommended be commissioned though in some instances junior to others.[90]

Both Lieutenant Colonel Hanley and Major Mahan returned to the regiment in early October, restored to rank after the cases of their absence without leave had been reconsidered. Meanwhile, the Ninth constructed a pleasant camp for itself, with shade trees planted so that it looked "like a grove of cedars." Brigadier General Judson Kilpatrick, commander of a division of Federal cavalry, visited the camp on October 5 and stayed with Guiney for an hour.[91]

A few day later, Guiney received a significant letter from Brigadier General Thomas Francis Meagher, who had resigned from the army.

[90] Patrick R. Guiney to Major William Rodgers, A.A.G. State of Massachusetts, Camp at Culpepper, October 4, 1863; letter located in the Ninth Massachusetts File in the Executive Department Letters, Massachusetts State Archives, Boston, Massachusetts.

[91] Regan diary, October 5, 1863.

Meagher had aroused the animosity of his countrymen by criticizing the Democratic Party, as discussed in the letter. Furthermore, Meagher's letter implies that Guiney shared his controversial views, which were unpopular with the bulk of the Irish population.

New York, 129 Fifth Ave

October 7th 1863[92]

My Dear Colonel,

Your hearty honest letter, from Culpepper, dated the 1st of this month, gratified me exceedingly.

The approval of intelligent and accomplished young Irishmen I have always esteemed—and I think I may include you in that category without being accused of an indulgence in flattery!

As for the great bulk of Irishmen in this country, I frankly confess to an utter disregard, if not a thorough contempt, of what they think or say of me in my relations to the questions and movements that are supported or designed to affect the fortunes of this nation, or actually do so. To their own discredit and degradation, they have suffered themselves to be bamboozled into being obstinate herds in the political field, contracting inveterate instincts, following with gross stupidity and the stoniest blindness certain worn-out old path-ways described for them by their drivers, but never doing anything worthy of the intellectual and chivalrous reputation of their race. Democrats they profess themselves to be from the start—the instant the baggage-smashers and cut-throat lodging-house-keepers lay hands on them—and Democrats they remain until the day of their deaths, miserably and repulsively regardless of the conflicting meanings that name acquires through the progressive workings of the great world about them. To have been a Democrat in the days of Andrew Jackson was to have been an American citizen in the boldest and proudest interpretation of the word. It was to have been a devoted friend of the country, whether it was right or wrong, and to the extent of being a fierce and relentless enemy of all who were not for it in the fullest measure of its growth and glory. Now-a-days to

---

[92] For information on the Irish-American community's reaction to Meagher's letter, see preface.

be a Democrat, is to be the partisan of a selfish and conscienceless faction, which under the captivating pretexts of the State-Rights, Habeas Corpus, and the popular claims and rights of the kind, would cripple the national power, play with the wildest or wickedest recklessness with the hands of every foe who would see that power laid low, either to gratify his jealousy or vengeance, or bolster his mean condition on the wreck furnished him by its overthrow. Sadly, and almost savagely, have I noted this of late; and hence the energy (if I can claim that quality for my public actions) with which I have broken loose from what might have been considered any imprescriptible associations and traditions in public life. In doing so, I have discarded with the haughtiest insensibility and disdain the "Irish opinion" of this country, having come to the conclusion that it was passed redemption, and, therefore, passed consideration or respect. That such an "opinion" should be in a state of the most violent fermentation against me, in consequence of my letter to the Union Committee of Ohio, was to be expected; and that, with the estimate that formed of it, this circumstance would affect me in the least, could not be reasonably conjectured.[93]

All this I am led to write, because you may have seen in some of the "organs" of that "opinion," strictures on the letter in question; and I am desirous of marking my appreciation of your approvals and that of your officers and men, by giving my notion,

---

[93] In July, 1863, Meagher received an invitation to visit Ohio and speak in support of the state Union Committee and gubernatorial candidate John Brough. However, on September 23 he wrote a letter cancelling the engagement, citing urgent business in Washington. This lengthy letter argued that electing Brough "vindicates and fortifies the National Government," while voting for his opponent, Clement Vallandingham, will "strain every nerve to perplex and shake and dislocate the Union, and invigorate, while they inflame, the spirit of Rebellion." The letter was printed in several newspapers including the *Irish American*, which interpreted it as an assault on New York's Democratic Governor Horatio Seymour, who did not enjoy the best relations with Lincoln. The New York paper differentiated between support for the Union and for the Lincoln administration, and claimed that "Meagher is equally in error, and that he represents neither the feelings nor the sentiments of his countrymen. . . ." Furthermore, many Irish-Americans were suspicious of Union leagues and presumably resented Meagher's association with them. *The Pilot* denounced them as "associations of the basest politics" led by "unscrupulous, cunning men" working not for the preservation of the Union but for the re-election of Lincoln and the propagation of abolitionism. *Irish American*, October 3, 1863. *The Pilot*, April 11, 1863. Robert G. Athearn, *Thomas Francis Meagher: An Irish Revolutionary in America* (Boulder: University of Colorado Press, 1949), pp. 128–29.

very distinctly and emphatically, of the condemnation of others, and the inveterate and irredeemable element from which it emanates.

I shall reserve myself, however, on this subject until I see you in camp—promising myself the very great pleasure, as I do, of passing my friends in the Army of the Potomac a visit between this and Christmas.

I beg you to remember me most cordially to the officers of the gallant and glorious old 9th Massachusetts.

And with sincere esteem
remain
Most Cordially Yours
Thomas Francis Meagher

Colonel Guiney
9th Mass. Vols.
Army of the Potomac

General Lee crossed the Rapidan River on October 9 in a maneuver designed to flank Major General Meade's right and menace Washington, but the Army of the Potomac mobilized to counter the threat. On October 10 the Irishmen received orders to move and advanced to Raccoon Ford, but received instructions to return to camp and march the following day. The Ninth passed through Culpepper next morning, forced to endure the catcalls and jeers of several locals. While serving as rear guard, the V Corps formed in line of battle against a suspected Confederate attack. Nothing happened, however, and the Ninth crossed the Rappahannock at Jones' Ford and bivouacked near the old Beverly Ford campground.[94]

The armies engaged in maneuvering the next few days, with much marching and countermarching along the way. October 16 found the Ninth in bivouac in Centreville, and by October 19 the regiment had marched onto the old Second Manassas battlefield, where they unknowingly camped among the bodies and skeletons of hastily buried men. The men of the Ninth shifted to a less eerie position the next morning, upon realizing where they had slept. Early on October 20, Guiney led his regiment to a village called New Baltimore, where they waited until the 24th.[95]

[94] Regan diary, October 10, 11, 1863. Macnamara, *Ninth Regiment*, p. 347.
[95] Macnamara, *Ninth Regiment*, pp. 348–49.

New-Baltimore Va.
Oct. 21, 1863

My Dear Jennie:

After a long intermission in the mail, one arrived here tonight containing your favor of the 11th inst. It seems at its writing, you knew nothing of the fact that we had broken our camp at Culpepper and were on the move. But so it was, and ever since we have scarcely had a night's rest. After going near Washington, Lee retreated and we in turn pursued him to this point—which is near Warrenton. He is now beyond the Mountains and the Rappahannock. Whether the campaign is over, I am unable to say—it looks so, but appearances are apt to be deceptive in War. Most of the time I have enjoyed good health—had one [t]urn, and am now well again. My sickness occurred at Fairfax C. H. I had to dismount and go one-side in a wood where I suffered very much for about an hour. Dr. Sullivan remained with me and it is owing to his kindness and treatment that I recovered so quickly.

During our retreat and subsequent advance the corps did not fall in with the enemy at all. Indeed the whole thing would remind you of the old game of "hide-and-go-seek"—Lee being "tag" at one time and Meade at another. We slept a portion of one night on the battle field of Bull Run—the sight of the unburied skeletons was horrible. The air seemed heavy with the odor of death.

I enclose you a letter from General Meagher which I wish you to keep safely for me. We are all well here and in very good spirits. I will write you again so soon as we settle down. If you do not like those pictures—do not purchase. I have lost the "proofs." Love to my dear Loolie and kindest regards to Father Whelan and Lizzie.

Guiney

Camp at
New Baltimore, Va.
Oct. 22, 1863

My Dear Jennie:

This morning I received a whole lot of letters from you and one from Loolie.

There is some prospect of our staying here some few days to come—perhaps for weeks.

Like the scene in the song of "O Susana," "everything is still." The only trouble is we cannot get anything to eat except <u>hard</u> bread and beef just quivering between life and death. This neither improves our tempers or digestion, nor love of the locality. We are all getting a little savage as you will observe when we go home. The Dr. [Sullivan], by the way is not included in this remark for I perceive that he is becoming more sentimental—talks more than is usual of the moon and matrimony. You had better tell his mother that he is in love with some young lady in Chelsea. His case is so bad that I do not think he will recover.

I gave that <u>Carte de visite</u> of Sarah to Gen. Griffin—he remembers her well and speaks in glowing terms of her father—she, he says, was a little girl at the time he knew them.

Enclosed you will find picture of Gen. McClellan and Lady for your album. When all your visitors are gone, I should like to go home a ten days—cannot bear a crowd <u>at home</u>.

Guiney

On October 24 the regiment broke camp and undertook a muddy march to Auburn, remaining here until October 30. The Ninth then proceeded to Three Mile Station, and stayed there until November 7.[96]

Head Quarters 2d Brigade
1st Div. 5th Corps
Army of the Potomac
Oct 31, 1863[97]

John A. Andrew
  Governor of Massachusetts

Governor:
  I see by the Boston papers that one or more Massachusetts regiments are to be sent home to recruit and, I suppose, in a general

---

[96] Macnamara, *Ninth Regiment*, p. 349.

[97] This letter is located in the Ninth Massachusetts File in the Executive Department Letters, Massachusetts State Archives, Boston, Massachusetts.

way to encourage volunteer enlistments in the state. As there is now a lull in active operations and no indications to warrant any very robust hope in their speedy resumption, I respectfully suggest to Your Excellency that the "Ninth" be ordered on the service named.

If this suggestion should be favorably acted upon by the War Dept. I feel sanguine that most of my old command would reenlist and that a new Ninth could soon be sent into the field with full ranks.

I make this suggestion with a view to the interests of the service, and feeling convinced of its practical utility.

Whether myself and the other officers of the regiment should remain in service is a secondary question and one that can be determined by future circumstances.

> I have the honor
> to be
> Your   Excellency's   Obt.
> Servt.
> PR Guiney Col
> 9th Mass. Vols.

> Camp Near
> Warrenton Junction, Va.
> Nov. 1, 1863

My Dear Jennie:

This morning I was gratified by the receipt of yours of the 28th inst. I had been expecting a letter from you for some days before and one days further delay on your part would have entitled you to a prodigious scolding. Just in time! I am rather inclined to kiss you more than to say a single cross word. Little trifles sometimes make immense differences "Don't they Dear?"

I suppose I encouraged you too much as to the prospect of my visit—There is no way in which I can claim a Leave of Absence just now—but so soon such things are rendered possible I will be with you. This is all I meant to have said to you in my former letter on that point.

We continue to move about from place to place and for what

particular purpose or uses is incomprehensible to all but proph-
ets and Brigadiers! One would think that Meade's object had
some relation immediate or remote to the solution of the perpet-
ual motion problem—or perhaps he fears his Army might become attached to Localities and in that way jeopardize their love
for the whole United States of America. No danger of this last, as
our affections embrace not only the United States—but Mexico
and several other small places on the Continent! This is not the
last American War of this Generation—there are at least two more
on hand.

Neither Flynn nor Phelan have arrived here yet—all those here
are well + in pretty good spirits. I stop with the Regmt. although
in command of Brigade—there is something genial about the
Ninth after all.

Just as soon as you read this I wish you would take Loolie right
up in your arms and kiss her hard for me.

For yourself, Dear, accept whatever of heart words can convey
and was left to me by you originally and believe me,

Ever yours,
Guiney

*Breaking camp on November 7, the Fighting Ninth joined its corps in
support of Major General Sedgwick's VI Corps, engaging the Confederates
at Rappahannock Station. The next day the Massachusetts men tramped
to Kelly's Ford and crossed the river, only to recross it on November 9 to
guard the railroad between Morrisville and Bealton Station. They remained on duty here for ten days.*[98]

Camp Near Bealton, Va.
Nov. 12, 1863

My Dear Jennie:

This is quite a lazy day—we are lying still in camp by the road
side and time hangs heavily upon us—not even the shaggy visage
of fabled guerillas breaking in to disturb the monotony to which

---

[98] Macnamara, *Ninth Regiment*, p. 350.

the crack of his rifle would be a relief and a gratifying contrast. I have nothing to do. You may think it strange that it is only now, under such circumstances, I sit down to converse with you Dear Jennie. Why should I not at all times, in the midst of duties and conflicts, write to her on whom I <u>do</u>, and ever must, rely for my happiness here? Why should the head have such mastery over the heart? But so it is love. The <u>certainty</u> of being loved—although it is the very sweetest thing in life—makes us more or less careless about it, and we sacrifice, (at least I often do) the duties which love and home impose, to the less important duties of every day life in the army. <u>Postponement</u> in affairs of the heart, indeed in religious matters, is too much our inclination—while we are always ready to accept and wrestle with the other duties and incidents as they occur. God loves us and we know it, and are careless. Those of our bosom love us and we know it, and are careless. The <u>world</u> does <u>not</u> love us and we know it, and we must be vigilant, ever active and bold to keep our <u>status</u> in it. Hence, Dear, I am sometimes apparently neglectful in writing to you—but if I never wrote you my thought and hope for the future, are by your side and around you.

I received a letter from you this morning in which our meeting in Virginia or at home is looked upon as probable and soon to come. I wish I could comfort myself by thinking so too—but that realization is so doubtful and distant that I am afraid to even hope. I do not think it possible under existing regulations for you to come here. Indeed if it were possible—as I am satisfied that no proper "Winter Quarters" will be allowed this army—it would not be pleasant for you to be here. Some people say that when they have company <u>misery</u> is not half so miserable to them, but I am certain that if you were here without proper comforts—I should feel worse than if alone. I applied some <u>weeks</u> ago for Leave of Absence to [Major] Gen. Meade but I have not heard from it since—if matters become quiet again he may let me go. On this subject I guess we had better make up our minds—as Gen. Meade said of his plan of battle at Gettysburgh—to "<u>let</u> the thing develop itself."

All our friends in the Ninth are in good spirits, and in fact the whole regiment is jovial, prompt, and remarkably healthy.

The command of the Brigade which devolved upon me was purely temporary and owing to the illness of [Brigadier] Gen.

Griffin. He is still in Washington. Old Sweitzer commanded the division, if you please, but a general was assigned to the Div. afterwards, so Sweitzer is now back to his Brigade, and I to the Ninth.

I honestly think I ought to be appointed a Brigadier General—in which capacity a portion of the world, at least, would hear from me—but I indulge no hopes as I have no influential political friends. Still, I feel convinced that Destiny is not done with me yet. These are stirring times and <u>new</u> arrangements will be made by swift events.

Guiney

Head Quarters 9th Mass.
Camp Near Bealton, Va.
Nov. 15, 1863

My Dear Jennie:

Your very kind letter of the 8th inst. came to hand this morning. This is the second I have received of that date. It gives me great pleasure to know that you + Loolie are so well. Indeed I had preciously heard that you were in the best of spirits. The Dr. told me of a visit yourself and Capt. F. made to Chelsea—<u>I don't know about this sort of thing but you are the best judge</u>.

We are again expecting a move—where to etc. we are all in happy ignorance. There has been some cannonading at the front to-day. If the weather holds good I have no doubt of a fight soon, and as the army is in good condition—I believe in our triumph.

Yours
P. R. Guiney

The Irishmen crossed the Rappahannock at Kelly's Ford on November 19 and marched to the vicinity of Brandy Station, remaining on picket duty here until November 24.[99]

---

[99] Macnamara, *Ninth Regiment*, p. 350.

Camp Near
Brandy Station, Va.
Nov. 19, 1863

My Dear Jennie:

Your very welcome and dear letter came to hand today. You see by the caption of this that we have moved again across the Rappahannock. My tent is just pitched—for how long, Heaven only knows—whether for months or hours. Flynn has not yet arrived he is still in Washington—so I cannot tell you "how I like my things." The weather is quite fine for the season. I wish for a storm I assure you, because I feel confident that Meade will let me go home when the roads get so bad that he cannot move his Army. This is the season of storms and I am anxiously looking for one, and watch the clouds every hour. I am totally unable to give you any advice about assuming the responsibilities of St. Joseph's Table at the Fair. Indeed My Dear, while I have very decided notions about the <u>brazen</u> <u>piety</u> required and exhibited at such places, yet I have such a horror of being advised myself on matters about which anyone is competent to judge, that I cannot, for the life of me, advise even my wife on the subject. I certainly would avoid such places—all public displays—if I were you. I fear my thoughts are rather <u>ancient</u> on this + kindred subjects—perhaps they are morbid and erroneous—so much do I distrust myself on such matters, although I <u>feel</u> intensely on these points, that I am ashamed, or rather, diffident about writing my views to you, my cherished, and certainly would not even hint them to another. It would be different if I were at home, or if you had relatives to accompany you. <u>Bluebeardism</u> is not dead yet, you see. But more anon—when I see you, I'll give you a "Coudle [candle?] Lecture" improved, revised and illustrated. I must not forget to say—that while I will not promise much aid in "gardening," I'll guarantee to drink the wine and eat the grapes etc.

Yours
P. R. G.

On November 24, the Ninth Massachusetts marched several miles in rain and mud, only to have the orders countermanded and they returned to camp. *Two days later, on the 26th, Major General Meade began his Mine Run campaign, attempting to turn General Lee's right flank. Guiney's regiment crossed the Rapidan River at Culpepper Ford to bivouac near Chancellorsville. On the 27th they reached New Hope Church to relieve of some cavalry skirmishing with the Rebels, and the men lay on their arms that bitter cold night, made worse since the men could not light fires for fear of attracting Confederate artillery. The Fighting Ninth moved to Robertson's Tavern the next day, and on the morning of the 29th they joined the V Corps on the east side of Mine Run. Major General Meade intended to strike a blow against General Lee's army opposite the creek on November 30, and the Ninth waited in line of battle until the attack was cancelled due to the strength of the Southern line. By December 1 the Irishmen withdrew, crossed the Rapidan at Germanna Ford, and went into winter quarters at Bealton Station on December 3. While here, they guarded a portion of the Alexandria and Orange Railroad against Confederate raids, especially from Colonel Mosby's guerillas.*[100]

At this time, *Guiney engaged the regiment in strict drill and regular Sunday morning inspections, while a hospital was erected.*[101] *Things were well in the Irish Ninth, and Guiney returned to Boston on leave, passing through Camp Convalescent near Alexandria on New Year's Eve to visit any of his men who were there.*[102]

---

[100] Macnamara, *Ninth Regiment*, pp. 351–54. Macnamara, *Bivouac*, pp. 242–43.
[101] Macnamara, *Ninth Regiment*, p. 356.
[102] Regan diary, December 31, 1863.

1864: "God gave me an opportunity . . . to shed my blood for our beloved Republic."

Guiney returned from leave in Boston and reassumed command of the Ninth Massachusetts on January 15, 1864.[1]

Camp
Jan. 21, 1864

My Dear Wife:

Your dear letter came to hand this morning and enclosed one from Loolie, my little pet. These were both the more gratifying, as I did not expect to hear from you until my first letter reached home.

Indeed I do not wonder, Love, that you are lonely. I am so, and it can not be otherwise with either of us for the time has come when you and I should be together. This separate existence is becoming unreasonable and unbearable as well as unnecessary. There was a time—Ah! a bitter time—when we could not help it. But now it is over or nearly so. God speed next June, after which I hope, Dear, to be ever with you.[2] I must confess that I need you near me—I need your influence in my efforts to become a better man. These horrible hell-born fellows, with whose contemptible natures I am ever coming in contact, are corrupting me and debasing me. They were busy while I was at home and have done everything in their power to injure me—of course without effect. But never mind—I'll wear them out until June.

In the mean time be happy, Dear, and keep our home so—the flowers blooming and the birds singing—so that all of Heaven will not fade from my eye nor vanish from my ear. Give kisses to Loolie for me.

Guiney

P.S. If the Traveller has not already published those remarks—Let the matter go. Have you received the deed back from Dedham yet—or arranged with Mr. Colburn?

P. R. G.

---

[1] Regan diary, January 15, 1864.

[2] The regiment was to be mustered out after three years of service on June 21, 1864. Macnamara, *Ninth Regiment*, p. 392.

Many ladies visited their husbands while the army remained in winter camp, and on the evening of January 29, a ball was held in their honor. All the officers and men of the brigade were invited, along with several local families that attended.[3]

On February 10 Jennie and some more officers' wives came to visit the Ninth and stayed for some time. Little Loolie accompanied Guiney's wife; much later, she recalled spending time in his log cabin, where officers would plant her on the table and toast her. The little girl got into mischief, once cutting some tent strings, and would sometimes amuse herself by hanging around a sentry, or taking some drumsticks for her own use. Guiney would warn her not to disobey a colonel, lest he court martial her. Guiney's daughter also remembered playing with Adjutant Phalen's two spaniels, and falling asleep on the knee of a captain who would tell her stories.[4]

Meanwhile, time passed in the winter camp, and soon the excitement of another St. Patrick's Day filled the regiment. At the entrance of each company street an arch of laurel, holly, and evergreen vines was erected, having in their center the company letter in a shield, a Maltese Cross (the V Corps' badge) above the shield, and a harp mounted with the regiment's number on top. On St. Patrick's Day, all Irishmen in the division were given leave to be in the Ninth's camp, as were many men from the army as a whole. The holiday commenced with Father Egan's service in the chapel, constructed of logs hidden from sight inside by cedar boughs. Following this, Guiney and M. H. Macnamara both delivered an address, and watched a mock parade held by officers 'promoted' from the ranks for the occasion. Foot and horse races and other games accompanied four rations of whiskey per man to make the day merry, and many officers and their ladies walked about with green sprigs on their clothing. At night a dinner was held, and a grand ball at division headquarters in a specially constructed tent wound up the day. The tent was decorated with rifles, crossed sabers, sashes of red, white and blue cloth, chandeliers made of bayonets, all the regimental colors of the division, and the flags of Massachusetts, New York, Michigan, and Pennsylvania, the four states represented in the division.[5]

On March 9, a new change came with the commissioning of Ulysses S. Grant as lieutenant general. Although Major General Meade remained in charge of the Army of the Potomac, Grant traveled with it and, in effect,

---

[3] Regan diary, January 20, 1864.

[4] Louise Imogen Guiney, "A Child in Camp" in *Goose-Quill Papers* (Boston: Roberts Brothers, 1885), pp. 120–23.

[5] Regan diary, February 22, March 16, 17, 1864. He called the chapel a she-bang—army slang for any non-canvas building.

acted as its commander. Grant reorganized the army on March 24 by consolidating it into three corps and, relieving Major General Sykes, gave V Corps to Major General Gouveneur K. Warren.[6]

Bealton, Va.
March 31, 1864

My Dear Jennie:

As we anticipated I am lonesome enough I assure you. The house is deserted—none to call and comfort me, but the inevitable rats! The poor fellows, as if aware of my forlorn condition gnaw more persistently than ever every night.

I sincerely hope you have arrived home without any inconvenience to yourself or Loolie or Lizzie. By the way, Capt. Phelan arrived here this afternoon and reports you all in good condition at Brown's Hotel.[7]

The enclosed letter came here this evening. There is nothing new going on—everything the same as you left. Father Egan has not come back yet.

My health is good + I am getting strong again.

Do not forget to give Miller Jessica about my boots. Tell Flynn to send back my Meershaum pipe.

Yours
P. R. Guiney
Col. etc.

---

[6] Second in his West Point class of 1850, Gouverneur K. Warren commanded troops during the Peninsula, Second Manassas, and Antietam campaigns. Promoted to major general, he became chief engineer of the army. In this capacity he stood on Little Round Top at Gettysburg on July 2, 1863, and saved the Federal left flank by taking action to prevent the success of a Confederate attack. With its regular commander Major General Winfield S. Hancock absent due to wounds, Major General Warren commanded II Corps until Lieutenant General Grant appointed him to direct V Corps. He led his divisions through the 1864 Overland campaign and the Petersburg siege, but personality conflicts with Grant and Major General Philip Sheridan led to his removal from command on the battlefield of Five Forks on April 2, 1865. Years later, a court of inquiry vindicated Major General Warren and criticized his relief. Warner, *Generals in Blue*, pp. 541–42.

[7] Phelan had been in Boston since last July on business connected with the draft. Regan diary, March 31, 1864.

Bealton, Va.
April 5th, 1864

My Dear Jennie:

I rather expected a note from you this evening but perhaps I was hasty in my hope; but tomorrow I shall expect to hear from you—you must tell me all about your trip home—about Loolie, the hens etc.

Things are pretty much as you left them—except that "Chris" [Plunkett?] is gone home for ten days. I tried to dissuade him but with his usual want of reason, he pressed me to let him off.

Our friends are well and the Dr. [Sullivan], Father Egan, Adjt. [Phalen] etc frequently speak of you and wish to be remembered to you.

How sadly, My dear Jennie: all our fears were realized in poor Loolie's case? Her visit was not so pleasant to herself or to us as it ought to have been.

My health is now good, and I hope you have fully recovered your strength. Poor Hanley is sick again. Lucky time! Just as campaign is about to open. He is going to Washington, and I shall be alone again in battle except the Adjt.—who, as usual, is worth all the rest put together.

It is raining very heavily here and this may delay Gen. Grant for some time, but I am satisfied that the only delay that can occur now must arise out of the weather—The intention is to go ahead![8] I set—for certain reasons, a very high price upon my life but I do sincerely hope that, before our time expires, a movement will be made which will result in capture of Richmond—though thousands fall. In respect to those who die it will be merely a matter of time. They would soon die anyhow! In the world's economy it will be all for the better.

I am very lonesome, My Dear and sometimes that inexpressible sadness comes over me which makes me seem to myself more like an insane person than a reasonable agent in this awful life—but Adieu Love—

Guiney

---

[8] It had rained since the first of April. Regan diary, April 5, 1864.

Bealton, Va.
April 7, 1864

My Dear Jennie:

Your note of the 4th came to hand just this moment. It was very kind, dear, and when I read it, I could not help thinking how unthankful I have been to God for blessing me with such a wife as you are; but it is my misfortune.

The enclosed letter from your brother John was addressed to me personally as you will see and since you will understand how I came to open it. But having once opened it I was curious enough to read it and one particular portion was very amusing. You will readily realize what portion that was.

I am very thankful of my dear little pet for her presents of flowers and kisses. If she and I live she will yet realize how much I can love.

June next will end my career in the Army—if matters do not change immediately, in the mean time. But a campaign is coming on and who can tell its results?

Yours, My Dear Wife
Ever and in all things
P. R. Guiney

The Fighting Ninth broke its winter camp on April 30 and discarded that which could not be brought along on the upcoming campaign— Grant's drive to Richmond. That day, the regiment marched to Rappahannock Station, where the entire V Corps bivouacked. On May 4, with Brigadier General Griffin's division in the lead, the corps advanced over the Rapidan River via Germanna Ford and camped that night a mile west of Wilderness Tavern on the Orange Turnpike, on the extreme right of the Federal Army. No one had realized yet that General Lee's army remained in the woods ahead, with Lieutenant General Richard S. Ewell's corps bivouacked two miles further down the pike.[9]

Major General Warren began to move his troops at 5:00 a.m. on May 5, with Brigadier General Griffin's division as the rear guard. Confederate skirmishers began pushing Griffin's pickets back, however, and he in-

---

[9] OR, vol. 36, pt. 1: 552. Macnamara, *Ninth Regiment*, pp. 369, 371.

formed his surprised corps commander; the Rebels were not supposed to be anywhere near here. After receiving another message from Griffin that Southern infantry was in his front, Warren ordered him to reconnoiter, and Griffin ordered Brigadier General Joseph J. Bartlett to probe up to Saunder's Field, where he confirmed the Rebel position. Griffin received directions to hold the turnpike and attack while the rest of V Corps came up in battle line to support him. Griffin waited before advancing, however, allowing the corps some time to form. At noon, he pressed forward, with Brigadier General Romeyn Ayres' brigade to the right of the pike, Bartlett on the left, and Colonel Sweitzer, including the Ninth, in support. To Griffin's left, and advancing with him, was Brigadier General James Wadsworth's division.[10]

Drawing near Saunder's Field, the Federal officers reformed the lines broken up by the dense woods through which the men advanced. Some Rebels initially fell back before Wadsworth's force, but Griffin's men encountered staunch resistance from Major General Edward Johnson's Confederate division. With bugles sounding through the air, the Federals swept forward into the blazing line. Ayres confronted Brigadier General George H. Steuart's brigade, and Bartlett struck Brigadier General John M. Jones's Virginians. Colonel Sweitzer's brigade straddled the turnpike, with the Thirty-second and Twenty-second Massachusetts to the right and the Sixty-second Pennsylvania, Fourth Michigan, and Ninth Massachusetts on the left, in that order. As the Federal offensive disintegrated, Rebels captured two cannon of Captain George B. Winslow's battery of the First New York Light Artillery and decorated them with a Southern banner to annoy the bluecoats. With the goal of recapturing them, Guiney led his regiment into the storm of bullets.[11]

The Irishmen sprung forward with a yell, and almost instantly, powerful volleys drove them back. In this maelstrom, Guiney was hit, a bullet tearing into his left eye. The regiment, now under Lieutenant Colonel Hanley, had to retreat, having lost twelve officers and 138 men in a period of ten minutes. Colonel Sweitzer, not having seen this, ordered the Ninth back into the fray. Lieutenant Colonel Hanley explained, "We have been in, and just come out!" but the brigade commander simply commanded, "Well, take 'em in again." Hanley was about to comply when one of

[10] Wainwright, *A Diary of Battle*, pp. 349–50. Gordon C. Rhea, *The Battle of the Wilderness May 5–6, 1864* (Baton Rouge: Louisiana State University Press, 1994), pp. 98, 100–101, 104, 139, 143.

[11] Wainwright, *A Diary of Battle*, p. 351. Macnamara, *Ninth Regiment*, p. 372. Rhea, *The Battle of the Wilderness*, pp. 141–42, 144, 169.

Griffin's staff officers rode up and announced, "General Griffin's orders are not to take the 9th in again," as the division commander had observed the slaughter of the Massachusetts regiment. With relief, the Irishmen received a reprieve, and Sweitzer apologized the next morning that he had not realized the punishment the regiment had endured.[12]

The next day, the V Corps was not substantially engaged and Brigadier General Griffin held line in the Federal center, straddling the turnpike on the eastern edge of Saunder's Field. The division had lost 1,748 men in this thick woods and undergrowth simply known as the Wilderness.[13] *The Ninth lost 150 men here, and it was Guiney's last battle. His regiment would serve through the upcoming campaign under Hanley's command until mustering out on June 21.*[14]

The bullet had entered above Guiney's left eye, destroying it and the surrounding bone. Brought to a hospital, he lay unconscious with what seemed a mortal wound until he regained consciousness and insisted on a painful operation to remove the lead slug. While in the hospital at Fredericksburg, Guiney managed to scrawl, on the back of a casualty list that he had mistaken for an envelope, a brief request to his doctor that his wife be informed of his condition. The handwriting is extremely shaky, but his thoughtful presence of mind under such duress and pain is impressive and touching.

Fredericksburg
May 11, 1864[15]

Doctor,

I have just risen up and torn your envelope to ask a favor of you.

Please send word to Mrs. Guiney in Rox. that I am in a fair way to recover—have lost my left eye etc.

PRGuiney
Col 9th

---

[12] Macnamara, *Ninth Regiment*, pp. 372–73. Flynn, *The Fighting Ninth*, pp. 40–41. Egan, reprinted in Corby's *Memoirs*, p. 336. Rhea, *The Battle of the Wilderness*, p. 170.

[13] Flynn, *The Fighting Ninth*, p. 41. Rhea, *The Battle of the Wilderness*, p. 436.

[14] From May 8–19, 1864, the Battle of Spotsylvania, the regiment would further lose another hundred and one men. OR, vol. 36, pt. 1: 142. Macnamara, *Ninth Regiment*, p. 392.

[15] This note is located in the Casualty Reports, Ninth Massachusetts Volunteer Infantry file, Massachussetts National Guard Military Museum, Worcester, Massachusetts.

Guiney was sent to Washington on May 12 and returned home to what he called the "angel-like" care of his beloved Jennie.[16] *He wrote the following letter from home. Despite the pain and disfigurement of the wound, it is evident that he looked forward to his future and Grant's eventual victory.*

Roxbury, Mass.
June 2, 1864

My dear Mrs. Shaw:

After an absence of three years, I am once more with my family. My career (?) in the army, I hope has been such as you would wish it to be, useful and honorable. Up to the battle of the Wilderness, I had not been wounded although meeting with what are termed "narrow escapes" in many a battle. Now, at last, I am proud to say—and I know you will participate in this pride—God gave me an opportunity and of which I availed myself, to shed my blood for our beloved Republic. This is a source of great pleasure to me and one in which the pain and consequences of my wound are entirely lost. One other source of pleasure though, is deeper and gives more satisfaction to my heart, and that is the conviction that I have many times assisted in the damage and discomfiture of the Enemy. That Enemy is now driven to the wall and I hope Grant will <u>press</u> <u>him</u> <u>to</u> <u>it</u> until a rebel throat is unable to shout for "Quarters!" You may think this a little bloodthirsty, but it makes one feel so to lose nearly all the blood he had, in the Wilderness. I have nothing for the foe but <u>hate</u> now, as I am unable

---

[16] The minie ball had entered above the eye and passed downward toward Guiney's jaw; the incision made to remove the slug was about a half inch in front of his ear. The bullet destroyed Guiney's eye and penetrated his front sinus. Dead bone was discharged from the wound. Stenson's duct, located below the cheekbone, was severed in removing the ball, creating a salivary fistula which continued to discharge saliva for a year. One day this discharge unexpectedly ceased with a sensation of an "electric thrill"; this feeling was renewed whenever, in shaving, a razor touched near the area. As late as 1870 Guiney still suffered dizziness from the effects of the wound, and he sometimes needed to grasp onto a rail to support himself. While still practicing law in court, he occasionally had to bathe his head during recess, in order to relieve the discomfort. Joseph K. Barnes, *The Medical and Surgical History of the War of the Rebellion (1861–65)* (Washington, D.C.: Government Printing Office, 1875), p. 330. Louise Guiney, "Patrick Robert Guiney," 41.

to fight anymore and my regiment is to come home in a few days—its term served.

My wound is still suppurating, and on account of a fracture of my skull, my head troubles me. My eye is gone—and, on the whole, I am very much used up. Time though, with the angel-like tenderness with which I am cared for at home, will improve me sufficiently to recommence the practice of my profession. How strange has been my fortune! You know the commencement. The end is not yet.

My compliments to Mr. Shaw—and believe me my dear friend,

Ever Truly Yours,
P. R. Guiney

EPILOGUE: THE GOOD KNIGHT OF BOSTON

Guiney, his health shattered, preceded the Ninth Massachusetts home. Jennie met him in Washington and brought him back to Roxbury. Young Louise felt taken aback at his condition and appearance, and later recalled of the homecoming,

> It was my earliest glimpse of the painful side of the war, when he stood worn, pale, drooping, waiting recognition with a weary smile, at the door of the sunny little house we all loved. Instantly, heedless of any persuasive arms or voices, I slipped headlong, like a startled seal from the rocks, and disappeared under the table. Such was my common mode of receiving strangers; and here, indeed, was a most bewildering and appalling stranger. In vain my soldier called me by the most endearing names; even the whimsical nomenclature of camp-life failed to convince me that this was no imposition. I shut my disbelieving eyes, and crouched on the carpet. For two long hours I did not capitulate, and then but warily. What was this spectre with whom I must not perch, whose head, bound in bandages, I must not handle? What was he, in place of my old-time comrade, blithe and boyish . . .?[1]

Meanwhile, after three years of service, the Ninth Massachusetts Volunteers returned home as well. On June 10 the men packed their gear and Brigadier General Griffin and Colonel Sweitzer, with division and brigade flags fluttering behind them, addressed and took leave of the Irishmen. Men of the division then crowded around to bid farewell to acquaintances and friends who had fought by their side on many a battlefield. Cheers filled the air for President Lincoln, Lieutenant General Grant, Major General Meade, Brigadier General Griffin, Colonel Sweitzer, the Ninth Massachusetts, the Army of the Potomac, the Union, the Red Cross, and the V Corps. And then, excited at going home and

---

[1] Louise I. Guiney, "A Child in Camp," 125–26. Cullen, *The Story of the Irish in Boston*, p. 248.

saddened at leaving army buddies, the Fighting Ninth started for White House Landing on the Pamunkey River, to return home as heroic defenders of the Union.[2]

The next day they boarded the steamer *Kayport* as strains of "Johnny Came Marching Home" sounded through the air, and nightfall found the 250 battle-hardened veterans anchored at the mouth of the Potomac River. The regiment reached Washington on June 12 and, via railroad, Baltimore on the 13th and Philadelphia early the next day. Here they received a delicious breakfast at the Union Volunteer Refreshment Room, complete with tablecloths, fresh rolls, butter, bacon, tea, and coffee. At the head of a large table was a shield emblazoned, "Welcome Home." Arriving in New York later that day, anxious people crowded around the men as they boarded a train for Boston, trying to gather the latest news from the front.[3]

Finally, the regiment had its homecoming on June 15, and though still recuperating, Guiney mustered his strength and turned out to meet his men. Throngs of people—mothers and sweethearts, fathers and friends—anxiously pushed forward to see the long-awaited men at the depot early that morning. The Ninth paraded through a hot, steamy Boston with Guiney riding at its head, his appearance prompting loud, repeated cheers. Patriotic citizens lined Boston's streets, and decorations and flags brightened the way as the Irishmen marched to have dinner at Faneuil Hall, decorated with the names of Colonel Cass, Guiney, and the principal battles of the Ninth in medallions draped with the colors of the United States and Ireland. Family and friends packed into the galleries, and Mayor Lincoln and Massachusetts Adjutant General William Schouler gave brief welcoming remarks, after which Guiney addressed the regiment.[4]

Following dinner, the soldiers retired to the Columbian Association's hall for a reception, complete with toasts, cheering, and music. The Roxbury Reserve Guard, 50 men under Captain Edward Wyman, wishing to honor Guiney, escorted the colonel home after the affair. A carriage of four white horses bore Guiney in the company of Mayor Lewis of Roxbury, as the honor guard

---

[2] Regan diary, June 10, 1864.
[3] Regan diary, June 11, 12, 13, 14, 1864.
[4] Regan diary, June 15, 1864. *The Pilot*, June 25, 1864. Macnamara, *Ninth Regiment*, pp. 407–408.

marched by its side. Upon reaching his house on Shawmut Avenue, Wyman thanked Guiney for his service to the Union, and Guiney responded with gratitude and modesty at the unexpected honor paid him.[5] The following week, on June 21, the regiment gathered on the Boston Common, to be mustered out of service by Lieutenant W. S. Arnold of the Eighteenth United States Infantry.[6]

Guiney needed more time to convalesce, with "his fine constitution shattered, his spirited beauty ruined by the loss of his left eye and the deep scar in the cheek, with only his courage and his wife's never-faltering care to sustain him, he patched up, in a measure, his civil existence. . . ."[7] He also began receiving a military pension of $22.50 a month, granted on October 13, 1864.[8]

Despite his physical condition, Guiney spoke on behalf of President Lincoln before the 1864 election, giving the speeches at Institute Hall and Dorchester discussed in the introduction of this volume.[9] Lincoln defeated Democratic candidate Major General George McClellan, ensuring prosecution of the war to its victorious conclusion, but the nation was stunned when John Wilkes Booth assassinated the President only a few days following Lee's surrender at Appomattox. Despite the differences between President Lincoln and the Irish-American community, *The Pilot* called for everyone to set aside partisan feelings and recall the labors for which President Lincoln was martyred.[10]

The Civil War altered relations between Irish Catholics and Yankee Protestants. The participation of the Irish had torn down some of the obstacles separating them, and the common ground of war experience eased tensions.[11] In a speech before the 1868

---

[5] *The Pilot*, June 25, 1864.

[6] Regan diary, June 21, 1864.

[7] Louise I. Guiney, "Patrick Robert Guiney," 41.

[8] Patrick R. Guiney Pension Record, National Archives, Washington, D.C.

[9] Thomas H. O'Connor cites Guiney and Meagher as having helped attract Republican attention to the Irish community. Guiney scrapbook, 2. *Daily Advertiser*, October 7, 1864, in Guiney Scrapbook, 12–13. O'Connor, *The Boston Irish*, pp. 96–97.

[10] *The Pilot*, April 22, 1865.

[11] Irish-Americans also benefitted economically during this period, enjoying a gradual decline in unemployment. Inventions such as the sewing machine allowed expansion into areas of work once solely performed by skilled craftsmen. Several construction projects begun before or during the Civil War, such as the Boston City Hospital, a new Catholic cathedral, the Jesuit Church of the Immac-

presidential election, Guiney suggested that the accomplishments of the Irish regiments wiped away nativist prejudice against the Irish. He challenged his audience: "Go up to the State House and you will find the torn and faded banners of the Ninth Regiment, and so long as they remain there no man will ever be heard to say that the Irish people living in Massachusetts are enemies of the republic."[12]

When Assistant District Attorney for Suffolk County Henry F. French resigned his position to accept the presidency of the State Agricultural College, Governor Andrew nominated Guiney for the position on May 17, 1865, at the request of Judge Russell and other leading lawyers. However, lingering prejudice led several members of the legislature to try to thwart the appointment because of Guiney's ethnicity. A bill to reduce the office to that of a clerkship passed the Massachusetts Senate but failed in the House of Representatives, and Guiney assumed his duties under District Attorney George P. Sawyer.[13] He also maintained his commission as colonel of the Ninth Regiment in the first division of Massachusetts Militia, and on April 28, 1865, John A. Marcy issued an order appointing Guiney Major General and Commandant of the Massachusetts chapter of the United States Veteran Military League.[14]

On May 26, 1866, President Andrew Johnson and Secretary of War Edwin Stanton signed a brevet promotion making Guiney a brigadier general "for gallant and meritorious service during the war," with rank to date from March 13, 1865.[15] Pleased with the honor, Guiney went on to run for Federal office a few months later. Nominated by the Workingman Party at its convention at Faneuil Hall, Guiney ran to represent the Third Congressional District of Massachusetts. *The Pilot*, which regretted his opposition

---

ulate Conception, expansion of the Boston business district, and development of the South End, provided additional jobs for Irish labor. With the actual outbreak of the Civil War, some women went to help manufacture ammunition at the Watertown arsenal or other factories, while the men helped staff iron foundries and shipyards turning out guns, cannon, shells, and ships for the Union war effort. Baum, "The 'Irish Vote' and Party Politics in Massachusetts," 118. O'Connor, *The Boston Irish*, 92–93.

[12] Guiney scrapbook, 7, 14.

[13] *The Pilot*, May 27, 1865; March 31, 1877.

[14] Commissions for both offices can be found in the Rare Book Room of Dinand Library, College of the Holy Cross.

[15] Commission can be found in the Rare Book Room of Dinand Library, College of the Holy Cross.

to Major General McClellan's 1864 presidential bid, nonetheless praised Guiney's bravery, service, high-minded ideals, and honor, and described him as a conservative Republican.[16]

The Workingman Party supported an improved moral, intellectual, and social culture for the nation's workers, besides such practical measures as an eight hour work day. In a speech at Institute Hall in Roxbury, Guiney expressed his vow to fight for laborers' rights, especially considering his youth spent working in factories. He called for bipartisan support from both Democrats and Republicans to promote the interests of the common American citizen, and he expressed anger at such cases as the Amoskeag Manufacturing Company of Manchester, New Hampshire, which recently issued 80 percent dividends to stockholders but not so much as a cent increase in its workers' wages.[17]

In one oration Guiney explained of his political views, "But some old party-liner may say how can Democrats vote for you who are a Republican? Let me tell such a man that I am a better Democrat than he is—a Democrat in the true sense of that magic word."[18] Although Guiney was cheered at such assemblies and his speeches earned praise by area newspapers for both content and eloquence, he was defeated in a three-way race by Republican Ginery Twinchell. The president of the Boston and Worcester Railroad, Twinchell went on to serve in Congress for three terms (March 4, 1867 to March 3, 1873) before returning to the railroad industry.[19]

A few months later, Guiney sadly learned of the death of his friend Brigadier General Thomas F. Meagher, leader of the Irish Brigade during the Civil War. Serving as acting governor of Montana Territory, Meagher had been drinking on July 1, 1867 at Fort Benton. He fell from the deck of a steamboat into the Missouri River and mysteriously drowned, his body unrecovered. Guiney announced the news in a general order to the Ninth Massachusetts Militia, and expressed sorrow at his passing. He ordered his officers and men to wear badges of military mourning and for the

---

[16] *The Pilot,* October 13, 1866.

[17] Guiney Scrapbook, 8–10.

[18] Guiney scrapbook, 10.

[19] Ginery Twinchell received 6,076 votes, Democrat William Aspinwall 2,544, and Guiney 437. Boston *Herald,* November 7, 1866. *Biographical Directory of the American Congress* (United States Government Printing Office, 1980), p. 1934.

regiment to attend a public meeting in Faneuil Hall on July 25 to commemorate Meagher. Here, the regimental flags hung draped in mourning, and Guiney joined other prominent citizens in addressing the gathering.[20]

Through all this time, Guiney's health remained troublesome after his wounding in the Wilderness. On October 8, 1867, Guiney reported that he still suffered great pain from the wound, that it made it very difficult for him to concentrate mentally, and that the vision in his right eye had also deteriorated a great deal. In the spring of 1868, citing bronchial trouble as an impediment to performing his obligations, he resigned his commission as colonel of the Ninth Massachusetts Militia, despite a unanimous request from the regimental officers that he reconsider.[21] His head wound persisted in causing him pain, and sometimes he felt so dizzy that he needed to grasp nearby objects for support. While engaged in court, he would occasionally have to bathe his head in an effort to relieve some of the pain and disorientation.[22]

Despite these difficulties, Guiney roused himself to support Lieutenant General Ulysses S. Grant in the 1868 presidential contest. During one oration, Guiney exclaimed,

> It has been said to you that I, having been a democrat, rallied to the defence of the country in common with the patriotic masses of the people irrespective of party. Had I not done that I should not have been a true democrat. I was a democrat then and I am tonight; but the trouble is that the great bulk of the democratic party therein went into rebellion against the country that received my father and his children. . . . I believed with Stephen A. Douglas when he exclaimed, "There is no more a democratic or a republican party in this country. The people are divided into two parties, patriots and traitors." I served in the army and never dreamed that I had changed my politics a particle, but when I came back and settled down, to my astonishment some of my friends—dear friends, too—said, "What, are you not a democrat still?" "Yes,"

---

[20] Regan diary, July 25, 1867. Ninth Massachusetts Volunteer Militia General Order No. 6, July 18, 1867, in Guiney scrapbook, 15. Warner, *Generals in Blue*, p. 318.

[21] Form for an increase in pension, October 8, 1867, in Patrick R. Guiney Pension Record, National Archives, Washington, D.C. Patrick R. Guiney to the Officers of the Ninth Regiment M. V. M., Boston, April 6, 1868, reprinted in Guiney Scrapbook, 11.

[22] Barnes, *The Medical and Surgical History of the War of the Rebellion*, p. 330.

said I, "but not of this party, that has been playing tug-boat and speaking trumpet for the southern Confederacy during the four years we have been fighting them." The republican party have got all that was good for anything, all that was truly democratic, in the old democratic party. If to rally to the defence of the flag, when assailed, is not democratic, I have mistaken the whole career and spirit of Andrew Jackson.

Guiney continued, saying the actions of the Irish regiments in the war destroyed nativism but also warned, "Now I say to the people of Irish birth or extraction, that to vote against General Grant, against the magnificent results of the war, against liberty as personified by the republican party is to vote to take away a part of the glory and credit which the Ninth Regiment bled to achieve."[23]

In another speech, Guiney said that the chiefs of the rebellion still led the Democratic party, while those of the Union headed the Republicans. He attacked the institution of slavery and, while admitting that there were well-meaning men in both parties, Guiney criticized the Democrats for denouncing the war as a failure in 1864 and for acting to aid the rebellion (i.e., the New York City and Boston draft riots). Furthermore, he claimed that the Republican party and the Federal army were intertwined, that there existed a "union of hearts between the two." Guiney concluded by calling Grant the "triple harmony of loyalty, liberty and victory."[24] Nonetheless, in Massachusetts, the Irish voted for Grant's Democratic opponent two to one, while native-born voters supported Grant at a rate of six to one.[25]

In 1869 Guiney's salary as assistant district attorney was $2,100. But health problems prompted his sudden resignation in October of that year, and he returned to private practice, acting as attorney and consultant in several cases.[26] Mentioned as a possible candidate for district attorney, Guiney's poor health prevented his consideration of occupying the demanding post. Instead, Gui-

---

[23] Guiney scrapbook, 13–14.

[24] Draft of one of Guiney's speeches in support of Ulysses S. Grant and written in Guiney's hand, located in the Rare Book Room of Dinand Library, College of the Holy Cross.

[25] Baum, "The 'Irish Vote' and Party Politics in Massachusetts," 133.

[26] Moorfield Storey, private secretary to Senator Charles Sumner since 1867, succeeded Guiney. M. A. DeWolfe Howe, *Portrait of an Independent: Moorfield Storey 1845–1928* (Boston: Houghton Mifflin Company, 1932), p. 132.

ney ran for the office of Register of Probate and Insolvency for Suffolk County in November 1871, and *The Pilot* endorsed his nomination as a fitting honor to his service and race.[27] He won the election and took his oath on December 5 of that year, happy to be back in public service again.

Guiney remained involved with church activities as well. Pope Pius IX called for laity to organize in the spirit of loyalty to the Catholic Church, and this inspired the foundation of the Catholic Union of Boston in March 1873. Prominent Irishmen served among its first officers, and Guiney joined three other members to compose the Committee on Nominations. The Union's objectives were to further the interests of the Church, Catholic education, public schools and institutions, and other charitable work. It helped obtain freedom of worship for inmates in state penal institutions and residents of reformatory and charitable houses. Furthermore, the organization sponsored a festival in the Music Hall from November 11–13, 1873, featuring several addresses on issues pertinent to Catholic Americans.[28]

Meanwhile, Guiney enjoyed a high reputation earned from his Civil War service. Patrick Ford wrote to Guiney to thank him for a photograph and sketch sent via the Boston correspondent for the periodical *Irish World*. Ford wanted to include the image in a cluster of photographs around a likeness of the eminent Irishman Major General Philip Sheridan. "There is no other man whose portrait I had rather give in the cluster round Sheridan than yours," Ford wrote, "Indeed I have postponed all the portraits until the issue after next on your account."[29]

By 1874 Guiney was receiving a salary of $3,000 a year for his position, but Judge of Register and Probate Isaac Ames caused problems for him.[30] Guiney wanted to increase office efficiency by hiring paid clerks under official oath and responsibility, reforming the looser system in place. Also, since the Register was responsible for the office and its responsibilities, Guiney pro-

---

[27] *The Pilot*, November 11, 1871; March 31, 1877.

[28] Theodore Metcalf was the first president of the organization, and Patrick Donahoe enjoyed the rank of First vice president. *The Pilot*, November 22, 1873. Cullen, *The Story of the Irish in Boston*, pp. 160–62.

[29] Patrick Ford to Patrick R. Guiney, New York, July 19, 1873.

[30] S. N. Gifford and George A. Marden, *Commonwealth of Mass. Manual for the Use of the General Court* (Boston: Wright & Potter, State Printers, 1874), p. 229.

posed that the he, instead of the judge, be able to control it and appoint subordinate assistants. Ames balked at such reform and increased organization, while Guiney continued to lobby for it.[31]

Guiney remained involved in Irish-American affairs; he served as Chair of the Committee of Arrangements for a banquet honoring the Centennial of Irish patriot Daniel O' Connell. As such, Guiney wrote to invite the prominent abolitionist William Lloyd Garrison to attend the banquet, to be held at the Revere House in Boston on August 5, 1875. Although Garrison declined, his reply was read by the toastmaster at the banquet.[32] It is significant that Guiney contacted Garrison, considering the hostility which most Irish-Americans felt toward abolitionists in general and Garrison in particular.

Roxbury, August 3, 1875

P. R. Guiney, Esq

Dear sir—I am gratified to receive through you, from the Committee of Arrangements, an invitation to participate in the O'Connell Centennial Banquet, to be given in this city on the evening of the 5th inst; for, though not an Irishman by birth, no son of Erin holds a higher appreciation than I do the memory and service of the great Irish Liberator. While circumstances will prevent my attendance, I gladly avail myself of this opportunity to recognize him afresh as among the foremost champions of liberty and equal rights in any land or age. Certainly, the millions of Irishmen on their native soil, and the millions of them in this and other lands, have special reasons for remembering him with pride and gratitude, admiration and affection, as the ablest, most eloquent, and potential advocate of "Justice for Ireland" against centuries of wrong and oppression. If he did not live to see the accomplishment of all that he aimed to secure, it was not owing to any lack

---

[31] Patrick R. Guiney to Editor of the Boston *Post*, Boston, October 27, 1873. Patrick Robert Guiney, *General Guiney's Reply to Henry W. Paine, Esq., Before the Committee on Probate and Chancery of the House of Representatives March 20, 1875* (Boston: M. H. Keenan, Printer, 1875).

[32] Patrick R. Guiney to William Lloyd Garrison, Boston, July 30, 1875; this letter is located in the Boston Public Library Rare Book and Manuscript Collection, Boston, Massachusetts. Garrison's reply is in the Holy Cross Guiney Collection.

on his part of vigilance, zeal, courage, energy or devotion; for, animated by the most patriotic incentives and sustained by the noblest principles, the trumpet-tones of his voice were ceaselessly heard, demanding a full and prompt redress of grievances no longer tamely to be born.

Yet he was incomparably more than a technical, geographical Irishman. In one of his many inspirational speeches he nobly said—"I have no superfluous tears to shed for Ireland, and shall show my love of my country by continuing my exertions to obtain for her justice and good government; but I feel that I have something Irish at my heart, which makes me sympathize with all those who are suffering under oppression and forces me to give to universal man the benefit of the exertions which are the consequence."

Hence, O'Connell was not only the champion of Catholic Emancipation and Repeal, but he sympathized with the downtrodden and oppressed in every land, especially those whose fate was the most deplorable, because they were registered with goods and chattels, cattle and swine. "Man cannot have property in man," he exclaimed; "slavery is a nuisance to be put down, not to be compromised with; and to be assailed without cessation and without mercy by every blow that can be levelled at the monster." As early as 1825—half a century ago—he presented himself on an Anti-slavery platform as the advocate of unconditional emancipation; and, joining hands with Wilberforce and Clarkson, Brixton and Brougham, and their associates, he did his full share in effecting the liberation of eight hundred thousand bondsmen under the British Crown.

On my first visit to England in 1833, he honored me with his personal friendship, warmly espoused the object of my personal mission, and expressed in vehement terms his astonishment, sorrow and indignation that such a nefarious system as chattel slavery should be tolerated in a land, proud of its Declaration of Independence, and boastful of its free institutions. As long as he lived, he did not fail to rebuke us in scathing language for our own shocking inconsistency as a republic; at the same time saying, "We honor all that is really good in America, and would have it all on our side in this glorious struggle. Let us unite and persevere, and, by the blessing of God and the aid of good men, freedom will ere long, wave her triumphant banner over emancipated America, and we shall unite with the whole world to rejoice in the result."

It is for "emancipated America" to honor the memory of him whose constant desire was for her purification and ever increasing prosperity. It is for the whole world to accord a conspicuous place to his statue in the pantheon of its noblest champions of freedom and humanity.

Yours for liberty for each, for all, and for ever.

Wm. Lloyd Garrison

Guiney also felt a little lonely at this time, as Louise went away to boarding school. She attended Elmhurst Academy of the Sacred Heart in Providence, Rhode Island, from 1873 to 1879, starting at age twelve. Guiney kept up correspondence with her, always addressing her as "My Dear Pet." He was often sick at this time; in March, 1876 both he and Jennie were ill with influenza, and he suffered from a cough in October of that year. The letters recall that they went to Mass every week and remembered Louise in their prayers, and he often inquired into her studies and academic pursuits with avid, genuine interest in her well being and activities. When she was sick he prescribed her to drink the juice of Florida oranges he sent, jokingly referring to himself as "Doctor Guiney." Recalling his own youth, he assured her, "You may whisper every note in the whole gamut of your sensibility in the ear of Papa and be sure of his sympathy in every one."[33] And, with the bittersweet emotions of any loving father, he realized that his cherished little girl was becoming a young woman, although he remembered playing with her in childhood not too long ago.[34]

Despite his sickness, Guiney persisted in one of his favorite pastimes—smoking cigars. Whimsically writing his daughter, he asked "Mama scolds awfully about my smoking too much—do you sympathize with her or with poor persecuted me?"[35] He used a cigar case that Father Egan gave him, having received it from a dying Southern officer whom he ministered to in the Wilder-

---

[33] Patrick R. Guiney to Louise I. Guiney, March 2, 28, July 26, October 25, December 5, 1876.

[34] Patrick R. Guiney to Louise I. Guiney, January 23, 1877.

[35] Patrick R. Guiney to Louise I. Guiney, July 26, 1876.

ness.[36] Guiney wrote his daughter in January 1877 that, "I am as big a nuisance as ever, smoking, lying around loose, and fussing as usual, yawning, and wishing, generally that Lulie was at home to comfort."[37]

In his letters, Guiney expressed concerns for the political situation of the Republic at this time. He feared corruption in the 1876 election, and hoped Democrat Samuel J. Tilden would win the Presidency and Charles F. Adams, United States Minister to Great Britain during the Civil War, the Massachusetts governorship. He wrote Louise that he was "an independent with democratic proclivities," and that he would vote for Tilden not necessarily because he was better, but because he thought the election would secure long-awaited peace in the country.[38] Of the disputed contest, Guiney declared, "Our beloved country is in danger, nay in actual peril of its life. The people have just lawfully elected a President of the United States, but the corrupt sort of fellows who have the counting of people's votes in Florida, South Carolina and Louisiana, defy law, justice and truth, and declare that Hayes got the most votes." He continued with regret at his condition, "My heart is nearly broken at the sight, the more so that I am unable to draw my sword again in its [the Republic's] defence."[39] However, the situation did not come to war. In an arrangement over the contested election, Hayes was declared winner in return for easing harsh Radical Republican Reconstruction policies toward the South. Meanwhile, Adams lost the Massachusetts gubernatorial race to Alexander H. Rice.

In what would be his last letter to Louise, Guiney wrote her on Saint Patrick's Day, joyously penning, "Glory to Old Ireland forever! The Saint himself doesn't need it." He continued by informing her that he would celebrate moderately, and would "tip a tankard to the health and happiness of the girl I love—in Elmhurst."[40]

On March 21, 1877—the last day of his life—Guiney sat at his office desk, with daffodils in a glass before him. Earlier that day, between one and two p.m., he dined with Judge Norton, as had

---

[36] Patrick R. Guiney to Louise I. Guiney, February 26, 1877.
[37] Patrick R. Guiney to Louise I. Guiney, January 23, 1877.
[38] Patrick R. Guiney to Louise I. Guiney, September 29, November 7, 1876.
[39] Patrick R. Guiney to Louise I. Guiney, November 23, 1876.
[40] Patrick R. Guiney to Louise I. Guiney, March 17, 1877.

been a custom of his. At 5:30 he left his office and visited the barber's room at the St. James Hotel. Afterward, he was crossing Franklin Square to his house when he coughed up a bit of blood to his lips, and he knew death drew near. Nobly, Guiney took off his hat, knelt by a tree, and died. A child who knew Guiney ran from his playing to reach his soldier friend, but was too late— Guiney had passed from this earth. Two passing citizens recognized him and carried the lifeless body to his home at 48 East Brookline Street. An obituary recognized him as a true Catholic and Irishman, a devoted family man and citizen of his adopted country.[41]

Funeral services were held at his parish on Harrison Avenue, the Church of the Immaculate Conception. The one hundred and forty rifles of the Ninth Battalion, commanded by Lieutenant Colonel Strachen, assembled and marched to Guiney's residence while mourners gathered there for the funeral procession. Members of the Fighting Ninth, legal colleagues, delegations from the Loyal Legion and the Irish Charitable Society—upwards of forty carriages—joined in escorting the hearse. As a band played a slow dirge and hundreds of spectators solemnly watched, the body was borne to the church. Inside, elaborate floral arrangements bedecked the church, some in the shape of an Irish lyre, the V Corps' Maltese cross, a shield, and a regular cross, all given to commemorate Guiney's life. Father Joseph O' Hagan, now serving as president of Guiney's beloved College of the Holy Cross, delivered the Requiem while the Ninth's former chaplain, Father Thomas Scully, acted as deacon. Father Robert Fulton, S.J., Rector (and later President) of Boston College, proclaimed a farewell eulogy, professing that "General Guiney's I regard as a very perfect character. He conformed himself not only to what is lawful, but to what is great and fitting." Afterward, the cortege reformed and the body was brought to rest at Holywood Cemetery.[42]

On April 4, the Military Order, Loyal Legion, United States of Massachusetts recognized Guiney's service, virtue, and character, and honored his passing. The Catholic Union of Boston followed

---

[41] Louise I. Guiney, "Patrick Robert Guiney," 42. *The Pilot*, March 31, 1877. The house on the corner of East Brookline Street and Harrison Avenue has since been demolished for the construction of the South End Housing Project. Henry G. Fairbanks, *Laureate of the Lost* (Albany: Magi Books, 1972), p. 1.

[42] Louise I. Guiney, "Patrick Robert Guiney," 42. *The Pilot*, March 31, 1877.

suit on May 2, honoring his duty and fidelity, and deemed him one of the nation's "bravest and most patriotic defenders."[43]

After leaving Elmhurst, Louise joined her mother to live in Auburndale. She kept her father's sword and spurs and a regimental scarf mounted on the wall of her study beside the flag which had draped his coffin. She never married, but supported Jennie and traveled with her to England and Ireland. Following Guiney's death, Jennie received a pension of thirty dollars a month, but required and received an increase after becoming very ill. After July 17, 1906, she was disabled and confined to her bed or room, suffering from double pneumonia, hepatitis, and an inflammation of the gall bladder. Guiney's beloved wife joined him in death on February 5, 1910, having never remarried. Louise became an accomplished poet; she died in 1920.[44]

Patrick Robert Guiney is not a famous man of American history, nor did he aspire to be. He came over to this country as an Irish immigrant to start a new life with his family. He went on to become a lawyer, he commanded a regiment in the epic struggle of the nation's history, and afterward, set out to serve as a government official in a time of discrimination and hostility against Irish Catholics. An educated man who enjoyed such authors as Horace, Guiney also understood the common people, from which he had his roots. Devoted to Church and country, his greatest passion remained his family—the devotion of his beautiful, beloved Jennie and the smile of his little daughter. With a sense of conviction, he wrote in the album of a young girl that "One's own consciousness of a good action done is the glory and satisfaction of life."[45] He believed this, and made it the credo by which he conducted his life.

Perhaps the words of his daughter, written for a magazine published by Holy Cross, provide the most fitting conclusion of Patrick Guiney's life. She wrote,

---

[43] Military Order, Loyal Legion, United States Tribute, Boston, April 14, 1877, in the Rare Book Room of Dinand Library, College of the Holy Cross. Guiney scrapbook, 25.

[44] On February 25, 1907, Congress granted Jennie Guiney a pension of fifty dollars a month. Patrick R. Guiney Pension Record, National Archives, Washington, D.C. Henry G. Fairbanks, *Louise Imogen Guiney* (New York: Twayne Publishers, 1973), pp. 18–21.

[45] Louise I. Guiney, "Patrick Robert Guiney," 40.

His thirteen years of constant pain, the life 'hidden with Christ in God,' a strange exchange for the outlook of his masterful youth, he endured not without thanksgiving and a certain ultimate satisfaction. He did, indeed, achieve much, though not quite as he had planned; and he may have felt himself, as he was, one of those pioneers who, by sheer force of lovely character, rather than by specific deed or word, broke a way for the maligned Catholic faith in New England. He had distinct charm of manner, and a gracious, almost endearing bearing; these things both indicated and concealed the 'flint and iron' of which his purposes were made. He loved wit and laughter, but not a tenth so well as he loved seriousness. His friends, his books, and the open air, (where his later attitude was that of a quiet but not uncompensated spectator, as he drilled at Green Hill a company composed of martial small boys and his own young Amazon,) were his refuge and delight. His memory is altogether wholesome. Where he stands it is clear air. Whenever the Church and the state have the final roll-calls, and count in, though with so different understanding, their elect who 'hungered and thirsted after justice,' the good knight of Boston who was my father will be remembered.[46]

[46] Louise Guiney, "Patrick Robert Guiney," 42–43.

WORKS CITED

Unpublished Sources

John A. Andrew Collection, Massachusetts Historical Society, Boston, Massachusetts.

Boston Public Library Rare Book and Manuscript Collection, Boston, Massachusetts.

Casualty Reports, Ninth Massachusetts Volunteer Infantry file, Massachusetts National Guard Museum, Worcester, Massachusetts.

Joshua Chamberlain papers, Library of Congress, Washington, D.C.

College of the Holy Cross Registration Book, Dinand Library Archives, College of the Holy Cross, Worcester, Massachusetts.

Patrick Robert Guiney Military Service Record, National Archives, Washington, D.C.

Patrick Robert Guiney papers, Dinand Library Rare Book Room, College of the Holy Cross, Worcester, Massachusetts.

Patrick Robert Guiney Pension Record, National Archives, Washington, D.C.

James F. McGunnigle Military Service Record, National Archives, Washington, D.C.

Timothy O'Leary Military Service Record, National Archives, Washington, D.C.

National Archives, Record Group 94: Ninth Massachusetts Infantry Regimental Order and Letter Book, Washington, D.C.

Ninth Massachusetts File in the Executive Department Letters, Massachusetts State Archives, Boston, Massachusetts.

Timothy Regan Diary, owned by Kenneth Pluskat.

Newspapers

Boston *Herald*
Boston *Pilot*
Boston *Post*
The Catholic News
Cologne *Gazette*
New York *Herald*
New York *Irish American*
Roxbury *City Gazette*

BOOKS AND ARTICLES

Acts and Resolves Passed by the General Court of Massachusetts in the Year 1861. Boston: William White, Printer to the State, 1861.

Acts and Resolves Passed by the General Court of Massachusetts in the Year 1863. Boston: Wright & Potter, 1863.

Annual Report of the Adjutant-General of the Commonwealth of Massachusetts . . . For the Year Ending December 31, 1862. Boston: Wright & Potter, 1863.

Annual Report of the Adjutant-General of the Commonwealth of Massachusetts . . . For the Year Ending December 31, 1863. Boston: Wright & Potter, 1864.

Athearn, Robert G. *Thomas Francis Meagher: An Irish Revolutionary in America.* Boulder: University of Colorado Press, 1949.

Austerman, Wayne. "Armor for the Soldier," in *Civil War Times Illustrated,* vol. 26, no. 9 (January 1988): 34–37.

Barnes, Joseph K. *The Medical and Surgical History of the War of the Rebellion (1861–65).* Washington, D.C.: Government Printing Office, 1875.

Baum, Dale. "The 'Irish Vote' and Party Politics in Massachusetts," in *Civil War History,* vol. 26, no. 2 (June 1980): 117–42.

The Boston Directory . . . For the Year Commencing July 1, 1860. Boston: Adams,Simpson & Company, 1860.

Burton, William L. *Melting Pot Soldiers: The Union's Ethnic Regiments.* Ames: Iowa State University Press, 1988.

A Catalogue of the City Councils of Boston 1822–1890; Roxbury 1846–1867; Charlestown 1847–1873. Boston: Rockwell and Churchill, 1896.

Connelly, Patrick J. *Islands of Boston Harbor 1630–1932.* Dorchester, Mass.: Chapple Publishing Company, 1932.

Conyngham, David P. *The Irish Brigade and Its Campaigns,* Lawrence F. Kohl, ed. 1867; reprint, New York: Fordham University Press, 1994.

Cullen, James Bernard, ed. *The Story of the Irish in Boston.* Boston: James B. Cullen & Company, 1889.

Davis, William C. *Battle at Bull Run.* Baton Rouge: Louisiana State University Press, 1977.

Davis, William C. *Duel Between the First Ironclads.* Baton Rouge: Louisiana State University Press, 1975.

Davis, William T. *Professional and Industrial History of Suffolk County in Three Volumes: Volume I: History of the Bench and Bar.* Boston: The Boston History Company, 1894.

Dowdey, Clifford. *Lee.* 1965; reprint, Gettysburg: Stan Clark Military Books, 1991.

Dunn, Richard S. *Sugar and Slaves The Rise of the Planter Class in the English West Indies, 1624–1713.* New York: W. W. Norton, 1972.

Egan, C. L. Untitled narrative published in William S. Corby, *Memoirs of Chaplain Life*. Lawrence Frederick Kohl, ed. reprint, New York: Fordham University Press, 1992.

Fairbanks, Henry G. *Laureate of the Lost*. Albany: Magi Books, 1972.

Fairbanks, Henry G. *Louise Imogen Guiney*. New York: Twayne Publishers, 1973.

Flynn, Frank J. *The Fighting Ninth for Fifty Years and the Semi-Centennial Celebration*. No date.

Foner, Eric. *Free Soil, Free Labor, Free Men: The Ideology of the Republican Party Before the Civil War*. reprint, New York: Oxford University Press, 1995.

Frawley, Mary Alphonse. *Patrick Donahoe*. Washington, D.C.: The Catholic University of America Press, 1946.

Furgurson, Ernest B. *Chancellorsville 1863*. New York: Alfred A. Knopf, 1992.

Gannon, Robert I. *Up to the Present: The Story of Fordham*. Garden City: Doubleday & Company, Inc., 1967.

Gibson, Florence E. *The Attitudes of the New York Irish Toward State and National Affairs 1848–1892*. New York: Columbia University Press, 1951.

Gifford, S. N., and George A. Marden. *Commonwealth of Mass. Manual for the Use of the General Court*. Boston: Wright & Potter, State Printers, 1874.

Gould, James M. *History of the First-Tenth-Twenty-Ninth Maine Regiment*. Portland: Stephen Berry, 1871.

Guiney, Louise Imogen. "A Child in Camp," in *Goose-Quill Papers*. Boston: Roberts Brothers, 1885: 117–29.

Guiney, Louise Imogen. "Patrick Robert Guiney," in *The Holy Cross Purple*, vol. 3, no. 1 (June 1896): 37–43.

Guiney, Patrick Robert. *General Guiney's Reply to Henry W Paine, Esq., Before the Committee on Probate and Chancery of the House of Representatives March 20, 1875*. Boston: M. H. Keenan, 1875.

Handlin, Oscar. *Boston's Immigrants 1790–1880 A Study in Acculturation*. Cambridge:Belknap Press of Harvard University, rev. and enl. ed., 1979.

Headley, P. C. *Massachusetts in the Rebellion*. Boston: Walker, Fuller, and Company, 1866.

Hernon, Joseph M., Jr. *Celts, Catholics & Copperheads*. Ohio State University Press, 1968.

Howe, M. A. DeWolfe. *Portrait of an Independent: Moorfield Storey 1845–1928*. Boston: Houghton Mifflin Company, 1932.

Johnson, Allen, and Dumas Malone, eds. *Dictionary of American Biography* 22 vols. and index. New York: Charles Scribner's Sons, 1928–37.

Levine, Edward M. *The Irish and Irish Politicians*. Notre Dame, Ind.: University of Notre Dame Press, 1966.

Long, E. B. *The Civil War Day by Day*. Garden City, N.Y.: Doubleday & Company, 1971.

Lord, Robert H. et al. *History of the Archdiocese of Boston in the Various Stages of its Development*. 3 vols. New York: Sheed & Ward, 1944.

Macnamara, Daniel George. *The History of the Ninth Regiment Massachusetts Volunteer Infantry*. Boston: E. B. Stillings & Company, 1899.

Macnamara, Michael H. *The Irish Ninth in Bivouac and Battle*. Boston: Lee and Shepard, 1867.

McPherson, James M. *Battle Cry of Freedom*. New York: Oxford University Press, 1988.

Manarin, Louis H., and Weymouth T. Jordan, Jr., eds. *North Carolina Troops 1861–1865: A Roster*. 13 vols. Raleigh: North Carolina Division of Archives and History, 1966–93.

Massachusetts Soldiers, Sailors, and Marines in the Civil War. 8 vols. and index. Compiled and published by the Adjutant General of Massachusetts, 1931–37.

Moore, Frank, ed. *The Rebellion Record*. 12 vols. New York: G. P. Putnam, 1861–68.

O'Connor, Thomas H. *Fitzpatrick's Boston 1846–1866*. Boston: Northeastern University Press, 1984.

O'Connor, Thomas H. *The Boston Irish: A Political History*. Boston: Northeastern University Press, 1995.

Official Military Atlas of the Civil War. Washington, D.C.: Government Printing Office, 1891.

Parker, Francis J. *The Story of the Thirty-Second Regiment Massachusetts Infantry*. Boston: C. W. Calkins & Co., 1880.

Pfanz, Harry W. *Gettysburg: Culp's Hill & Cemetery Hill*. Chapel Hill: The University of North Carolina Press, 1993.

Pfanz, Harry W. *Gettysburg: The Second Day*. Chapel Hill: The University of North Carolina Press, 1987.

Porter, Fitz John. "The Battle of Gaines' Mill and its Preliminaries," in *Century Magazine* vol. XXX, no. 2 (June 1885): 309–24.

Powell, William H. *The Fifth Army Corps*. New York: G. P. Putnam's Sons, 1896.

Reese, Timothy J. *Sykes' Regular Infantry Division, 1861–1864*. Jefferson, N.C.: McFarland & Company, 1990.

Rhea, Gordon C. *The Battle of the Wilderness May 5–6, 1864*. Baton Rouge: Louisiana State University Press, 1994.

Rice, Madeleine Hooke. *American Catholic Opinion in the Slavery Controversy*. New York: Columbia University Press, 1944.

Ryan, Dennis P. *Beyond the Ballot Box: A Social History of the Boston Irish*,

1845–1917. Rutherford, N.J.: Fairleigh Dickinson University Press, 1983.

Sears, Stephen W. *To the Gates of Richmond The Peninsula Campaign.* New York: Ticknor & Fields, 1992.

Silbey, Joel H. *A Respectable Minority: The Democratic Party in the Civil War Era 1860–1868.* New York: W. W. Norton & Co., 1977.

State Temperance Committee. *Address of the State Temperance Committee to the Citizens of Massachusetts on the Operation of the Anti-Liquor Law.* Boston: no publisher, 1853.

State Temperance Committee. *Massachusetts Anti-Liquor Law; with an Analysis and Exposition.* Boston: State Temperance Committee, 1852.

Todd, Gary L. "An Invalid Corps," in *Civil War Times Illustrated,* vol. XXIV, no. 6 (December 1985): 10–19.

United States Congress. *Biographical Directory of the American Congress 1774–1927.* Washington, D.C.: United States Government Printing Office, 1928.

Wainwright, Charles S. *A Diary of Battle.* Allan Nevins, ed.; reprint, Gettysburg: Stan Clark Military Books, 1993.

The War of the Rebellion: A Compilation of the Official Records of the Union and Confederate Armies. 128 Vols. Washington, D.C.: Government Printing Office, 1880–1901.

Warner, Ezra J. *Generals in Blue: Lives of the Union Commanders.* Baton Rouge: Louisiana State University Press, 1964.

Warner, Ezra J. *Generals in Gray: Lives of the Confederate Commanders.* Baton Rouge: Louisiana State University Press, 1959.

INDEX